Being Possible

Being Possible

—— Stephen Dozeman ——

RESOURCE *Publications* · Eugene, Oregon

BEING POSSIBLE

Resource Publications
An Imprint of Wipf and Stock Publishers
199 W. 8th Ave., Suite 3
Eugene, OR 97401

www.wipfandstock.com

PAPERBACK ISBN: 978-1-7252-8790-7
HARDCOVER ISBN: 978-1-7252-8791-4
EBOOK ISBN: 978-1-7252-8792-1

For that ideal reader suffering from an ideal insomnia.

Contents

Introduction

In an interview regarding his book *Capitalism and Desire*, Tracy Morgan asked author Todd McGowan why he'd chosen to write his book focusing on the theories of Lacan instead of, say, Klein. He thought about it for a moment, and said that might've been good, but in the end shrugged and said that Lacan is who he's read, so he wrote using Lacan. I imagine I'll encounter a similar question if this ever finds a publisher, although my situation is a bit different. Using Heidegger, not just to analyze *the human condition*, but to open up the possibility for political change has always been fraught, and only more so since the publication of the *Black Notebooks*, private journals he kept throughout his life, including the period of his involvement with the Nazi party. Having initially found myself fascinated with Heidegger's thought in college shortly before the *Notebooks* were published and translated meant I only had a brief period of time to enjoy *Being and Time* with a sense of innocence before I was suddenly forced to answer questions I didn't yet have answers for. In this way, it was a lot like the time I was first trying on womens clothing and painting my nails when my mom walked in *without knocking* and I suddenly had to answer the question 'What are you doing!?' long before *I* even knew (interestingly enough, this was also my parents reaction to my reading Marx's *Capital*, although they never expressed any of this urgent confusion when I started reading Heidegger). At numerous points I wondered if I ought to follow the paths set down by others and pursue this project via some other, less problematic figure. Every time I stumbled on a new book or writer doing a similar-yet-slightly-different thing via Foucault,[1]

---

1. Brown, *Undoing the Demos*.

1

Agamben,[2] Marx,[3] Gramsci,[4] Lacan[5] or even Jung,[6] or some synthesis of these figures[7] or via some new methodology such as transindividuality,[8] bioacoustic resonance,[9] or Christian theology[10] I was often tempted to stop and try rewriting the whole thing based on that new text, a less-than-stellar way of maintaining focus on the topic at hand. Writing became a weird and sometimes desperate act of restraint, trying to stay focused on *this* thing right here and now. My hope is this text makes some unique contributions, partly as a more theoretically accessible work, as well as offering some new angles that I haven't seen covered in this way before, although anyone who gets to the end of this book and finds themself wanting more should of course go ahead and follow the footnotes to any of the books just mentioned. I've benefited immensely from all these writers, even if they often had me feeling somewhat alone much of the time, with the exception of the occasional intellectual and political comrades who shared a belief in the emancipatory potential of Heidegger's thought.[11] The question of Heidegger's politics still weighs heavily on me, and deserves a more thorough treatment than it receives here, and I even considered simply picking up Sartre's *Being and Nothingness* or Gadamer's *Truth and Method* and simply using one of those less problematic thinkers for this book, but it struck me as both too much work for too little payoff, as well as being a sort of bad-faith act to avoid biting some difficult bullets. However, even having read some of the *Black Notebooks* and finding myself troubled by the implications, I'm still confident in the possibility of a political existentialism, even one committed to more progressive principles

2. Kotsko, *Neoliberalism's Demons*.

3. Harris, *Kids These Days*.

4. Brons, *The Hegemony of Psychopathy*.

5. Tomsic, *The Capitalist Unconscious*; McGowan, *Capitalism and Desire*; DeLay, *Against*.

6. Fontelieu, *The Archetypal Pan*.

7. Finkelde, *Excessive Subjectivity*; Johnston, *Prolegomena* Vol 1; Johnston, *Prolegomena* Vol 2.

8. Read, *The Politics of Transindividuality*.

9. James, *The Sonic Episteme*.

10. Boer, *Deliverance From Slavery*.

11. Vattimo and Zabala, *Hermeneutic Communism*; Zabala, *Being at Large*; McCumber, *Metaphysics and Oppression*. The more progressive approach to Heidegger actually goes back quite some time, even including some of his own students (see for example Herbert Marcuse's *Heideggerian Marxism*), as well as a number of of attempts to synthesize the more broad existentialist themes with a Marxist approach (see for examples Fritz Pappenheim's *The Alienation of Modern Man* or Istvan Meszaros' *The Work of Sartre*).

of LGBTQ+ rights, antiracism or Communism. This project is possible. It's not what this book does.

This book grew out of a talk given in 2018 I gave at a small conference at Boise State University, run by a small group of students. The conference was centered around Jordan Peterson, a Canadian psychologist who'd exploded in popularity in the last couple years, enamored by some and loathed by others. I'd heard of the conference while living at a small study fellowship near Vancouver, where I was doing my own recovery from a severe mental breakdown suffered in late 2017. I sent in a paper proposal, less because I thought they'd accept it but because it couldn't hurt to try and it would be a small emotional boost that I was at least willing to put myself out there. I then promptly forgot about it.

Several months later, I received an email saying I'd been selected as one of the presenters. At first I thought of turning them down, feeling unqualified, but a friend convinced me that I should actually take advantage of the opportunity, and several months later I gave a short talk in Boise that received some semi-helpful criticism and a few more encouraging comments. I personally felt fine about it, but had more I wanted to say. I'd partly been limited by time, but also because I didn't want to tread on other speakers territory, and the result was I didn't bring Žižek in as much as I would've liked (at first he was allegedly going to show up, and I had no interest in talking about Žižek to an audience that included Žižek himself, but then a Žižekian discussion was left to Peter Rollins), and also had a lot of 'context' I felt would be helpful to add.

This book then started as a critique of Jordan Peterson, although it grew in a variety of ways I didn't expect it to over time. In the process of writing it, I stumbled upon a set of new ideas, problems and questions, and if I can manage it, I hope to explore in later writings. This book is admittedly ambitious, synthesizing Heidegger and Marx as a critical analysis of late capitalism, and then jumping off this to see how Peterson fails to properly address our dilemma, concluding then with a Žižekian critique of Peterson. The result is a book that itself spans a *lot* of territory, and could have easily been a 1,000-page tome (and maybe the 2nd edition will be). For now, my hope is that this book serves several purposes for different audiences. For those already committed to an emancipatory leftist politics, the first eight chapters can be skimmed (or skipped entirely), as it will likely not offer much beyond a new way of describing what you already know. I do think my reading of Peterson is more detailed than most critical readings that have been offered to date, and hope that it will serve as a helpful critical reading of his work. For those who've found themselves enamored with Peterson in recent years, this book is unapologetically critical of both Peterson's core philosophical positions as well as his recent forays into politics, but I hope it will be clear that I've read him closely, and my criticism will not be based on off-hand comments made in interviews, but on a close reading of his core theoretical work. My hope is that I'll offer a new perspective not just on Peterson and what he's wrong about, but the way in which he is, whether sincerely or in deliberate bad faith, closing off our understanding of our current situation, as well as what we can do about it. This project was inspired not just by seeing Peterson flounder about in recent years, but also watching progressives struggle to offer any sort of serious counter to his work.[12] This didn't go unnoticed. In his oft-cited article on Peterson, Nathan J. Robinson reflected on Peterson's enormous popularity, concluding that

> here the left and academia actually bear a decent share of blame. Why is Jordan Peterson's combination of drivel and cliché attracting millions of followers? Some of it is probably because alt-right guys like that he gives a seemingly scientific justification for their dislike of "social justice warriors." Some of it is just that self-help always sells. Another part of it, though, is that academics have been cloistered and unhelpful, and the left has failed to offer people a coherent political alternative. Jordan Peterson is right that people are adrift and in need of meaning. Many of them lap up his lectures because he offers something resembling insight, and promises the secrets to a good life. It's not actually insight, of course; it's stuff everybody already knows, dressed up in gobbledegook. But it feels like something. Tabatha Southey was cruel to call Jordan Peterson "the stupid man's smart person." He is the desperate man's smart person, he feeds on angst and confusion. Who else has a serious alternative? Where are the other professors with accessible and compelling YouTube channels, with books of helpful advice and long Q&A sessions with the public? No wonder Peterson is so popular: he comes along and offers rules and guidance in a world of, well, chaos.[13]

This sentiment was echoed in a similar fashion by George Monbiot, who argued that neoliberalism's ideological effectiveness was that it told a rather compelling and convincing story, closing us off epistemologically and

---

12. I'll try and make the case that Žižek's opening statement, while brief, does offer hints of a more serious critique of Peterson, but I should also say that there have been some valuable offerings in terms of critical response, (to name just a couple, Burgis, et al, *Myth and Mayhem*; Burston, *Psychoanalysis, Politics and the Postmodern University*, ch. 7; Nichols, "Postmodernism in the Twenty-First Century") although these have tended to be the exception rather than the rule.

13. Robinson, "The Intellectual We Deserve," para 101.

politically from considering alternatives.[14] This book is an attempt both at unpacking the story we've been told and offering a different one, with an implied 'alternate ending' in the final chapter.

Žižek's critique of Peterson was, in typical Žižekian fashion, a bit scattered and seemed to lack a single thesis, but it did contain *hints* at something I'll unpack, particularly around the central topic in both their work on the nature of the human subject and it's capacity to respond to difficult conditions. Both come from a psychoanalytic perspective here, but take it in wildly different directions. Petersons more conservative Jungian approach has his subject bearing the burden of their life as Christ bore the cross, as all the world's mythology reminds us.[15] Žižek's Freudo-Lacanianism (synthesized with German Idealism and Marxism) advocates for a more radical political subjectivity where the X marks not the treasure we've lost and need to rediscover, but "the loss of this loss itself."[16] Their underlying ontologies point towards different political orientations, the point of contention perhaps best illustrated by their use of lobsters as a symbolic image meant to illustrate either the necessity or contingency of reality.[17] This book then steps up in the spirit in which they both in their own ways say we often need to shift our perspectives to better understand the world around us, and could perhaps be summarized as an attempt to answer the question 'What is the meaning of lobsters?'

The book has three main sections. Chapters 1-3 will offer an introduction to the main themes of Heidegger we'll be engaging with, the first two focusing on his worldly Dasein and the third on his developments in his essays on art and technology. Chapters 4-8 develop Heidegger further as a critical analysis of late capitalist subjectivity and its attendant aspirations and anxieties, and the fundamental disjoint that occurs between them. Chapter 6 will be a sort of interlude, offering an introduction to the basics of Marx, as a way of 'materializing' Heidegger, so that we're not left with a perspective too detached from reality. Chapter 9 will be a close and critical reading of Jordan Peterson's work, with chapter 10 relying on Žižek to criticize and overcome his limitations.

14. See Monbiot, *Out of the Wreckage.*

15. "I came to a more complete, personal realization of what the great stories of the past continually insist upon: the centre is occupied by the individual. The centre is marked by the cross, as X marks the spot. Existence at that cross is suffering and transformation - and that fact, above all, needs to be voluntarily accepted." (Peterson, *12 Rules for Life*, xxxiii).

16. Žižek, *Disparities*, 78.

17. See Peterson, *12 Rules for Life*, ch. 1; Žižek, "Jordan Peterson . . .", 12.

One last thing should be brought up; research for this project was compiled through 2018-19, and the book was written late-2019 and through the middle of 2020. At the time of this writing, COVID is still ravaging the world (especially in the US with its combination of precarity and lack of adequate healthcare), protests are occurring over police violence, fascism and reactionary politics are on the rise and a controversial (potentially illegitimate) presidential election is looming. This book doesn't engage with any of this, or the disaster of a presidency that is Donald Trump, partly because they are all happening in real time and I lack the journalistic skills to keep up, but also because my hope is that this book digs a bit deeper, showing that many of our political problems are more foundational than this or that particular instance.

I'm indebted at this point to a few people. Feedback and encouragement has come in a variety of forms from Michael Alex, Matt Beukema, Jamie Lombardi, Caroline Holland, and Tijmen Landsdaal. A separate and special 'thank you' is owed to Reuben Niewenhuis, who has proven to be one of my most careful and critical readers over the years, as well as one of my best friends. Other thanks is owed to Marshall Poe and Tracy Morgan, my editors at the New Books Network where I've hosted a number of interviews. Their welcoming attitude, helpful feedback and high tolerance for my constant emails asking them minor questions goes beyond what I deserved. I also owe a thanks to everyone who has done an interview with me; even if your book isn't cited in what follows, know that I remember and learned from our conversation, and appreciate your willingness to trust a total stranger to be in charge of getting the word out about your book. Another enormous thanks goes to my therapist, for helping me wrestle with the problems that matter. A final thanks goes to Liz, Clarke, Julia, Sam and Sara-Beth for showing me that life can be worth living, something I'd forgotten for quite some time until you all let me in.

Chapter 1—**Clearing the Ground**

He was not at all used to philosophizing, and yet felt some
urge to do so.

—Thomas Mann, *The Magic Mountain*

Born in 1889 in Messkirch, Germany, Martin Heidegger's life, for all the scandal and controversy that plagues it, is in many respects fairly banal. He grew up in a small town, had a brief interest in joining the Jesuits but couldn't for health reasons, so he went to university, showing a brief interest in mathematics and theology before finally turning to philosophy. His early work reflected this interest, with much of his early work engaging with the discourse at the time on Thomas Aquinas (although in his conversion from Catholic to Protestant, Augustine would take precedence), and his habilitation thesis focusing on the philosopher and theologian Duns Scotus. In the 1920's, his attention would expand to include much Greek philosophy, as well as shifts towards the growing field of phenomenology under Edmund Husserl.[1] One can also detect some of his early inclinations towards existentialism, especially considering much of his early development occurred in parallel with Karl Jaspers,[2] although he would later deny the label.[3] However, his response to Husserl would turn out to be a slow-but-steady radicalization of his predecessor, synthesizing his phenomenological method with the ideas of more historically inclined thinkers such as Wilhelm Dilthey.[4] While one can trace the development of much of his early thought through the various essays and lectures he gave throughout the 1920's, we're going to

---

1. For a look at his early development throughout the 1910's and 1920's, see Van Buren, *The Young Heidegger* and Sheehan, "Reading A Life."

2. See Heidegger, "Comments on Karl Jaspers *Psychology of Worldviews*."

3. Heidegger, "Letter on Humanism."

4. See West, *Continental Philosophy*, ch. 4 and Kisiel, "The Paradigm Shifts of Hermeneutic Phenomenology."

move straight to *Being and Time*, where a variety of his early developmental influences would come together.

Being and Time has a well-earned reputation for difficulty, and it's not helped if one is reading it in translation, since so much of Heidegger's efforts involve deep-dives into the etymology of various key terms and phrases, much of which doesn't translate well into English.[5] Beyond that, Heidegger's prose has a certain intensity to it which can scare off casual readers. Jokes and humor or a comforting fireside manner to welcome the reader in are absent; instead, the text starts off with a quote from Plato's Sophist: "For manifestly you have long been aware of what you mean when you use the expression '*being*'. We, however, who used to think we understood it, have now become perplexed."[6] Heidegger continues: "Do we in our time have an answer to the question of what we really mean by the word 'being'? Not at all. So it is fitting that we should raise anew *the question of the meaning of Being*. But are we nowadays even perplexed at our inability to understand the expression 'Being'? Not at all. So first of all we must reawaken an understanding for the meaning of this question."[7]

'The question of Being' is an esoteric sounding project, made stranger still by the capitalization of the word Being. This isn't actually as unusual as it seems; the word in German, *Sein*, along with the other substantive *Seiend* are always capitalized in German. By capitalizing it, the translators are simply distinguishing between various grammatical difficulties, although anyone who doesn't bother reading the translators footnotes available on the first page of the text will no doubt be compelled to think of *Being* in ways that mystify rather than clarify their understanding of the rest of the text, especially in the first pages, where he tries to reanimate the question of what it means for something to be. He takes time to do this, running through a list of reasons one might raise for objecting to raising the question at all, such as Being being the "most universal concept"[8] or being "indefinable" or "self-evident."[9] But it's to this very self-evidence of the concept he draws our attention: "everyone understands 'The sky *is* blue', 'I

---

5. I'll generally be relying here on the first translation, by John MacQuarrie and Edward Robinson, although sometimes Stambaugh's translation will be brought in to help clarify difficult terminology. Scholars tend to find Stambaugh's translation to be less accurate or precise, but it is helpful as a supplement and is, in my personal opinion, generally a bit more clear and easy to read. Pagination offered will always be to the numbers found in the margins of both editions, and which refer to the German original.

6. Heidegger, *Being and Time*, 1.

7. Heidegger, *Being and Time*, 1.

8. Heidegger, *Being and Time*, 3.

9. Heidegger, *Being and Time*, 4.

am merry', and the like. But here we have an average kind of intelligibility, which merely demonstrates that this is unintelligible. It makes manifest that in any way of comporting oneself towards entities—even in any Being towards entities—there lies *a priori* an enigma. The very fact that we already live in an understanding of Being and that the meaning of Being is still veiled in darkness proves that it is necessary in principle to raise this question again."[10] What he is trying to tease out is the way that we are immersed in a certain understanding of things that is simultaneously obvious and yet 'veiled in darkness'. This shows us how we are in a strange dilemma, that of trying to analyze something that is simultaneously obvious to the point where it's ridiculous to even question it, and hidden in obscurity. This dilemma, Heidegger thinks, is not simply due to the concept itself being a difficult one to wrap our heads around, but because the question itself is often formulated inappropriately. The appropriate formulation, he thinks, means making all of its elements transparent, so no hidden baggage gets brought in, and this will involve a high level of focus on one particular element of the question: the questioner.

> If the question about Being is to be explicitly formulated and carried through in such a manner as to be completely transparent to itself, then any treatment of it in line with the elucidations we have given requires us to explain how Being is to be looked at, how its meaning is to be understood and conceptually grasped; it requires us to prepare the way for choosing the right entity for our example, and to work out the genuine way of access to it. Looking at something, understanding and conceiving it, choosing, access to it—all these ways of behaving are constitutive for our inquiry, an therefore are modes of Being for those particular entities which we, the inquirers, are ourselves. Thus to work out the question of Being adequately, we must make an entity—the inquirer—transparent in his own Being.[11]

Being and Time is then largely an attempt to get a firm grasp on this questioning entity, us, as a way of better understanding the question itself. This requires wiping the slate clean on a number of levels, and this is part of why he picks a seemingly odd name for his 'subject': "This entity which each of us is himself and which includes inquiring as one of the possibilities of its Being, we shall denote by the term '*Dasein*.'"[12] As with the capitalized-Being, the untranslated term Dasein has the potential to mislead uncautious

---

10. Heidegger, *Being and Time*, 4.

11. Heidegger, *Being and Time*, 7.

12. Heidegger, *Being and Time*, 7.

readers into thinking this is some special word unheard of outside of Heidegger, although it's actually a fairly common term in German philosophy, finding use even from some of Heidegger's predecessors such as Kant or Hegel. It literally translates as Being-there, although the translators note that "in traditional German philosophy it may be used quite generally to stand for almost any kind of Being or 'existence' which we can say that something *has*, in everyday usage it tends to be used more narrowly to stand for the kind of Being that belongs to *persons*."[13] By picking this term, his goal is to get to a more everyday understanding of what it means to be human. Later chapters will focus on big existential questions, the ones we ask when we realize we're not going to be here forever, or when we're feeling a bit lonely or insignificant, and we start to ask the classical philosophical questions such as 'Why am I here?' and 'What should I do with my life?' But Heidegger wants to understand those questions as emerging out of a particular sort of entity, Dasein (us), that has a particular way of inhabiting the world that leads it to eventually start asking those questions. He makes this transition for the 'big questions' to more everyday existence in series of passages on the sciences, writing

> The basic structures of any such area have already been worked out after a fashion in our pre-scientific ways of experiencing and interpreting that domain of Being in which the area of subject-matter is itself confined. The 'basic concepts' which thus arise remain our proximal clues for disclosing this area concretely for the first time. And although research may always lean towards this positive approach, its real progress comes not so much from collecting results and storing them away in 'manuals' as from inquiring into the ways in which each particular area is basically constituted—an inquiry to which we have been driven mostly by reacting against just such an increase in information.[14]

He continues:

> The real 'movement' of the sciences takes place when their basic concepts undergo a more or less radical revision which is transparent to itself. The level which a science has reached is determined by how far it is *capable* of a crisis in its basic concepts. In such immanent crises the very relationship between positively investigative inquiry and those things themselves that are under interrogation comes to a point where it begins to totter. Among

13. Heidegger, *Being and Time*, 7 note 1.
14. Heidegger, *Being and Time*, 9.

the various disciplines everywhere today there are freshly awak-
ened tendencies to put research on new foundations.[15]

He then wanders through a number of scientific fields, including math, phys-
ics and even theology, all of which are responding to new information that
challenges not just the old data but the very presuppositions and categories
we used to organize said data. This is remarkably close to the theory of science
developed several decades later by Thomas Kuhn, who argued that science
always operates within certain paradigms which inevitably break down due
to new data, leading to a more fundamental 'paradigm shift' in how data is
collected and interpreted. A number of comparisons between the two have
been made,[16] as both see scientific inquiry as depending on closing off the
deeper structures it depends upon. The two diverged, however, in that "Kuhn
endorsed this closing off of ontological inquiry, whereas Heidegger did not."[17]
Heidegger's project then is to get 'below the sciences', to study what we could
convolutedly call the 'pre-ontic ontologies': "The question of Being aims
therefore at ascertaining the *a priori* conditions not only for the possibility
of the sciences which examine entities as entities of such and such a type,
and, in so doing, already operate with an understanding of Being, but also for
the possibility of those ontologies themselves which are prior to the ontical
sciences and which provide their foundations."[18] There's a subtle addition happening here in this passage that's worth noting. While we've already alluded to
the way Heidegger wants to get below the more technical scientific theories to
a more everyday understanding of human beings, he also wants to get a look
at 'the possibility of those ontologies themselves'.

There's a lot happening in these first few pages, so it may be worth paus-
ing to try and unpack things with a now infamous example. On February 12,
2002, Secretary of Defense Donald Rumsfeld, when discussing intelligence
about possible chemical weapons in Iraq, referred to three types of knowledge: "there are known knowns; there are things we know we know. We also
know there are known unknowns; that is to say we know there are some
things we do not know. But there are also unknown unknowns—the ones we
don't know we don't know." In Heidegger's view, science deals with things we
know, known knowns, to discover things we don't know, known unknowns.
On top of these two, science occasionally makes surprise discoveries, things
we didn't even know that we didn't know. However, what Rumsfeld misses

15. Heidegger, *Being and Time*, 9.

16. Caputo, *Hermeneutics*, 57-62; Thomson, *Heidegger on Ontotheology*, 115; Dreyfus, "Heidegger's Ontology of Art."

17. Rouse, "Heidegger's Philosophy of Science," 177.

18. Heidegger, *Being and Time*, 11.

that Heidegger is interested is the fourth category of unknown knowns, things we don't even know that we know. While the first three categories deal with facts, this fourth category deals with the underlying assumptions that make engaging with those facts possible. Underneath our explicit understanding of the world is a much more subtle, implicit understanding, one that Heidegger thinks is fundamental to Dasein, writing that "*Understanding of Being is itself a definite characteristic of Dasein's Being.* Dasein is ontologically distinctive in that it *is* ontological."[19] He continues:

> Here "Being-ontological" is not yet tantamount to "developing an ontology". So if we should reserve the term "ontology" for that theoretical inquiry which is explicitly devoted to the meaning of entities, then what we have had in mind in speaking of Dasein's "Being-ontological" is to be designated as something "pre-ontological". It does not signify simply "being-ontical", however, but rather "being in such a way that one has an understanding of Being".[20]

This passage shows the shift he's trying to make by using the term Dasein, as opposed to person or subject; rather than think of people as having a single, fixed essence, Dasein "can comport itself in one way or another, and always does comport itself somehow . . . "[21] but the how itself is always one possibility among others. "Dasein has either chosen these possibilities itself, or got itself into them, or grown up in them already."[22] His somewhat abstract language obscures a more basic point he's trying to make, namely that Dasein's existence isn't some fixed thing, but is instead born (he'll later use the word 'thrown') into a series of possibilities for how one should lead their life. This problem of what one should do with their life has become more pronounced in modernity, where birth is less determinative of what one does, but even in places where one is born into a more strict society, one is not in some metaphysical sense born as a carpenter, but is born into the possibility of being a carpenter, although it's up to each Dasein to decide if it will then live out the life of the carpenter, or do something else such as running away and joining the circus. [23] So core to Dasein's existence is not some eternal thing, but instead the fact that it discovers its existence in an already-designed world of possibilities that it can either seize or reject, and it's out

19. Heidegger, *Being and Time*, 12.

20. Heidegger, *Being and Time*, 12.

21. Heidegger, *Being and Time*, 12.

22. Heidegger, *Being and Time*, 12.

23. "Only the particular Dasein decides its existence, whether it does so by taking hold or by neglecting." (Heidegger, *Being and Time*, 12).

of this series of everyday possibilities and understandings that the more complicated scientific theories and ontologies emerge out of; "whenever an ontology takes for its theme entities whose character of Being is other than that of Dasein, it has its own foundation and motivation in Dasein's own ontical structure, in which a pre-ontological understanding of Being is comprised as a definite characteristic."[24] So any proper understanding of the sciences, including the proper understanding of the question of Being, will require a 'fundamental ontology,' an "ontological analytic of Dasein in general,"[25] for "the question of Being is nothing other than the radicalization of an essential tendency-of-Being which belongs to Dasein itself—the pre-ontological understanding of Being."[26] 'Pre-ontological' is a weird word, and it assumes you already know what 'ontology' is. One of the most succinct definitions Heidegger gives is in a much later essay on Kant, where he says the fundamental question ontology addresses is "What are beings, in general, as beings? Considerations within the province of this question come, in the course of the history of philosophy, under the heading of ontology."[27] Iain Thomson gives a very clear explication of this passage:

> Heidegger's main point here is that metaphysics functions as ontology when it searches for the most general ground of entities; it looks for what component element all entities share in common. Ontologists understand the *being* of entities in terms of that entity beneath or beyond which no more basic entity can be 'discovered' or 'fathomed'; they then generalize from their understanding of this 'exemplary entity' to explain the being of all entities. This exemplary entity thus comes to play the ontological role 'giving the ground' to all other entities; that is, this basic ontological entity becomes identified as that kind of entity in whose being all other entities share and by which they are thus unified or composed.[28]

So ontology is the study of *what is*. However, Heidegger has a slightly different use of the term. To provide an example, when one thinks of asking what exists, one often thinks of the age-old question of whether or not God is real. This is usually one of the key questions in introductory philosophy courses, as well as more advanced ones in philosophy of religion and metaphysics. Heidegger's study of ontology is less interested in this. Instead, he's

24. Heidegger, *Being and Time*, 13.
25. Heidegger, *Being and Time*, 14.
26. Heidegger, *Being and Time*, 15.
27. Heidegger, "Kant's Thesis About Being," 340.
28. Thomson, *Heidegger on Ontotheology*, 14.

interested in how the answer creates large shifts in what *everything else* is. If God exists, that means Ze created everything, including us. That means we exist *as God's creation*, which is a very different way of thinking about ourselves and the world around us compared to a more mechanistic or scientific view, where we exist as a result of various evolutionary factors and processes. Heidegger's interest, at least in *Being and Time*, isn't even interested in this yet, as these two ontologies, religious and scientific, are at this level too explicit and formal. He's interested in the more everyday sort of ontology, the ways in which Dasein always proceeds with its life with an ontological view implicitly assumed: "In Dasein itself, and therefore in its own understanding of Being, the way the world is understood is, as we shall show, reflected back ontologically upon the way in which Dasein itself gets interpreted."[29] So our way of seeing the world always assumes an implicit ontological worldview, even if we've never set foot in a philosophy class, and that understanding is then reflected back on how we see and understand ourselves. What's more, the ways in which Dasein understands itself and its world are not as universal as we might be tempted to think, as "this understanding develops or decays along with whatever kind of Being Dasein may possess at the time."[30] However, Heidegger believes there may be some underlying structures to the various ways Dasein can *be*, although getting at this underlying structure is difficult. There is always the danger that one might impose one's own assumptions into an area where they don't apply, or assuming certain particular cultural assumptions or practices are universal. So how does Heidegger propose we get past our own ontological assumptions to the underlying core? He explains at length:

> To put it negatively, we have no right to resort to dogmatic constructions and to apply just any idea of Being and actuality to this entity, no matter how 'self-evident' that idea may be; nor may any of the 'categories' which such an idea prescribes be forced upon Dasein without proper ontological consideration. We must rather choose such a way of access and such a kind of interpretation that this entity can show itself in itself and from itself. And this means that it is to be shown as it is *proximally and for the most part*—in its average *everydayness*. In this everydayness there are certain structures which we shall exhibit—not just any accidental structures, but essential ones which, in every kind of Being that factical Dasein may possess, persist as determinative for the character of its Being. Thus by having regard for

29. Heidegger, *Being and Time*, 15-16.
30. Heidegger, *Being and Time*, 16.

the basic state of Dasein's everydayness, we shall bring out the
Being of this entity in preparatory fashion.[31]

So *Being and Time* will be a study of the underlying structures of Dasein in
its everyday navigating of the world. This will give us a better understanding
of the structure of the question of Being in general, so it is still intended as a
provisional jumping off point for the larger question he's trying to ask.

It's at this point in the book where he adds the second half of the
books title, turning to time and temporality "as the meaning of the Being
of that entity which we call 'Dasein.'"[32] When Heidegger speaks of temporality, however, he means something a bit different (as usual). The normal
way of thinking of time is in strictly measured terms, a series of seconds,
minutes and hours that add on and allow us to differentiate between them.
But for Heidegger, temporality is a fundamental part of being Dasein, not
simply in the sense that we persist in time, exist for a certain number of
moments, but that the past and future determine us in the present in ways
it doesn't for other beings. His discussion of temporality and it's relation to
Dasein moves through some discussion of Kant, Descartes and then goes
back to early Greek philosophy, which is where he starts pulling out some
really radical transitions in our thinking that make his point regarding the
importance of temporality more clear. For example, "the treatment of the
meaning of Being as παρουσία [presence] or ουσία [beings], which signifies,
in ontologico-Temporal terms, 'presence'. Entities are grasped in their Being
as 'presence'; this means that they are understood with regard to a definite
mode of time—the '*Present*.'"[33] And then there is the hidden element of the
traditional definition of humans which comes from Aristotle, that man is a
ζῷον λόγον ἔχον, usually translated as *rational animal*. However, Heidegger
notes some alternatives hidden by that translation; "λόγον is derived from
the same root verb λέγειν ('to talk', 'to hold discourse'); he identifies this
in turn with νοεῖν ('to cognize', 'to be aware of' 'to know'), and calls attention to the fact that the same stem is found in the adjective διαλεκτικός
('dialectical')."[34] To turn back to Heidegger's own words,

> λέγειν [discourse] is the clue for arriving at those structures of
> Being which belong to the entities we encounter in addressing

31. Heidegger, *Being and Time*, 16-17.

32. Heidegger, *Being and Time*, 17.

33. Heidegger, *Being and Time*, 25. Whenever possible, I'll include Heidegger's
Greek with the translated term in brackets. A Greek-English lexicon is frustratingly
absent from the MacQuarrie/Robinson translation, although the Stambaugh translation has one in the back.

34. Heidegger, *Being and Time*, 25 note 3.

ourselves to anything or speaking about it. This is why the ancient ontology as developed by Plato turns into 'dialectic'. As the
ontological clue gets progressively worked out—namely, in the
'hermeneutic' of λόγος—it becomes increasingly possible to
grasp the problem of Being in a more radical fashion . . . That
is *why* Aristotle 'no longer has any understanding' of it, for
he has put it on a more radical footing and raised it to a new
level. λέγειν itself—or rather νοεῖν [thinking, representation]
. . . —has the Temporal structure of a pure 'making-present' of
something. Those entities which show themselves in this and for
it, and which are understood as entities in the most authentic
sense, thus get interpreted with regard to the Present; that is,
they are conceived as presence (οὐσία).[35]

In other words, by reading ancient Greek philosophy very closely, Heidegger has found that in its very linguistic structure, being is temporal at
its very core. There is no existence without temporality. However, he believes that things have gotten off-track, and temporality as a fundamental
quality of Dasein has been buried over. Recovering this, Heidegger says,
will require a special method, so it's at this point in the text that he turns
our attention to phenomenology. While Heidegger was brought to phenomenology by his mentor and predecessor Edmund Husserl, Heidegger
would still add many of his own twists to phenomenology,[36] and he starts
by splitting the term up into its two component parts: "'phenomenon' and
'logos'. Both of these go back to terms from the Greek: φαινόμενον and
λόγος."[37] Let's start with the first of these.

"The Greek expression φαινόμενον, to which the term 'phenomenon'
goes back, is derived from the verb φαίνεσθαι, which signifies 'to show
itself'. Thus φαινόμενον means that which shows itself, the manifest."[38] So
phenomenon are here attached to visibility, but Heidegger goes further
by pointing out that the beginning of the term φαινόμενον "comes from
φαίνω—to bring to the light of day, to put in the light. Φαίνω comes from
the stem φα-, like φῶς, the light, that which is bright—in other words,

---

35. Heidegger, *Being and Time*, 25-6.

36. While Heidegger borrowed the term and certain key elements from Husserl,
and even dedicated the first edition of *Being and Time* to Husserl, they had substantial
disagreements brewing throughout the 1920's, which would eventually lead to a total
break when Heidegger joined the Nazi Party in 1933 (Husserl was Jewish). For more
on the relationship between them and their thought, see Crowell, "Heidegger and
Husserl"; Boedeker, "Phenomenology"; Carman, "The Principle of Phenomenology."

37. Heidegger, *Being and Time*, 28.

38. Heidegger, *Being and Time*, 28.

that wherein something can become manifest, visible in itself."[39] Things start to get a bit more complicated, however, as he starts to distinguish 'phenomenon' from 'appearances'. Heidegger points out that the latter term, while very conceptually close to the former, is itself a deeply layered one with multiple possible meanings:

> the expression 'appearance' itself can have a double signification: first, *appearing*, in the sense of announcing-itself; and next, that which does the announcing—that which in its showing-itself indicates something which does not show itself. And finally, one can use 'appearing' as a term for the genuine sense of 'phenomenon' as showing-itself. If one designates these three different things as 'appearance', bewilderment is unavoidable.[40]

But then, to add to the already confusing term, he adds a fourth possible definition:

> this bewilderment is essentially increased by the fact that 'appearance' can take on still another signification. That which does the announcing—that which, in its showing-itself, indicates something non-manifest—may be taken as that which emerges in what is itself non-manifest, and which emanates from it in such a way indeed that the non-manifest gets thought of as something that is essentially *never* manifest.[41]

There's a lot to unpack, but what Heidegger is trying to tease out is the fact that phenomenon may not directly show themselves, as in the case of certain sorts of illnesses, which often 'announce themselves' by way of certain symptoms. In cases such as this, the appearance simultaneously announces the thing while also covering it up. This covering-up will in some cases be as a result of the announcement being a 'mere semblance', when something appears to be something but in actuality isn't, but in other cases certain phenomenon only show themselves indirectly via an 'announcement'. So while appearances are that which show themselves, phenomenon are that which show themselves via indirect surrogates, such as illnesses appearing via symptoms. However, as with appearances, phenomenon can be broken down into several types, which William Blattner helpfully breaks down: "*phenomenon in the ordinary sense* (that which shows itself to our sense, objects of perception), the *formal conception of the phenomenon* (the concept of a phenomenon, but in which we do not specify anything about what shows itself), and the

39. Heidegger, *Being and Time*, 28.
40. Heidegger, *Being and Time*, 30.
41. Heidegger, *Being and Time*, 30.

phenomenological conception of the phenomenon (that which is latent in what shows itself and thereby enables what shows itself and thereby enables what shows itself to show itself)."[42]

This brings us to the second portion of phenomenology, the λόγος. This term often gets rendered today as –logy, as in 'biology' or 'theology', so is usually meant to indicate a certain field of study. Heidegger at first renders it as 'discourse', but then adds some other possible definitions: reason, judgment, concept, definition, ground or relationship.[43] However, he immediately moves to start making other connections in the Greek, writing "λόγος as 'discourse' means rather the same as δηλοῦν: to make manifest what one is 'talking about' in one's discourse . . . The λόγος lets something be seen (φαίνεσθαι) . . . "[44] One should note that the very word φαινόμενον (phenomenon) starts with the characters (φα- pronounced *pha*) which mean 'bright' or 'shining'. So while phenomenon shine and show themselves, discourse allows them to be seen in their brightness. He also connects λόγος to σύνθεσις (synthesis), although he clarifies that "Here 'synthesis does not mean a binding and linking together of representations, a manipulation of psychical occurrences where the 'problem' arises of how these bindings, as something inside, agree with something physical outside. Here the σύν has a purely apophantical signification and means letting something be seen in its *togetherness* with something—letting it be seen *as* something."[45] This leads into Heidegger's rethinking of truth, which will be one of the largest shifts he'll try to enact in his rethinking of the subject. Since λόγος is a 'letting-something-be-seen', it doesn't fall under the standard assumptions about truth or falsity, where a proposition is either true or false depending on whether or not it corresponds to reality. Instead, Heidegger wants to push us towards another way of understanding truth, one that is more integrated to the various Greek elements he's slowly been unpacking over the last few pages:

> here everything depends on our steering clear of any conception
> of truth which is construed in the sense of 'agreement'. This idea
> is by no means the primary one in the concept of ἀλήθεια [truth].
> The Being-true' of the λόγος [speech] as ἀληθεύειν [Being-true]
> means that in λέγειν [discoursing] as ἀποφαίνεσθαι [showing]
> the entities *of which* one is talking must be taken out of their
> hiddenness; one must let them be seen as something unhidden

42. Blattner, *Heidegger's* Being and Time, 29.
43. Heidegger, *Being and Time*, 32.
44. Heidegger, *Being and Time*, 32.
45. Heidegger, *Being and Time*, 33.

(ἀληθές [true]); that is, they must be *discovered*. Similarly, 'Being false' (ψεύδεσθαι [being-false]) amounts to deceiving in the sense of *covering up*: putting something in front of something (in such a way as to let it be seen) and thereby passing it off *as* something which it is *not*.[46]

The key in this passage is in the Greek word for *truth*, ἀλήθεια, which Heidegger is instead retranslating as *unhiddenness*. The first character, ἀ, is meant to be privative, as in un- or not-. The word also contains the verbal stem –λαθ- which means 'to be concealed', so the Greek word for truth is literally un-concealed or un-hidden. This demands we rethink what it is when we are talking, discoursing, or even trying to write a book about something. It is not simply a matter of asserting a series of propositions that happen to be true; a good speaker or writer has to work to weave their facts into a cohesive whole, so that one doesn't simply upload information, but sees how and why that information is important and what its implications might be.

To pull this all together then, what is *phenomenology* in Heidegger's sense? We saw that phenomenon are things which shine and show themselves, and discourse works to let those things be seen, to uncover them, so with all this in mind Heidegger's definition, "to let that which shows itself be seen from itself in the very way in which it shows itself from itself"[47] should be (relatively) clear. Phenomenology is a way of looking at things, letting them be seen and the way they show themselves. This sets in apart from other fields of study, such as theology or biology, which have their objects of study established beforehand. Phenomenology is instead a method, a way of looking at things. But what is it looking at? What is this "that which shows itself" he's referring to? He answers, "Manifestly, it is something that proximally and for the most part does *not* show itself at all: it is something that lies *hidden*, in contrast to that which proximally and for the most part does show itself; but at the same time it is something that belongs to what thus shows itself, and it belongs to it so essentially as to constitute its meaning and its ground."[48] He continues: "Yet that which remains *hidden* in an egregious sense, or which relapses and gets *covered up* again, or which shows itself only '*in disguise*', is not just this entity or that, but rather the *Being* of entities . . . "[49] Things are still likely a bit unclear, so let's try and unpack what he's saying.

46. Heidegger, *Being and Time*, 33.
47. Heidegger, *Being and Time*, 34.
48. Heidegger, *Being and Time*, 35.
49. Heidegger, *Being and Time*, 35.

Bearing in mind that Heidegger's thinking of truth is a bit different than normally conceived; entities are shown, uncovered, via various sorts of discourses. Various sorts of entities require different 'tools', or types of discourse, in order to be properly uncovered. So if one wants to study a novel, one will likely use the various interpretive methods offered by literary studies to unpack it, whereas those methods would be totally inappropriate for diagnosing a weird looking rash that appeared after a camping trip, and vice-versa. But Heidegger is interested in what makes all these particular ways of seeing function; what's the underlying way in which sight sees what it sees? This is what the Being of entities is, the *ground* on which they rest so they can properly 'shine', and in order for the ground or foundation to function as such, it needs to disappear. For example, when one is lost in a good book or movie, one forgets that one is reading or watching, simply getting lost in the spectacle. In order for that to work, the screen and speakers need to 'disappear'. If the screen is scratched or a speaker is broken or the words on a page are smeared and hard to make out, one loses that sense of immersion. And the big point Heidegger is trying to make is that we are always 'forgetting' about Being, the way entities come forward and are made visible for us, and this forgetting is the very condition required for them being made visible in the first place. Heidegger's goal, then, is to study this way in which entities 'appear', along with the inverted ways in which some things need to disappear for appearance to even occur.

This leads us to the final element of this section, the idea of covered-up-ness. This fits in with the rest of the analysis thus far, with truth as uncon-cealment and discoursing as showing needing an inversion which Heidegger supplies: "Covered-up-ness is the counter-concept to 'phenomenon.'"[50] Covered-up-ness, like phenomenon and appearances, has several possible forms. Being 'undiscovered' is one, where something "is neither known nor unknown."[51] However, more interesting to Heidegger is when phenomenon are *buried over*:

> This means that it has at some time been discovered but has deteriorated to the point of getting covered up again. This cov-ering-up can become complete; or rather—and as a rule—what has been discovered earlier may still be visible, though only as a semblance. Yet so much semblance, so much 'Being'. This covering-up as a 'disguising' is both the most frequent and the most dangerous, for here the possibilities of deceiving and mis-leading are especially stubborn. Within a 'system', perhaps, those

50. Heidegger, *Being and Time*, 36.
51. Heidegger, *Being and Time*, 36.

structures of Being—and their concepts—which are still available but veiled in their indigenous character, may claim their rights. For when they have been bound together constructively in a system, they present themselves as something 'clear', requiring no further justification, and thus can serve as the point of departure for a process of deduction.[52]

This passage, I would argue, is one of the most important ones in Heidegger's work, not just for understanding *Being and Time*, but for thinking his work as a whole. The process he is indicating here, and which will be elaborated at greater length throughout the rest of his life in various ways, is how certain things can be *partially* covered up; certain things are seen, but improperly. Again, religion provides a helpful example. Most Christians in the west today attend church semi-regularly on Sundays, may occasionally pray before a meal, and on even more rare occasions read their Bible. This approach to religion has it isolated from the rest of one's life; it's held arm's length apart from the rest of one's life, which is usually spent doing a job that has little to do with one's 'faith'. Withholding judgement regarding whether this is good or bad for now, special attention would need to be paid by any modern commentator trying to study ancient religious texts. They were written in a very different context and with very different people in mind. Studying classics doesn't just mean doing a close reading of ancient books with modern presuppositions in mind; the work of scholars in classics, history and anthropology departments involves recreating the world in which the text was produced. When this isn't done, various fragments of the original text are brought forward, but they are improperly seen. The modern Bible provides a weirdly on-point example in the very way it's printed today, with numbers splitting the text up into chapters and even verses. People today memorize and quote the Bible, even getting tattoos of specific verses, which covers up the text as it was originally written as a whole. This leads to a host of problems as people often justify their beliefs with specific verses while missing the underlying spirit of the text as a whole, which of course gets even more confusing when one remembers the specific books had numerous authors in numerous contexts which were put together long after they were all written. The fact that the text is a sort of Frankensteinian creation doesn't mean one must simply abandon it, but that truly understanding it means unpacking the various assumptions that are holding it together. When verses are ripped out of their original context, presented as isolated propositions, they are bound to be misunderstood, but this misunderstanding is, in Heidegger's view, a

---

52. Heidegger, *Being and Time*, 36.

partial covering-up; they are seen, but seen inadequately (bear in mind that for Heidegger, seeing is always 'seeing-as'[53]).

This covering-up is the first of two types Heidegger outlines; misunderstanding ancient texts is an 'accidental' one, but there is also a covering-up which is 'necessary' "grounded in what the thing discovered consists in. Whenever a phenomenological concept is drawn from primordial sources, there is a possibility that it may degenerate if communicated in the form of an assertion. It gets understood in an empty way and is thus passed on, losing its indigenous character, and becoming a free-floating thesis."[54] This is a covering-up that is actually *necessary* for certain sorts of understandings. Religion, again, provides an example. Poetry and art offer examples of where things need to be partially covered in order to be properly seen; if one looks up the plot of a film on Wikipedia, for example, they haven't really engaged with it; they've instead reduced it to a set of plot-points, perhaps with a few 'symbols' thrown in, and are now treating it like a puzzle that simply needs to be put together. This approach obviously misses what can sometimes be the most important part of a film; the cinematography, or the color palette, or the actors performances. This approach also misses some of the best parts about poetry; the rhythm of the words, the ways they work together, ebbing and flowing. But getting at these aspects means *holding back* from grasping them too firmly; allowing them to be properly seen means properly excavating them, allowing yourself to get lost in them, perhaps rereading or rewatching them and taking the *experiential* part of them seriously. As Heidegger puts it, "The idea of grasping and explicating phenomena in a way which is 'original' and 'intuitive' is directly opposed to the *naïveté* of a haphazard, 'immediate', and unreflective 'beholding.'"[55]

With this, Heidegger comes to his conclusion about his phenomenological method which we've been working ourselves towards.

> In explaining the tasks of ontology we found it necessary that there should be a fundamental ontology taking as its theme that entity which is ontologico-ontologically distinctive, Dasein, in order to confront the cardinal problem—the question of the meaning of Being in general. Our investigation itself will show that the meaning of phenomenological description as a method lies in *interpretation*. The λόγος of the phenomenology of Dasein has the character of a ἑρμηνεύειν [understanding interpreting] through which the authentic meaning of Being, and also those

53. Heidegger, *Being and Time*, 33.
54. Heidegger, *Being and Time*, 36.
55. Heidegger, *Being and Time*, 37.

basic structures of Being which Dasein itself possesses, are *made known* to Dasein's understanding of Being. The phenomenology of Dasein is a *hermeneutic* in the primordial signification of this word, where it designates this business of interpreting.[56]

When Heidegger brings up the word 'hermeneutic', it's in a few different senses that need to be unpacked. The main sense already mentioned is in the way he'll be approaching Dasein, by interpretive descriptive, rather than analytic. However, there's also another sense he intends; he'll also be "working out the conditions on which the possibility of any ontological investigation depends,"[57] or in other words, he'll be unpacking the interpretive conditions of even carrying out such a study. Finally, his hermeneutic approach will be "an analytic of the existentiality of existence . . . "[58] What ties all these together is how he's actually radicalizing hermeneutics with this work. We've already seen how he's shifting our understanding of truth from correspondence to unconcealment, but this means rethinking the subject's relationship to truth. Hermeneutics originally came from religious studies, a series of methods for reconstructing and interpreting ancient religious texts, as we've already discussed. But Heidegger's shift is to push beyond the simple idea that texts require special methods of interpretation, but that Dasein is a fundamentally interpretive being. Cristina Lafont summarizes:

> To bring about this paradigm shift, Heidegger generalizes hermeneutics from a traditional method for interpreting authoritative texts (mainly sacred or legal texts) to a way of understanding human beings themselves. As a consequence, the hermeneutic paradigm offers a radically new understanding of what is distinctive about human beings: to be human is not primarily to be a rational animal, but first and foremost to be a self-interpreting animal. It is precisely because human beings are nothing but interpretation all the way own that the activity of *interpreting a meaningful text* offers the most appropriate model for understanding any human experience whatsoever.[59]

Heidegger's project then will be *showing* how Dasein does not sit outside it's world and look in, formulating theories about it and acting accordingly, but is instead always immersed in a world, with things appearing in such-and-such a way, as well as studying the ways in which this process of appearing and disappearing happens. This is what he means when he pushes

56. Heidegger, *Being and Time*, 37.
57. Heidegger, *Being and Time*, 37.
58. Heidegger, *Being and Time*, 38.
59. Lafont, "Hermeneutics," 265.

against the idea of phenomenology as a movement or doctrine and instead insists that "We can understand phenomenology only by seizing upon it as a possibility"[60] for "it is one thing to give a report in which we tell about *entities*, but another to grasp entities in their *Being*."[61]

Thus ends the introduction to *Being and Time*, which I've tried to summarize as clearly as I can. I felt compelled to start out this way to highlight the peculiarity of Heidegger's philosophical style and approach, as well as the underlying method. There are some concluding remarks that are worth highlighting, now that we've finished working through the text.

One thing one should notice is how his philosophical approach involves a process, working through various thoughtpaths to get to a final 'clearing', a central metaphor for his thinking. Heidegger had a cabin in the woods where he'd often go on long walks, and the scenery seems to have influenced much of his own thinking. Two anthologies of his essays have even been published in reference to this; *Holzwege and Wegmarken*, translated as *Off The Beaten Track* and *Pathmarks*. Meanwhile, the German word for clearing, *lichtung*, contains the German word for light, *licht*. His work is then a wandering through various paths in order to get to a place where things are able to 'shine' and be seen. Bulldozing down the whole forest isn't a possibility; one instead needs to work through various pathways, cutting through brush and tall grass, and possibly taking a hidden shortcut only known by those intimately familiar with the woods, in order to get to a place where the light cuts through the leaves at just the right angle to let us see the forest, and ourselves, in a whole new light. This is difficult work, and it should be clear by now why many accusations of 'mysticism' and 'obscurantism' have been thrown at Heidegger and his various followers over the years, but I hope it's clear by now that while his work is difficult, it's not nonsensical. A close reading of his work, with careful attention not to just to what he's saying but *why* and what led him various points, can offer up new pathways for thinking through certain problems. Sometimes what appeared to be a commonsense position is revealed to be a dead-end down the road, while a well-placed bush or boulder was covering a much more helpful trail.

But Heidegger isn't just interested in taking various paths to various clearings, but thinking about how it is we navigate pathways themselves, how we find ourselves following certain paths at the expense of others, or perhaps end up in a clearing that goes nowhere, and with no idea how we got here. As such, he's not simply providing us with a map, but a guide to hiking itself, the ways in which one foot gets put in front of the other, gets

60. Heidegger, *Being and Time*, 38.
61. Heidegger, *Being and Time*, 38-9.

caught on a root or loose stone. In the words of Taylor Carmen, "phenomenology consists precisely in letting the ordinarily *unseen* dimensions of what is seen *be seen*. And such *letting be seen* is an ineluctably interpretive or *hermeneutic* effort."[62]

It's my hope that this book, while often taking seemingly strange detours, will eventually get us somewhere new and more helpful for thinking about various contemporary social and political problems. It will take time, and I'll ask for patience as we work out the underlying logic of various issues, but if I am successful, it will pull through in the end.

62. Carman, "The Principle of Phenomenology," 101.

Chapter 2—**Worlds**

The moods we feel, always a part of us, are another fundamental way in which we relate to the world. We do not know
where they come from or what they mean, only that they
are always there.

—Karl Ove Knausgaard, *My Struggle Vol VI*

S o far we've set up the introductory scaffolding; now it's time to start
painting the surface. We've already unpacked how the Heideggerian
subject always finds itself *immersed* in the world around it, although a better
word for us to use would be *attuned*, or *in sync* with it's world. There are
several mechanisms by way of which this tune is produced.

Before unpacking *attunement* itself, a couple other layers deserve to be
addressed. A good place to start would be *intentionality*. At a very foundational level, Dasein exists in its surroundings not as one object among many,
nor as an external observer who sees its surroundings and formulates some
sort of abstract theorizing about them. This way of thinking about Dasein
actively covers up being-in, for "subject and Object do not coincide with
Dasein and the world."[1] Instead, Heidegger describes Dasein as being absorbed in the world, being concerned and fascinated with it.[2] Supposedly
'neutral' scientific observations, while useful in rarified instances, are a way
of 'holding-oneself-back'[3] from the world. This doesn't just go for the world
in general, but for individual entities, things. Again, Heidegger turns to the
Greek in order to rethink our relationship to the things we find ourselves
surrounded by: "The Greeks had an appropriate term for 'Things': πράγματα
[matter of concern]—that is to say, that which one has to do with in one's
concernful dealings (πρᾶξις [action])."[4] The things we encounter in our

1. Heidegger, *Being and Time*, 60.
2. Heidegger, *Being and Time*, 54 and 61.
3. Heidegger, *Being and Time*, 61.
4. Heidegger, *Being and Time*, 68.

concernful dealings he calls 'equipment', and we encounter them in a much more primordial way than we often assume. His famous hammer-example is helpful, as it points to our larger relationship with the world around us: "the less we just stare at the hammer-Thing, and the more we seize hold of it and use it, the more primordial does our relationship to it become, and the more unveiledly is it encountered as that which it is—as equipment."[5] So we don't learn about hammer's or kitchen tools or cars by staring and making observations; instead, we start hitting a nail, chopping vegetables and getting in the drivers seat to 'unveil' the things. Heidegger's 'truth-as-unconcealment' is still present, and hopefully in a more clear sense at this point; we are in a world where things are 'lit up' for us in such and such a way, so that we can properly engage with them. One might be tempted to say this leaves the world as a purely psychological phenomena, but that's not quite right. Heidegger himself was motivated to push against pyschologism, the reduction of all truth-statements being about one's psychological state-of-mind. He does want to maintain a certain amount of realism, although of a weaker sort than much modern philosophy. Instead, the world has what Heidegger calls 'totalities of significance', although one might prefer John McCumber's shorter 'script.' So the hammer and nail convey the script

1. Pick up the nail.

2. Position the nail, sharp end down, over the board.

3. Pick up the hammer with you other hand . . .

McCumber explains, "Unlike normal scripts, Heidegger's totalities of significance are usually unconscious—complexes of habits through which we move without thinking about it. Such scripts are not subjective in the sense that they are entirely in our heads; the short script above is expressed, for example, in the design and existence of such things as hammers and nails."[6] So while it is true that Heidegger isn't interested in a neutral description of the world, he isn't interested in pure psychological states either; he's interested in the way Dasein and its environment interact and feed into one another, both unsettled by the nature of the other. These sorts of scripts are a part of people as well:

> Dasein exists by taking herself to be a certain sort of person, for example, a professor. In order to fulfill this role, she must use certain tools (computers, offices, chalk, books) in certain ways. Most roles require both the Dasein to take herself to be that role

5. Heidegger, *Being and Time*, 69.
6. McCumber, *On Philosophy*, 161-2.

and others to take her to be it, or at least participate somehow; one cannot be a professor unconsciously or without the proper institutions, nor without students taking one to be a professor or in a society without an educational system. All of these factors and many more collectively make up one's world and are needed if one is to be that kind of person.[7]

Interestingly, this also leaves room for one to *fail* to be who one is. A teacher who doesn't command the respect or attention of their students, or who is simply incomprehensible to them, is in a certain way failing to be a teacher, even if they are the ones giving a lecture every class period. Being a friend or lover is a way of being with others, although one can fail to come through in the ways that make up that role. One may also at times have to choose which way they are going to be, as any young man who's been reminded that bros come before hoes can attest.

Another mechanism for attuning ourselves to our world is *language*. For Heidegger, language is connected to interpretation, which he connects back to understanding. Following Hubert Dreyfus,[8] Mark Wrathall gives us three layers to understanding: at the top, there are assertions, and at the bottom is primordial understanding, with interpretation in the middle.[9] We've already talked about understanding in regard to things like hammers; interpretation is a slightly more explicit form of understanding, such as when you can articulate why a particular hammer isn't working with a particular type of nail. When you say "This large mallet is too large to be effective for this small nail", you not only alert us to your oddly formal way of speaking, but you also demonstrate interpretation which Heidegger says is a 'development' of understanding: "In [interpretation] the understanding appropriates understandingly that which is understood by it."[10] So primordial understanding is knowing how to use a hammer, and perhaps having a 'feeling' of whether or not a particular hammer isn't suitable for the task at hand, while interpretation is making that understanding more explicit. To get to the top, assertions are then the more precise types of sentences, such as "Large mallets don't work well with small hammers." The lines can get blurry between these different layers, but what's important to note is that when we use language in our everyday lives, we are often relying on a more primordial understanding of the world around us. To return again to our

---

7. Braver, *A Thing of This World*, 172.

8. Dreyfus, *Being-in-the-World*.

9. Wrathall, "Heidegger on Human Understanding," 184.

10. Heidegger, *Being and Time*, 148.

terms from earlier, language relies on what is already unconcealed for us in a more primordial fashion, making it explicit.

In all this, language is never directly addressed until ¶34, in the wake of extended discussion of assertions and their relations to various forms of understanding. After showing that assertions are a rarified form of language, he brings it back to the more primordial everyday level, what he calls *discourse*, although one should note the German term *Rede* implies something slightly less formal, although it remains more formal than *talk*.[11] It is tempting to think that discourse might arise out of primordial understanding, but Heidegger insists they are equiprimordial. In its narrowest sense, discourse is often seen as a conversation, although it's usually intended to imply something broader. There is political discourse, which is seen as a sustained series of conversations all vaguely connected by similar topics and themes. It can span across different publications and channels, with cable news often starting segments with a "new report from the Washington Post". If one reads the original Post-story, it may cite "a new study from Harvard University", which is often seen as the foundation for the whole host of 'discourse' that will follow. People will discuss the study, as well as the way different other programs have discussed it, which will then be satirized on various satirical news shows (not to mention twitter). Discourse can also be centered on more specific things as well. There can be discourse around a particular film being released (or even a new trailer for the film). A provocative book or article can generate a discourse around it, with various people offering their takes on it.

However, Heidegger also thinks there is a broader way in which discourse operates; while it does often have objects it focuses on, there is a more general sort of discourse, an "In this more general kind of communications, the articulation of being with one another understandingly is constituted. Through it a co-state-of-mind gets 'shared', and so does the understanding of being-with."[12] This last fragment, being-with, is incredibly important for Heidegger. Common sense tells us that we are, well, ourselves, and other people are *other*. In what is by this point an almost cliché-move for Heidegger, he inverts our typical understanding of other people, and instead says that "They are rather those from whom, for the most part, one does *not* distinguish oneself—those among whom one is too."[13] Who we are, primordially and for the most part, is then largely indistinguishable from those around us. A literal example might help illustrate this concept in the

11. Heidegger, *Being and Time*, 161 note 1.

12. Heidegger, *Being and Time*, 162.

13. Heidegger, *Being and Time*, 118.

abstract. When I was younger, I was on a rowing team, and when a boat is functioning well, it becomes difficult to distinguish oneself from the rest of the boat; everyone is rowing in a highly synchronized fashion at a standard rate of 32-strokes-per-minute. Oars have to be dipped in the water at the exact same time in order to keep the boat balanced, and the stroke needs to be completed and we need to get back to the starting position at the same time as well. In the moments where an experienced team would work especially well together, you could actually feel the whole crew merge into a single unit. In cases like this, each one of us lost the *I*, the sense of 'mineness' to our being, save for instances where someone was out of sync with the rest of us. Heidegger is applying this to the whole of our lives; we experience ourselves as being-with others in various ways, including the ways we talk about certain things. We've seen this already in detail with Heidegger's reading of Greek philosophy in its original language; certain terms carry with them certain extra baggage that may not be intended but certainly can be effective in determining how we think and approach the world.

Parallel to discourse is how we as subjects situate ourselves towards it, by way of hearing and listening. Listening is a way of being-with (*Mitsein*) others. "Being-with develops in listening to one another, which can be done in several possible ways: following, going along with, and the privative modes of not-hearing, resisting, defying, and turning away."[14] These are ways of being towards our world, navigating within its designs, and it's more primordial than we often assume. "What we 'first' hear is never noises or complexes of sounds, but the creaking waggon, the motor-cycle. We hear the column on the march, the north wind, the woodpecker tapping, the fire crackling."[15] Hearing 'pure noise' is possible, but this itself is a very particular form of 'listening away', trying to abstract ourselves away from our ordinary dwelling within and alongside the world.[16]

All these mechanisms we've been discussing build up what we've already referred to as Dasein's attunement, although a better term might be mood. *Stimmung*, or *mood*, receives more attention from Heidegger than it has from most philosophers, and goes right along with the broader critique of self-transparent consciousness that defines much of *Being and Time*. Moods could be thought of as a more primordial version of a more conscious state-of-mind. He says mood is a sort of being-attuned,[17] and the original German, *Gestimmtsein*, gives us a clue to what he's actually getting

14. Heidegger, *Being and Time*, 163.
15. Heidegger, *Being and Time*, 163.
16. Heidegger, *Being and Time*, 164.
17. Heidegger, *Being and Time*, 134.

at. The word *Stimmung* actually usually refers to the tuning of an instrument, so being-attuned isn't just about the one isolated instrument or Dasein, but how that Dasein is in (or out of) sync with the rest of the world. In having or being in a mood, "Dasein is brought before its being as 'there.'"[18] Ordinarily, we only use the word mood to describe extreme variations, such as when we're especially happy or frustrated. However, Heidegger contends we always are in a mood, or have a way of being attuned to our surroundings and those around us. In a conversation among several people, for example, it's obvious when someone is sticking out of the group, making everyone else feel uncomfortable, but often we simply forget ourselves and the others *as* ourselves and the others, sinking into the conversation and forgetting everything else. This immersion is a sort of mood as well. And moods can open certain things up while closing others down: "The 'bare mood' discloses the 'there' more primordially, but correspondingly it *closes* it *off* more stubbornly than any *not*-perceiving."[19] In other words, if we're meeting someone for the first time while in a bad mood, we might notice their bad hair day or funny way of talking or interest in Bertrand Russell, and we might hold this against them. On the other hand, we might be in a particularly good mood and choose to not sweat the small stuff, giving us time to notice that there is a similar interest in seeing that new movie, leading us to exchange contact information so we can go see it next week.

It's tempting to think of moods as giving us a bias that keeps us from seeing things impartially, that "Dasein can, should, and must, through knowledge and will, become a master of its moods . . . "[20] This impartiality would only be partial, however, since "when we master a mood, we do so by way of a counter-mood; we are never free of moods."[21] And even so, this idea of (im)partiality implies a binary Heidegger is trying to push against, as Matthew Ratcliffe explains at length;

> In maintaining that moods constitute a sense of belonging to the world, Heidegger does not mean that one has a subjective state called a mood and that this somehow contributes to perception of one's spatiotemporal location in relation to other entities. To find oneself in a world is not, first and foremost, to occupy the perspective of an impartial spectator, neutrally gazing upon things from a particular space-time location. Rather, the world that we belong to is a significant realm, where things can have

18. Heidegger, *Being and Time*, 134.
19. Heidegger, *Being and Time*, 136.
20. Heidegger, *Being and Time*, 136.
21. Heidegger, *Being and Time*, 136.

a host of different practical meanings. An appreciation of these
meanings is inextricable from our actual and potential activities.
Finding oneself in the world is thus a matter of being practically
immersed in it rather than looking out upon it.[22]

Eventually, we'll discuss particular moods, but for now this description of
moods should suffice.

So to recap the story so far, Heidegger's project is a deconstruction of
the supposedly neutral subject that stands apart from the world, and is instead immersed in its surroundings, finding itself intrigued by them. And
the way the world reveals or shows itself to the subject is heavily dependent
on the subjects intentions, language and mood. The subject-object relation
is not one of neutral subjects encountering objects and listing properties to
itself about said object, but of encountering objects that are useful and useless regarding our intentions or completely broken; parts of them might
appear while others are obscured by the words we use to describe them;
the world might seem a hostile place during a moment of fear, or it might
seem welcoming when we feel safe and warm. All these add up to a way
Dasein is *tuned* like an instrument to fit in with a certain harmony produced by its surroundings. One can be 'out of tune' with their world, like
when people fail to read certain social queues, or fail to understand what
a particular tool is for. Dasein listens in on a sound (often several at once)
and produces its own tune (again, often different ones depending on their
context), trying to merge in a certain way with the sound being produced
by its surroundings. Even resistance reinforces the point Heidegger is trying to make. Trying to change the tune of the sound of one's surroundings
is still a way of responding to and navigating alongside (or against) certain
sounds. Dasein is never without a tune.

But beyond our individual experience of the world, in the wake of
Being and Time, Heidegger's thought would start moving towards broader
ways in which the world ebbs and flows, the way our experience of the world
isn't as universal as we often assume it is. Instead, the world we experience is
often dependent on various historical factors, and so are we. And it's to our
moment in history that we're going to start tuning into.

22. Ratcliffe, "Why Mood Matters," 158.

Chapter 3—**Epochs**

Where microscopes dominate our imagination, we feel that
the large wholes we deal with in everyday experiences are
mere appearances.

—MARY MIDGLEY, *THE MYTHS WE LIVE BY*

H eidegger's critique of technology that he would start to develop in the
1930's and 40's is well known, and in many respects still resonates with
us today. It's one of the places where he very directly confronts a contemporary social issue, and put in the context of the rest of his work, he's able
to offer up a diagnosis of contemporary society that goes a bit deeper than
most people. At first glance, it seems to run counter to his work on art that
he developed at around the same time, but a closer analysis of these two
themes shows that they are actually deeply intertwined, as both are connected with an underlying epistemological orientation. This chapter will then be
twofold: first, we'll look at how artworks work for Heidegger in setting up a
world, and then we'll look at what he means when he talks about us living in
a more 'technologically oriented' society. This will bring us to the end of part
I of the book, and from there we'll start applying his theories to our situation
in the early 21st century. Things will be significantly less abstract from there,
so just know that there's a light at the end of this tunnel.

Heidegger's middle period, generally considered to have started
shortly after *Being and Time* was finished and to have ended somewhere in
the 1940's,[1] saw him make a number of shifts, conceptually and themati-
cally as well as stylistically. While *Being and Time* does have some difficult

1. Early scholarship on Heidegger divided him only into an early and late period,
but as more work has been done on his later work, more precision has been needed.
While the lines between these periods are hazy, I generally follow Andrew Mitchell's
division of a "tripartite periodization of Heidegger's work: early (1912-1932, culminat-
ing in *Being and Time*, 1927), middle (1933-1944, centering on the *Contributions to
Philosophy*, 1936-1938), and late or 'post-war' (1945-1976, taking its orientation from
Insight into That Which Is (1949)." (Mitchell, *The Fourfold*, 6)

phrasing, it is a fairly organized text, with each section jumping off the last, and terms being defined and elaborated upon. His middle and late period, however, are characterized by being even more esoteric, at times reading as much like a religious-mystical text as a philosophical one. *Being* starts being spelled *beyng*, and we are told we need to learn to release ourselves into some ambiguous event. Underlying all this is an increasing sense of urgency in his writing, a sense of impending . . . something. Disaster? Salvation? Both? It can be difficult to tell, and it gets more disturbing when one bears in mind that this was during his time with the Nazi Party, which he joined and for a time actively supported. The connection between his politics and his philosophy has always been difficult to prove, but also hard to completely deny as well, and the recent publication of his *Black Notebooks*, where Jews are mentioned much more explicitly, has only reignited a series of old debates. While this won't be the place to discuss his politics in depth, it always needs to be kept in the background as we discuss the themes and threads that run throughout his work.

One of the key themes he would start to bring up is how worlds take place in history. The totality of significations, the ways things all appear and hang together, isn't the same for everyone at all times. Instead, different people in different times and places experience different worlds, even though they occupy the same earth. This comes to the forefront especially prominently in his essay 'The Origin of the Work of Art', first developed and presented in the mid 1930's.[2]

Heidegger's understanding of art stands apart from a number of other theories of art, developing what Iain Thomson calls a "post-aesthetic thinking about the work of art."[3] This actually fits with the rest of Heidegger's project we've been learning about; his deconstruction of the traditional subject/object relation in which subjects stand apart from objects and observe them, conceptualizing them in various ways. Instead, Heidegger wants to think about our experience with art as it happens during our immersion in the more fleshed out being-in-the-world he's already developed, and this means returning the question of *aletheia*, truth as unconcealment. He famously takes the example by Van Gogh of some peasant shoes. Like the hammer from *Being and Time*, the peasant shoes are not thought of as one object among many, but as equipment that shows up in a particular world: "The peasant woman wears her shoes in the field. Only here are they what they

2. The main essay was first presented in 1935, although a later note was added in 1956. I'll be using the edition available in *Poetry, Language, Thought*, although it was originally published in the translated anthology *Off The Beaten Track*, and can also be found in the *Basic Writings* anthology among many others.

3. Thomson, *Heidegger, Art and Postmodernity*, 42.

are. They are all the more genuinely so, the less the peasant woman thinks about the shoes while she is at work, or looks at them at all, or is even aware of them. She stands and walks in them. That is how shoes actually serve. It is in this process of the use of equipment that we must actually encounter the character of equipment."[4] And when we gaze at Van Goh's painting long enough, the whole context of the boots starts to come into focus.

> From the dark opening of the worn insides of the worn insides of the shoes the toilsome tread of the worker stares forth. In the stiffly rugged heaviness of the shoes there is the accumulated tenacity of her slow trudge through the far-spreading and ever-uniform furrows of the field swept by a raw wind. On the leather lie the dampness and richness of the soil. Under the soles slides the loneliness of the field-path as evening falls. In the shoes vibrates the silent call of the earth, its quiet gift of the ripening grin and its unexplained self-refusal in the fallow desolation of the wintry field. This equipment is pervaded by uncomplaining anxiety as to the certainty of bread, the wordless joy of having once more withstood want, and trembling before the impending childbed and shivering at the surrounding menace of death.[5]

What the painting does if it does its job well is it brings us into the world of the woman who wears these boots. We can feel the combination of sweat and water soaking her feet throughout the day, the slipperiness of the mud as she wanders around after a heavy rain. We can feel the fatigue across the long hours and the numb satisfaction after a hard day's work as she rests in front of the fire. But this equipmental character is experienced by the peasant without her actually realizing it, "she knows all this without noticing or reflecting."[6] She experiences her world without needing to reflect on it. What the work does for us is brings us to her level of understanding, to experience the world as she does, with all the physical and emotional sensations that come along with it. "Van Gogh's painting is the disclosure of what the equipment, the pair of peasant shoes, *is* in truth. This entity emerges into the unconcealedness of its being."[7] Art then is not about correspondence, for Heidegger; the accuracy of a painting to reality, impressive as it may be, isn't the basis on whether a work works or not as a work of art. Instead, it's a 'gathering', which he gets from the Greek word *sumballein*, or a symbol, although he translates it as a 'bringing together'. "In the work of

4. Heidegger, "The Origin of the Work of Art," 32.
5. Heidegger, "The Origin of the Work of Art," 33.
6. Heidegger, "The Origin of the Work of Art," 33.
7. Heidegger, "The Origin of the Work of Art," 35.

art something other is brought together with the thing that is made . . . The work is a symbol."[8] This is how he includes various other forms of art, such as architecture, which tend to not 'represent' some reality already there. Instead, in his example of a Greek temple, "It is the temple-work that first fits together and at the same time gathers around itself the unity of those paths and relations in which birth and death, disaster and blessing, victory and disgrace, endurance and decline acquire the shape of destiny for human being. The all-governing expanse of this open relational context is the world of this historical people. Only from and in this expanse does the nation first return to itself for the fulfillment of its vocation."[9] He continues,

> Standing there, the building rests on the rocky ground. This resting of the work draws up out of the rock the mystery of that rock's clumsy yet spontaneous support. Standing there, the building holds its ground against the storm raging above it and so first makes the storm itself manifest in its violence. The luster and gleam of the stone, though itself apparently glowing only by the grace of the sun, yet first brings to light the light of the day, the breadth of the sky, the darkness of the night. The temple's firm towering makes visible the invisible space of air. The steadfastness of the work contrasts with the surge of the surf, and its own repose brings out the raging of the sea. Tree and grass, eagle and bull, snake and cricket first enter into their distinctive shapes and thus come to appear as what they are. The Greeks early called this emerging and rising in itself and in all things *phusis*. It clears and illuminates, also, that on which and in which man bases his dwelling. We call this ground earth.[10]

So even in works that are not 'representations' something is still 'shown' to us. The temple makes the violence of the world all the more apparent, the way it stands against the storm both in triumphant resilience and trepidation. This brings us back to the classical Greek world, which is defined by individual mythic heroes standing against larger natural and divine forces well beyond their control. Reading the poems of Hesiod or Homer, for example, one finds a view of life that is in many ways somewhat pessimistic, with gods frequently toying with the lives of mortals at a whim, and with mortals simply holding on for dear life as fate tosses them about. As with Van Gogh's painting, the temple brings us into another world, shows us a different way of seeing things than we're used to.

8. Heidegger, "The Origin of the Work of Art," 19.
9. Heidegger, "The Origin of the Work of Art," 41.
10. Heidegger, "The Origin of the Work of Art," 41.

The struggle set forth by the temple, between architecture and nature, is echoed in the struggle between the peasant farmer and the ground she works on. This is actually crucial for Heidegger's understanding of what art does, since art sets forth a strife between two elements, world and earth. But aren't these two the same thing? Not here. We've already seen how *world* is to be understood in terms of our experiences and intentions, the way we navigate and understand our surroundings. It's the whole of what is unconcealed for us. *Earth*, then, "is that whence the arising brings back and shelters everything that arises without violation."[11] What does he mean by this? Well, as we've seen, art brings things into unconcealment, brings us into a new vision of the world. It shows us the material in a new light, causing it "to come forth for the very first time and to come into the Open of the work's world."[12] This is how Heidegger's theory of art is connected to his earlier work; it is less about a subject encountering an object and judging it to be some degree of beautiful or ugly, but instead about a subject's immersion in a particular understanding of the world, revealing and showing the world to the subject.

But in this revealing that art does, something always holds back. That something is the earth. He writes

> The world is the self-disclosing openness of the broad paths of the simple and essential decisions in the destiny of an historical people. The earth is the spontaneous forthcoming of that which is continually self-secluding and to that extent sheltering and concealing. World and earth are essentially different from one another and yet are never separated. The world grounds itself on the earth, and earth juts through the world. But the relation between world and earth does not wither away into the empty unity of opposites unconcerned with one another. The world, in resting upon the earth, strives to surmount it. As self-opening it cannot endure anything closed. The earth, however, as sheltering and concealing, tends always to draw the world into itself and keep it there.[13]

What Heidegger is drawing our attention to is the way art doesn't simply give us the world. Instead, in art, something is always pulling back, refusing to be totally disclosed. Van Gogh's painting is especially illustrative in this regard:

---

11. Heidegger, "The Origin of the Work of Art," 41.

12. Heidegger, "The Origin of the Work of Art," 45.

13. Heidegger, "The Origin of the Work of Art," 47.

If, following Heidegger, one attends long enough to the 'nothing surrounding this pair of farmers shoes,' meditating (with sufficient patience and care) on the 'undefined space' in Van Gogh's painting—the strange space that surrounds these shoes like an underlying and yet also enveloping atmosphere—one can notice that inchoate forms begin to emerge from the background but never quite take a firm shape; in fact, these shapes tend to disappear when one tries to pin them down. The background of the painting not only inconspicuously supports the foreground image of the shoes but, when we turn our attention to this ordinarily inconspicuous background, we can see that it continues to offer up other inchoate shapes that resist being firmly gestalted themselves.[14]

This is the strife that are sets up, showing something, but not everything. Anyone who's ever tried writing a poem or simply describing a rather intense or strange experience will be familiar with this; every word you use may come close, but never *quite* gets at what you're trying to express. This pulling back is the earth.

Heidegger doesn't see this limitation as a negative, however. In fact, it's one of the most interesting elements of being human, the inability to totally describe and understand it. It's this limitation that generates openness to new possibilities or alternative ways of thinking about something. Talk with your friends about a sufficiently complicated film and you'll likely get a few different thoughts and interpretations, even if everyone agrees that it's good.

Also noteworthy is the way in which Van Gogh's background is what pushes the shoes forward and makes them visible in the way that they are. They appear in a small patch of light against a dark background, but the darkness makes the shoes shine all the brighter in a small clearing of light. The word *clearing* is especially important for Heidegger. It appears in *Being and Time*, but here it comes forward to greater importance. The German word for clearing, *lichtung*, actually contains the German word for *light*, *licht*, so a clearing is more literally a place where things are illuminated, or in earlier terminology, unconcealed as in *aletheia*, connecting art further to Heidegger's Greek theory of truth, although it also connects all this back to the peasant shoes. Thomson explains:

> Here Heidegger has set up a genuine aporia—or better, an *Holzweg*, a 'forest path' or, more colloquially, a 'a path to nowhere.' It is not a coincidence that *Holzweg* is the title Heidegger gave to the book of essays that opens with 'The Origin of the Work

14. Thomson, *Heidegger, Art and Postmodernity*, 86-7.

of Art.' As Heidegger hints (in the otherwise empty page he had inserted into the book, before its first page), an *Holzweg* is a path through the woods made by foresters (and known to backwoods hikers as well as to the locals who follow these paths to gather their own firewood, as Heidegger himself did). Such a path eventually comes to an apparent dead-end, but this dead-end—seen differently—turns out to be a 'clearing' (or *Lichtung*) that is, a place in the forest from which the trees have been removed. Such a clearing thus offers an unexpected vista, an epiphany that, although it results only from walking a particular path for oneself, can nevertheless seem to come from out of the middle of nowhere.[15]

So in this particular work of art, Heidegger is trying to draw our attention to a number of things at once. The woman who wears the shoes wrestles to draw crops from the earth while Van Gogh as a painter wrestles to pull that woman's experience of being-in-the-world into disclosure, and in both cases, something will come forward while something else will hold back, such as when a crop fails to grow well or the color scheme isn't quite right. And then on top of all this, in looking at the work of art, we are then trying to draw some sort of meaning out of it, but the shadows both literally and figuratively refuse total disclosure. This is the essential strife Heidegger is talking about, and it applies on a number of levels, from art criticism to world navigation. Our world exists as a sort of clearing where things are 'lit up' in a number of ways, but there are also shadows that hold some things and possibilities back. And this isn't a fault, but instead a constitutive element of the human experience, to see some possibilities while missing others, to occupy a world where some things are readily apparent and others 'unthinkable.' But this illumination isn't just of things, but what Hubert Dreyfus calls the 'style' of a culture, a normally invisible set of behaviors and practices people carry out.[16] How we interact with our world has a certain style, one that becomes more apparent when we meet people from a different country, or even a different family. Meal times can be moments of both comfort in the familiar or confusion in something totally new. Whether or not you pray before a meal, sit at a table or in front of a TV, eat a home-cooked meal or go to a restaurant all reflect various styles, some traditional and others more modern or cosmopolitan. All this begs the question, however, what sort of world do we inhabit? What sorts of styles are we practicing? By nature, they would generally be invisible to us, invisible patterns of practice and thought that are

15. Thomson, *Heidegger, Art and Postmodernity*, 83.
16. Dreyfus, "Heidegger's Ontology of Art," 409.

so easy to navigate that they seem like commonsense, with other possibilities being closed off. It's to this topic that we now turn.

In the last pages of the art essay, Heidegger takes a brief look at Hegel's comments regarding art in the modern world, saying that art may not work for us in the modern age anymore.[17] There are a number of reasons to take this idea seriously, but for now it's worth turning to his thoughts on technology, which were in their early stages at the time his art essay was first published. Technology was actually a fairly common theme of discussion in Germany at the time,[18] and in line with many of his contemporaries and his other work, his reference point is Greek thought and terminology. References to technology can be found throughout his work in the 1930's, dotting his *Black Notebooks* and receiving several sections in his *Contributions to Philosophy*, a collection of fragments, aphorisms and paragraphs written from 1936-8, but his most famous statements on the topic took form of several essays appearing in the late 1930's and into the 1940's and 1950's. "The Question Concerning Technology", first presented in 1949 and then expanded in subsequent editions and publications,[19] is arguably the most important essay on the topic, and like his essay on art, contains some somewhat esoteric language that can obscure the underlying coherence.

As usual, his method is more cautious and meditative. The opening paragraph sets up a disruption of our expectations:

> In what follows we shall be *questioning* concerning technology. Questioning builds a way. We would be advised, therefore, above all to pay heed to the way, and not to fix our attention on isolated sentences and topics. The way is a way of thinking. All ways of thinking, more or less perceptibly, lead through language in a manner that is extraordinary. We shall be questioning concerning *technology*, and in so doing we should like to prepare a free relationship to it. The relationship will be free if it opens our human existence to the essence of technology. When we can respond to this essence, we shall be able to experience the technological within its own bounds.[20]

To unpack this a bit, Heidegger's goal in this essay is to get beyond our common assumptions about technology and achieve a free relationship, one without presuppositions, to the essence of technology. Heidegger's

17. Heidegger, "The Origin of the Work of Art," 78.

18. Greif, *The Age of the Crisis of Man*, 47-51.

19. I'll be using the edition in the short anthology *The Question Concerning Technology*, although this essay can also be found in the *Basic Writings* as well.

20. Heidegger, "The Question Concerning Technology," 3-4.

understanding of *essence* is a bit different than one might assume. The German term for essence, *die Wesen*, is quite close to *die Wesung*, or *essential occurrence. Wesen* is literally *to endure*.[21] Essence then is about the core of what is happening or being done, rather than the core of a thing that *then* acts or does. This even applies to the Dasein of *Being and Time*, which "finds 'itself' proximally and for the most part in *what* it does, uses, expects, avoids . . . "[22] Essence is then how something shows itself, a dynamic unfolding rather than a static presence. And with his thoughts on technology, as with art, Heidegger is less interested in the object and more how it orients us and our perception of our surrounding world.

Returning to some Greek themes we learned in the first lesson, Heidegger draws our attention to the word *uberlegen*, 'to consider carefully'. In Greek, this is *legein* or *logos*,[23] which as we saw in the first chapter is connected with bringing things into view, showing them.[24] He also connects *legein* to *apophainesthai*, bringing forward into appearance,[25] which he also connects to the Greek *poiesis*, bringing-forth.[26] This should all be familiar to us by now; Heidegger's trying to draw attention to the way in which our experience of the world is about particular ways of revealing affect the world, how our intentions, language and mood affect how something is brought forward. We also saw how art is a bringing-forward, an illumination of invisible elements of our world, a wrestling with reality to bring it into disclosure. At this point, however, many might pause and ask

> But where have we strayed to? We are questioning concerning technology, and we have arrived now at *aletheia*, at revealing. What has the essence of technology to do with revealing? The answer: everything. For every bringing-forth is grounded in revealing. Bringing-forth, indeed, gathers within itself the four modes of occasioning—causality—and rules them throughout. Within its domain belong end and means, belongs instrumentality. Instrumentality is considered to be the fundamental characteristic of technology. If we inquire, step by step, into what technology, represented as means, actually is, then we shall arrive at revealing. The possibility of all productive manufacturing lies in revealing.[27]

21. Heidegger, "The Question Concerning Technology," 9 note 7.
22. Heidegger, *Being and Time*, p. 119
23. Heidegger, "The Question Concerning Technology," 8.
24. Heidegger, *Being and Time*, 33.
25. Heidegger, "The Question Concerning Technology," 8.
26. Heidegger, "The Question Concerning Technology," 10.
27. Heidegger, "The Question Concerning Technology," 12.

He goes on to say that "Technology is therefore no mere means. Technology is a way of revealing."[28] This will likely seem strange to some, but he does back this up with his usual etymological deconstruction. The Greek word for technology, *technikon*, he connects to *techne*. Two points are drawn from this. First, "*techne* is the name not only for the activities and skills of the craftsman, but also for the arts of the mind and the fine arts. *Techne* belongs to bringing-forth, to *poiesis*; it is something poietic."[29] The terminology here should remind us of how poetry and art work; in every instance, one wrestles to bring something forward, although it resists total disclosure. There's an epistemological tug-of-war that constitutes how we navigate and try to understand our world, using the means we have at our disposal to bring things forward. This gets further developed in his second point, that "*techne* is linked with the word *episteme*. Both words are names for knowing in the widest sense."[30] He also connects *techne* to *aletheuein*,[31] bringing all this back to truth-as-unconcealment. This is all stuff we've seen demonstrated already however, both in *Being and Time* and "The Origin of the Work of Art"; a subject that knows things based on how they are revealed and brought forward, made visible in a clearing of intelligibility. But what's he getting at? If we remind ourselves that Heidegger is here inquiring regarding the essence of technology, the way it unfolds, it becomes clear that he's setting us up to see the way technology reveals the world, the way it "comes to presence [*West*] in the realm where revealing and unconcealment take place, where *aletheia*, truth, happens."[32]

But does this idea of technology still hold up today? Modern technology is fundamentally different compared to the classical Greek sort. Heidegger doesn't deny this, but he's trying to prepare us to see *how* it is different, by pointing to technology as a way of revealing the world. Modern technology also is a way of revealing, but of a different sort; "the revealing that holds sway throughout modern technology does not unfold into a bringing-forth in the sense of *poiesis*. The revealing that rules in modern technology is a challenging [*Herausfordern*],[33] which puts to

28. Heidegger, "The Question Concerning Technology," 12.

29. Heidegger, "The Question Concerning Technology," 13.

30. Heidegger, "The Question Concerning Technology," 13.

31. Heidegger, "The Question Concerning Technology," 13.

32. Heidegger, "The Question Concerning Technology," 13.

33. A note from the translator is worth recreating here: "*Herausfordern* means to challenge, to call forth or summon to action, to demand positively, to provoke. It is composed of the verb *fordern* (to demand, to summon, to challenge) and the adverbial prefixes *her-* (hither) and *aus-* (out). The verb might be rendered very literally as 'to demand out hither.' The structural similarity between *herausfordern* and *her-vor-bringen*

nature the unreasonable demand that it supply energy that can be extracted and stored as such."[34] He continues to unpack the implications of this
transition from *hervorbringen* (bringing forth) and *herausfordern* (challenging forth) with a number of examples:

> a tract of land is challenged into the putting out of coal and ore.
> The earth now reveals itself as a coal mining district, the soil as
> a mineral deposit. The field that the peasant formerly cultivated
> and set in order appears differently than it did when to set in
> order still meant to take care of and to maintain. The work of
> the peasant does not challenge the soil of the field. In the sow-
> ing of the grain it places the seed in the keeping of the forces
> of growth and watches over its increase. But meanwhile even
> the cultivation of the field has come under the grip of another
> setting-in-order, which *sets* upon nature. It sets upon it in the
> sense of challenging it. Agriculture is now the mechanized food
> industry. Air is now set upon to yield nitrogen, the earth to yield
> ore, ore to yield uranium, for example; uranium is set upon to
> yield atomic energy, which can be released either for destruc-
> tion or for peaceful use.[35]

It is tempting to say this is alarmism over nothing, that Heidegger is simply
an old man struggling to get with the times, and a thread of nostalgia can be
detected throughout much of his writings. However, quick dismissal misses
the deeper point he's trying to make. The problem he has with modern technology is not that it's getting more efficient or precise. Instead, he's trying to
connect the increased precision to the way we think about and see the world.
Technology as *techne*, connected to both *poiesis* and *episteme*, bring-forth
and knowing, is a way of knowing the world, forcing it forward with a level
of precision not allowed by a more artistic or poetic bringing-forth, which
is why it's a *challenging* forth, a demand. And this style changes the world
itself, which 'now reveals itself as' a pile of mere resources and products
waiting to be extracted. Even single parts of the world are fundamentally
changed by our intentions and frameworks used to bring it into disclosure.
One of Heidegger's classic examples is the Rhine River.

(to bring forth hither) is readily apparent. It serves of itself to point up the relation
subsisting between the two modes of revealing of which the verbs speak—modes that,
in the very distinctive ways peculiar to them, occasional a coming forth into unconcealment and presencing." Heidegger, "The Question Concerning Technology," 14 note 13.

34. Heidegger, "The Question Concerning Technology," 14.

35. Heidegger, "The Question Concerning Technology," 14-5.

> The hydroelectric plant is set into the current of the Rhine. It sets the Rhine to supplying its hydraulic pressure, which then sets the turbines turning. This turning sets those machines in motion whose thrust sets going the electric current for which the long-distance power station and its network of cables are set up to dispatch electricity. In the context of the interlocking processes pertaining to the orderly disposition of electrical energy, even the Rhine itself appears as something at our command. The hydroelectric plant is not built into the Rhine River as was the old wooden bridge that joined bank with bank for hundreds of years. Rather the river is damned up into the power plant. What the river is now, namely, a water power supplier derives from out of the essence of the power station. In order that we may even remotely consider the monstrousness that reigns here, let us ponder for a moment the contrast that speaks out of the two titles, 'The Rhine' as damned up into the *power* works, and 'The Rhine' as uttered out of the *art* work, in Holderlin's hymn by that name. But, it will be replied, the Rhine is still a river in the landscape, is it not? Perhaps. But how? In no other way than as an object on call for inspection by a tour group ordered there by the vacation industry.[36]

The world now appears as something to be used for various odds and ends, a pile of mere resources on call to be used whenever it's convenient for us. The resistance that the world offered up in artistic disclosure, that allowed things to come forward as meaningful in a particular way is gone. Worldly disclosure, the backgrounds and contexts that once made things what they were for us can't offer resistance to modern technology.

And people are not kept from this process as well. Heidegger's concern is that this sort of thinking slowly becomes pervasive, applying not just to thinking about crop yields and electric grids, but people as well, who find themselves treated as 'standing-reserve':

> The current talk about human resources, about the supply of patients for a clinic, gives evidence of this. The forester who, in the wood, measures the felled timber and to all appearances walks the same forest path in the same way as did his grandfather is today commanded by profit-making in the lumber industry, whether he knows it or not. He is made subordinate to the orderability of cellulose, which for its part is challenged forth by the need for paper, which is then delivered to newspapers and illustrated magazines. The latter, in their turn, set public opinion

---

36. Heidegger, "The Question Concerning Technology," 16.

to swallowing what is printed, so that a set configuration of opinion becomes available on demand. Yet precisely because man is challenged more originally than are the energies of nature, i.e., into the process of ordering, he never is transformed into mere standing-reserve. Since man drives technology forward, he takes part in ordering as a way of revealing. But the unconcealment itself, within which ordering unfolds, is never a human handiwork, any more than is the realm through which man is already passing every time he as a subject relates to an object.[37]

People are here turned into single nodes on a larger grid of various layers of data. 'How much energy can we get from this river?' conflicts with questions of 'Will this ruin it for the tourism industry?' The river doesn't have any value in itself; it's a series of contesting sets of numbers, and deciding which is more 'valuable'.

An objection alluded to earlier was that Heidegger is simply a grumpy old man annoyed about the 'kids these days' with their fancy television sets and radios, taking fancy trips on their fancy airplanes, while he continues to chop his own firewood in his cabin.[38] This is to miss the point of his objection. Heidegger is not opposed to precision in all cases; when I hire an architect or visit a doctor, I want them to be precise when deciding how much weight a building can hold and how much medicine to prescribe me. The problem is that this form of thinking can come to dominate areas where it's inappropriate. People not only think about isolated subjects in this more precise way, but start to think about everything, including themselves in such a fashion, and this doesn't need to be the intention on the subject's part. Remember, intentionality has a certain *un*intentionality to it; we're always already caught up in a collection of social and linguistic practices we carry out without ever thinking about it. "Wherever man opens his eyes and ears, unlocks his heart, and gives himself over to meditating and striving, shaping and working, entreating and thanking, he finds himself everywhere already brought into the unconcealed."[39] The danger of technological thinking is that we're starting to see everything in these overly reductive terms.

37. Heidegger, "The Question Concerning Technology," 18.

38. Heidegger actually made his own cabin, to which he'd often retreat to take long walks through the forest (all the metaphors about pathways of thinking and clearings make more sense when this is borne in mind) and was often visited there by guests, including Hans-George Gadamer, Jurgen Habermas and Terrence Malick. This has contributed, for both better and worse, to the image of an isolated mystic living in the woods who avoided the public whenever possible (Caputo, "A Commentary," 45), an image some have denounced as inaccurate.

39. Heidegger, "The Question Concerning Technology," 18-9.

To bring this chapter to a close, let's look at the intersection between art and technology in Heidegger's thought. Obviously, the two seem to point in opposite directions, with art wrestling with the world to bring it into disclosure, but leaving some of it hidden. It allows for a certain amount of mystery to be left, and enables us to occupy a meaningful clearing. Technology doesn't allow for such a clearing; instead, it cuts down the whole forest, which simultaneously allows us to see further while also ruining the view.

However, it should also be noted that Heidegger's critical analysis the two are rooted in the same frameworks that he developed in *Being and Time*. Art reveals the truth as *aletheia*, as "the unconcealedness of beings"[40] while technology also "comes to presence in the realm where revealing and unconcealment take place, where *aletheia*, truth, happens."[41] *Aletheia* is elsewhere connected with *techne* as "a mode of knowing . . . to have seen, in the widest sense of seeing, which means to apprehend what is present, as such."[42] *Techne* is also related to *episteme*; "Both words are names for knowing in the widest sense."[43] What becomes clear in reading these two essays is that the underlying question Heidegger is getting at is that our knowledge of things has a certain *way* about it, or what Dreyfus calls a *style*, and different worlds at different times and places have different styles. The work of art "doesn't merely *reflect* the style of a culture; it *glamorizes* it and so enables those in the culture to see it and to understand themselves and their shared world in its light . . . the temple opened a world for the Greeks by articulating their style. The Greeks' practices were gathered together and focused by the temple so that they saw nature and themselves in the light of the temple. Everything looked different once the style was articulated."[44] Great art of any period gathers together the various implicit beliefs and practices and renders them visible; the various ways of *knowing* and *seeing* are brought to light in a work of art. But technology is also a style, and while it may have brought us forward in some ways, it harbors danger in others. Two are worth pointing out.

The first is that the technological view will start to be applied inappropriately, as Albert Borgmann summarizes: "the scientific view, due to its prominence, obscures the moral and poetical force of nature. It follows that technology in its broad epochal sense is the temperament of an era that enables humans to grasp the lawful mathematical structure of nature and

40. Heidegger, "The Origin of the Work of Art," 49.

41. Heidegger, "The Question Concerning Technology," 13.

42. Heidegger, "The Origin of the Work of Art," 57.

43. Heidegger, "The Question Concerning Technology," 13.

44. Dreyfus, "Heidegger's Ontology of Art," 410-11.

that gives that structure a prominent, perhaps an unduly important, place in its culture."[45] Due to its precision, it is tempting to think that such precision makes it superior to other ways of thinking about things. The increasing emphasis on scientific education at the expense of various humanities is evidence of this, as well as thinking of cost-benefit analysis at times where it's simply inappropriate, or other moral frameworks are required to make difficult decisions. Heidegger's concern is that in thinking in overly systematic terms, we may be losing sight of what it is that makes us human, the ways we occupy meaningful clearings, navigate and inhabit worlds and engage with one another. We may also lose our sense of history as we forget that other worlds once existed, and that those who occupied them might have had other ways of seeing things. As someone who minored in art history in college, one thing that those lectures gave me was a much richer sense of the variety of worlds people can occupy, the multiple ways a single thing can be understood, practiced and expressed. Technology doesn't have variable styles; it asks to see the data, and it forgets the rest.

The second danger Heidegger sees is the way technological ways of seeing things might not simply be a passing phase; it might come to close off the very possibility of opening up new pathways, new forms of disclosure. In forgetting that we are by nature unconcealing beings, we may lose sight of the fact that technological precision isn't always the best way to approach things, or that it's the only way since *we may come to forget that it's a way at all.* The danger is that "our conception of *all* entities will be brought permanently into line"[46] with no resistance or alternatives possible. We've thus far been developing an account, in the abstract of the subject who attunes itself to a certain sound or background noise. What Heidegger's account of art gives us is a sense of how certain background noises are developed and take place, with some coming in and out of style at various times and places. What his account of technology adds to this is that we are being anesthetized to sound, taught to hear a single, perfectly timed rhythm, unable to be challenged by new sounds that might otherwise help us hear the world anew. And this will have consequences, many of which we are starting to see emerge. It's to this we now turn.

45. Borgmann, "Technology," 427.
46. Thomson, *Heidegger on Ontotheology*, 57.

Chapter 4 — **Brave New Clearing**

His work was, in its way, religious and, so far as he knew, unquestioning.

—THOMAS MANN, *THE MAGIC MOUNTAIN*

Heidegger's concern with our domination by a technological approach to existence would seem to lend itself to much of the discourse around subjectivity in late capitalism, and some such as Bernard Stiegler and Peter Sloterdijk have done so. A rather obvious connection seems to exist between Heidegger's techne-fied subject and what is often referred to as *Homo Economicus*, a subject driven to use rational means for the sake of accumulation. Heidegger's own critique of technology would naturally lend itself to this sort of project, finding itself in line with a number of other attempts to deconstruct the hyper-rationalized subject of late capitalism.[1] However, *Homo Economicus* has only been a part of the story, and the benefit of following along with Heidegger thus far is that we're in a position to think about the way people find themselves 'tuned in' to a certain world that *Homo Economicus* is believed to be impervious to, in its most extreme or idealized form. However, Heidegger's Dasein is much more enmeshed in its world, not simply standing apart from it but immersed in it, and always in a particular way with a particular set of affects and aspirations that open things up. It's with that in mind that I'll be offering up a modified vision of subjectivity under late capitalism, which we'll call *Homo Economartist*, a subject imbued at its core with a very particular desire; the desire to work!

To do this, we'll take Heidegger's claim seriously that works of art can help 'ground' a new sort of world and attendant set of subjects, establishing a particular paradigm for thinking about oneself and acting in such-and-such a way. Contra Heidegger, however, we'll expand our notion of what sorts of works are worth studying. Heidegger's idealism led him to believe

---

1. See for example Brown, *Undoing the Demos*; McCumber, *The Philosophy Scare*, ch. 3.

that the history of being was a history of various metaphysical systems, usually elaborated on in lengthy tomes. While this is *a* way of reading history, it neglects the force of everyday idle talk, much of which is carried through via news programs, blockbuster movies and novels, all of which can (unintentionally) carry a lot of philosophical weight that deserves unloading. It's with that in mind that we turn to Ayn Rand.

Rand is a somewhat odd figure in contemporary culture. Revered by some and despised by others, how you respond to her work will often say more about you than the work itself, and while I comfortably sit more closely to the 'despise' end of the spectrum, I do think reading her work is worthwhile, if only because it can tell us a lot about the world we inhabit. A close look at some of her life and work should make this apparent, and provide an entryway in talking about certain attitudes, particularly towards work and subjectivity, over the last several decades. In her 1943 novel *The Fountainhead*, Rand tells the story of Howard Roark, a daring architect who goes past all conventions to design a variety of buildings that are so unconventional that he even gets kicked out of the Architectural School of the Stanton Institute of Technology. In a scene early in the book, Roark talks with the Dean, who offers him a last chance to stay on board. Roark turns the offer down, saying he's not interested in simply doing what others have already done. He wants to do his own thing, follow the beat of his own drum and express himself through his architecture. The Dean isn't sure how to respond to this intense sense of independence.

"My dear fellow, who will let you?"

"That's not the point. The point is, who will stop me?"[2]

In spite of his boldness, Roark is let go without a degree, but it doesn't matter. He has no intention of working for one of the big firms that wants to see a fancy degree; he instead wants to go work for Henry Cameron, a washed up old architect who'd once been known for his experimental ambition, but is now seen as a laughingstock. By time Roark gets to Cameron, the old man is running a shabby office that pays poorly and hardly gets any commissions. Cameron is rude and often drunk, but Roark manages to get a job. Roark only makes enough money to rent a leaky apartment in the city, working long hours in exchange for poverty and abuse at the hands of his boss.

This is in stark contrast to his old college housemate Peter Keating, who graduates with honors and is offered a job right out of the gate at Francon and Heyer, one of the biggest and most prestigious architectural firms in the country. Keating isn't nearly as inventive as Roark, but he's far more

---

2. Rand, *The Fountainhead*, 11.

interested in the prestige of the job, perfectly happy to kiss ass and follow trends, and it does pay off. Keating gets the prestige and fame he desires while Roark slaves away in obscurity.

It's clear that for Rand, Roark is the archetypal hero, willing to stick to his own personal values rather than simply design the sorts of buildings the masses would have him do. Keating, on the other hand, seems at times to lack much of any personality at all; early in the novel, we find him wrestling with big decisions, and so he consults Roark, as well as his mother. In deciding whether or not to continue his education, or take the job Francon has offered him, his mother warns him that if he doesn't take the job, it'll simply be given to the next person in line, most likely someone named Shlinker.

"'No,'" he gulped furiously. Not Shlinker.'

'Yes,' she said sweetly. 'Shlinker.'"[3]

Keating's rise to fame set against Roark's slaving away in obscurity is then intended as a critique, although as we'll see one could easily be a bit confused what of. The isolated artist struggling against the pull of conformity is a fairly common theme, and runs throughout *The Fountainhead*, but it's always intertwined with other themes. Religion, oddly enough, comes up in a couple key moments, in spite of Rand's professed atheism. Roark himself is spoken of in near divine terms (or, depending on how you want to spin her ideology, *Ubermenschian*). Rand describes Roark's work[4] in a similar tone of praise as Giorgio Vasari might have used to discuss Michelangelo,[5] and even at one point describes it as a sort of religious expression. At one point, Roark is approached about designing a temple,

---

3. Rand, *The Fountainhead*, 24.

4. "They were sketches of buildings such as had never stood on the face of the earth. They were as the first houses built by the first man born, who had never heard of others building before him. There was nothing to be said of them, except that each structure was inevitably what it had to be. . .It was as if the buildings had sprung from the earth and from some living force, complete, unalterably right. . .not a line seemed superfluous, not a needed plane was missing. The structures were austere and simple, until one looked at them and realized what work, what complexity of method, what tension of thought had achieved the simplicity." (Rand, *The Fountainhead*, 7).

5. ". . .the most benevolent Ruler of Heaven mercifully turned His eyes towards earth, and, witnessing the hopeless quantity of such labours, the most fervid but fruitless studies, and the presumptuous opinion of men who were further from the truth than shadows from the light, He decided, in order to rid us of so many errors, to send to earth a spirit who, working alone, was able to demonstrate in every art and every profession the meaning of perfection in the art of design . . . " (Vasari, *The Lives of the Artists*, 414).

but a more openly humanist one dedicated to the human spirit in all its forms, rather than just one. Roark is hesitant at first;

> "'Mr. Stoddard, I'm afraid you've made a mistake,' he said, his voice slow and tired. 'I don't think I'm the man you want. I don't think it would be right for me to undertake it. I don't believe in God.' . . .
>
> 'That doesn't matter. You're a profoundly religious man, Mr. Roark—in your own way. I can see that in your buildings.'
>
> He wondered why Roark stared at him like that, without moving, for such a long time.
>
> 'That's true,' said Roark. It was almost a whisper."[6]

Elsewhere, Gail Wynand and Dominique Francon, characters close to Roark, discuss the almost spiritual awe they find when they see man-made projects.

> "'You've never felt how small you were when looking at the ocean.'
>
> He laughed. 'Never. Nor looking at the planets. Nor at mountain peaks. Nor at the Grand Canyon. Why should I? When I look at the ocean, I feel the greatness of man. I think of man's magnificent capacity that created this ship to conquer all that senseless space. When I look at mountain peaks, I think of tunnels and dynamite. When I look at the planets, I think of airplanes.'
>
> 'Yes. And that particular sense of sacred rapture men say they experience in contemplating nature—I've never received it from nature, only from . . . ' She stopped.
>
> 'From what?'
>
> 'Buildings,' she whispered. 'Skyscrapers.'"[7]

Later, when Wynand is talking to Roark, Wynand explains why he was hesitant to meet Roark, or any of his favorite artists.

> "'I never meet the men whose work I love. The work means too much to me. I don't want the men to spoil it. They usually do. They're an anticlimax to their own talent. You're not. I don't mind talking to you. I've told you this only because I want you to know that I respect very little in life, but I respect the things

6. Rand, *The Fountainhead*, 327-8.
7. Rand, *The Fountainhead*, 463.

in my gallery, and your buildings, and man's capacity to produce work like that. Maybe it's the only religion I've ever had.'
He shrugged. 'I think I've destroyed, perverted, corrupted just
about everything that exists. But I've never touched that.'"[8]

It should be clear by now that Rand holds personal artistic expression in very
high regard, treating it with an almost religious reverence. She also clearly
has a certain disdain for those who simply do things for attention or profit,
such as Keating, who at one point offers a somewhat drunk and rambling
antithesis to the more reverent approach to artistic expression;

"'I'll tell you if you want to know. [Roark] thinks you should take
your shoes off and kneel, when you speak of architecture. That's
what he thinks. Now why should you? Why? It's a business like
any other, isn't it? What's so damn sacred about it? Why do we
have to be all keyed up? We're only human. We want to make a
living. Why can't things be simple and easy? Why do we have to
be some sort of God-damn heroes?'"[9]

The mixing of spirituality and work isn't unique to Rand by a long stretch,
as well as the hostility towards the more sterile, bureaucratic approach of
Keating and the other major firms.

Interestingly, the very same year Rand published *The Fountainhead*
was the same year that Abraham Maslow would publish his famous essay
"A Theory of Human Motivation"[10] which gave us his famous 'hierarchy of
needs,' with the basics such as food and shelter at the bottom, and a deeper
sense of self-actualization at the top.

Full human potential was possible only if all basic needs had
already been met, and Maslow explained human activity in
terms of this basic *hierarchy of needs*. As individuals fulfill their
basic survival needs, they will naturally seek safety, then esteem,
and finally, at the apex, individuals will strive for what Maslow
dubbed *self-actualization*.[11]

While Rand naturally wouldn't have developed her novel in response to
Maslow's theories, they do clearly share similar ideas about the inherent
value of work and its relation to some deeper form of human expression.
Maslow wasn't as intentionally political as Rand was, but it's also clear that
his work did have political implications. By connecting his own theories to

8. Rand, *The Fountainhead*, 542.

9. Rand, *The Fountainhead*, 362.

10. Maslow, "A Theory of Human Motivation."

11. LoRusso, *Spirituality, Corporate Culture, and American Business*, 25.

the religious idea of 'calling' or 'vocation',[12] Maslow adjusts how we think of work: "Work appears here as self-evident, a ubiquitous aspect of human experience that transcends cultural and historical boundaries. Moreover, Maslow privileges the intrinsic rewards of work over its material benefits, and depicts the activity of work, regardless of context, as a moral good, insofar as it expresses the latent potential of an individual."[13] Work is it's own reward, and it's connected to some of the most foundational elements of our humanity, in Maslow's view. While this might appear to be self-evident and lacking in any real political implications, it actually is a rather loaded idea. LoRusso continues,

> Maslow's theory not only psychologizes work, but it presents a mode of human subjectivity that upholds cultural norms, modes of production, and political perspectives favorable of Western capitalism. . . The actualizing self reiterates capitalist norms because it translates business goals—productivity and growth—as qualities of the individual psyche. Work represents the apex of human action, and 'to prevent [actualizing individuals] from working would be as cruel a punishment as could be imagined.' Consequently, efforts to lessen the necessity for work prove to be self-defeating because they will destroy the very foundation upon which human potential rests. This logic implicitly renders leftist policies, from Social Security to National Labor Relations, particularly suspect and idealize a laissez-faire social order.[14]

Maslow's thoughts on work go hand-in-hand with Rand's; it's seen as the most fundamental element of many people's lives, the place in which they get to 'self-actualize' their innermost values and convictions. Whether Maslow intended to or not, the story he told about human nature does back up a certain political ideology and organization at the expense of alternative possibilities.

LoRusso's analysis lets us see where this attitude went in the decades following Maslow's work, especially as it co-opted the political and cultural dissent of the 1960's. A 1973 report entitled *Work in America: Report of a Special Task Force to the Secretary of Health, Education and Welfare*, managed to turn much of the dissent into a reanimated vision of free market capitalism. This was in spite of it's supposedly new age lingo about the

---

12. Language that also found heavy use in Max Weber's analysis of attitudes towards work in his *The Protestant Ethic and the Spirit of Capitalism*. See Weeks, *The Problem With Work*, ch. 1.

13. LoRusso, *Spirituality, Corporate Culture, and American Business*, 26.

14. LoRusso, *Spirituality, Corporate Culture, and American Business*, 26.

importance of fulfillment and authenticity in the face of the deadening effects of bureaucracy, which had been the main targets of various critiques
over the last couple decades.

> Work in America helped to make the counterculture safe for
> American capitalism. It acknowledged and reformulated the
> demands of protestors for existing institutions. Indeed, nearly
> a decade earlier, reform of work had been an integral compo-
> nent at the genesis of the student movements. . .Yet the report
> turned these concerns on their head, redeploying a vehement
> leftist condemnation of capitalism as its defense. Young Ameri-
> cans simply desired a return to a purer capitalism, to the kind of
> rugged individualism afforded their ancestors before the rise of
> bureaucracy and 'organization men.'[15]

This is one of the key themes of the AMC television series *Mad Men*, a show
which depicts a decade of slow-but-sure cooptation of various social and
political movements being turned into commodities. Many have accused
the show of featuring characters that fail or refuse to change, although this
is exactly the point; that by the end, all of them are in the same place that
they started, just with a new coat of paint. It's been occasionally claimed that
the women are actually the stars of the show, since they're the only ones
who grow, but the show is ambiguous here. If we take Peggy Olson to be
emblematic of the larger tale of women entering the workforce as a display
of feminism, the show clearly has mixed feelings about how we might remember and think about this. One should remember that Peggy herself
never claimed to be political; when she briefly dates a radical anti-imperialist
journalist, she tells him straight up that she doesn't see herself as political.
Her movement upward is about career ambitions, not politics, in spite of
how history might depict it retrospectively. And the show has mixed feelings
about the meaning of her success; one of the final scenes of her shows her
walking confidently into one of the top advertising agencies, sunglasses over
her eyes, cigarette dangling from her lips, and under her arm a framed poster
of a Japanese woodcut of an octopus performing oral sex on a woman who
is lying on her back. At first glance, this appears to be a depiction of femi-
nisms triumphant moment, although a lot depends on perspective here; one
could simply flip the picture sideways to get a woman being dragged into the
depths by the kraken-esque corporation (one that had recently ejected her
friend Joan when she raised a complaint about sexual harassment). Peggy

---

15. LoRusso, *Spirituality, Corporate Culture, and American Business*, 49.

might've broken the glass ceiling, but the show seems skeptical of whether 'organization women' is a large step forward.[16]

The most savage critique the show makes, however, comes at the end of the last episode. Don Draper, the main main character, has driven from New York all the way to California, and spends the last episode at a retreat on the Pacific coast, which has throughout the series been a place he often went to emotionally recover from the more stuffy businesslike New York. The retreat involves a number of people from various backgrounds, although a number are clearly from a similar place as him; middle managers who needed to get out of the office for a few days. The final scene shows him meditating on the side of a beach when an idea strikes. The next and final thing we see is the now famous 1971 hilltop ad for Coke, the implication being that he had his epiphany for the big ad while meditating there. A number of people have pointed out that characters throughout the episode were dressed in ways that can be seen in the ad, although the assimilation of various motifs goes further than this. One can think of the retreat itself as a commodification of both the religious movements such as the one Paul Kinsey joined, or the commune Roger Sterling's daughter Margaret left for. Both were attempts at a radical revision of society, now turned into a weekend retreat for 'organization men' to come take a long weekend at. In the end, all the dissent and desire for something more has been assimilated into a short tv-jingle to sell us pop. From communes to coca-cola, it's the real thing!

And yet this is where the contradiction comes in; Keating's perspective we read earlier, that architecture should simply be treated as a business without all the artistic heroics, is actually a fairly banal capitalist view that things ought to be done for profits at the expense of artistry, yet Rand claimed to be defending capitalism against other ideological forces (mostly variations of Communism) throughout her work. How do we make sense of this?

A hint may actually be found in Rand's own life. She experienced the Bolshevik revolution in Russia through the eyes of a young child, and it was at times a rather terrifying experience for her as she struggled to make sense of all the changes going on, including her father losing the pharmacy due to nationalization, as well as the workers suddenly gaining social status previously unseen. Everything was flipped upside down for the young Alissa (Ayn's childhood name), made more difficult by her young age at the time, as Lisa Duggan writes;

---

16. A more extensive discussion around 20th century transitions and debates between gender and work can be found in Weeks, *The Problem With Work*, ch. 4.

She had no framework for understanding what was happening other than the raw experience of loss. She was not aware of the injustices that motivated the Bolsheviks or the workers and peasants who supported them. She had no access to their aspirations, fantasies, and desires. All Alissa saw was resentment, envy, theft, bullying, and the exercise of illegitimate power by people who did not deserve it and could not exercise it rationally. She rewrote the vast canvas of social, economic, and political conflict underlying the Bolshevik revolution—between Russians and non-Russians, poor peasants and landowning kulaks, workers and bosses, nationalists and internationalists, Christians and Muslims, Marxists and populists—into a stark melodramatic clash between worthy individuals and the mob.[17]

It ought to be totally understandable that Rand's way of understanding the enormous changes going on around her were in overly simplistic terms. However, Duggan continues that this view of worthy individuals (such as Roark) and the mob (who clamor for Keatings) became deeply rooted; "she stuck to it and elaborated it for the rest of her life."[18]

This overly simplistic worldview of binaries would be resolidified as a coping mechanism during a rather difficult time in her life when she came to the United States and went to work in Hollywood. In the late 1920's, as films started to incorporate talking, Rand struggled to find work due to her heavy accent. What's more, she found many of her heroes to be 'box office chasers', pursuing scripts they felt they could sell rather than trying more creatively ambitious works. In other words, she was searching for a Roark in a sea of Keating's. The fact that capitalism demands profits, which narrows what sort of films can be made, apparently didn't deter Rand's love of capitalism; instead, she doubled down on her previous beliefs.

The reality of Hollywood as a land of hardscrabble business dealings that now affected her negatively dented her glittering fantasies of pure individual creative achievement. She reacted not by reorganizing her perceptions in accordance with her experience, but rather by attacking the people around her as disappointments and failures. It wasn't the dynamics of capitalism that were to blame for 'box office chasing'; instead, mediocre and morally compromised people betrayed the ideal of capitalism as the best engine of creativity.[19]

17. Duggan, *Mean Girl*, 18.
18. Duggan, *Mean Girl*, 18.
19. Duggan, *Mean Girl*, 37.

What should be increasingly clear is that for Rand, capitalism isn't a mode of production and distribution; it is much more deeply connected for her with various romantic ideas about work and creative expression. It's an affective-capitalism, not in the sense of emotional labor that many feminist critics have brought attention to, but in the sense that traditional forms of labor ought to be imbued with an affective quality or coat of paint.

The transition to neoliberalism has been connected to Rand's ideas already in the realm of economics,[20] but we can also see that it works at the level of personal subjectivity as well. As we learned with Heidegger, we always exist in a clearing of ideas, values and dispositions, and Rand's novels show that ideas about work and politics don't just work at the macro-level but at micro-levels as well. That work is seen as a form of spiritual and personal expression isn't politically neutral, and it helps us make sense of some social and political transitions that would come in the wake of the economic issues we discussed earlier.

The critique of more banal businessman such as Keating is exemplary of what sociologists Luc Boltanski and Eve Chiapello call the *artistic* critique, as opposed to a *social* one. The former emphasizes freedom and creativity, as well as detachment from material possessions, while the latter is concerned with the egoism of private bourgeoise interests, and the massive amounts of poverty that follows it along if left unchecked.[21] Both these critiques were in play throughout the 1960's, but the thesis of the book is that the social critique slowly died out, while the artistic critique of capitalism was appropriated by capital itself. Demands for personal autonomy were recognized in the form of weakened union participation and leaner, more flexible firms. While these could have certain advantages in dealing with increased levels of competition in a globalized economy,[22] the more flexible firm needed a new sort of subject, one redesigned from the ground up to inhabit the newer, more modern firm. David Harvey draws indirect attention to this in his outlining of a basic theory of neoliberalism: "Neoliberalism is in the first instance a theory of political economic practices that proposes that human well-being can best be advanced by liberating individual entrepreneurial freedoms and skills within an institutional framework characterized by strong private property rights, free markets, and free trade."[23] What's

20. Duggan, *Mean Girl*, ch. 4.

21. Boltanski and Chiapello, *The New Spirit of Capitalism*, 38.

22. Boltanski and Chiapello note that the management discourse of the 1960's barely mentions the third world; by the 1990's many Asian countries (especially Japan) were not only large sources of competition, but also inspiration which western firms were trying to imitate. (Boltanski and Chiapello, *The New Spirit of Capitalism*, 72).

23. Harvey, *A Brief History of Neoliberalism*, 2.

hidden in plain sight here is an idea of human well-being, one we've already seen that revolves around work as a form of personal expression. The result is that capitalism managed to turn some of its most salient critiques into some of its most salient defenses. As in the novels of Ayn Rand, many defenses of capitalism now rest on the idea that things like competition and certain forms of labor are ideal, and living up to these ideals would require an entirely new kind of subject.

We've seen how, for Rand and others, there was a desire in the middle of the 20th century to go beyond the stale monotony of the predictable career paths that were available. New ideas about what life should look like abounded, and new language helped articulate those ideas. We learned from Heidegger that we're always embedded in certain linguistic practices that reveal the clearing we occupy, but that language obscures as much as it reveals. We live in a world now where certain things seem obvious because they're so easy to say, but other things can be a bit more difficult to articulate.

For example, Dasein is always-already *thrown* into a particular set of conditions which help determine its lifestyle and choices. Being born in ancient Greece, we would be citizens occupying a *polis*, but in the wake of the neoliberal turn, this no longer seems to exist.

Instead, people born today instead get different words to describe themselves and their existence. This is the idea driving John Patrick Leary's excellent little book *Keywords: The New Language of Capitalism*. Organized like a little dictionary, Leary's book looks at a collection of buzzwords that have become incredibly popular in orienting people today. For example, kids in school today are taught civics and about social responsibility, but increasingly prevalent is teaching kids how to be *entrepreneurs*. "'Entrepreneurship' is more than 'business'—it is a way of life. Weber argued in *The Protestant Ethic and the Spirit of Capitalism* that American capitalism gave the impulse to seek profit the virtue of a vocation or a 'calling.'"[24] The idea that we're supposed to turn our careers into something we're passionate about fits with the analysis of Rand we already gave, the idea that we should be Roark's, in it for the love of the activity, with money as a weird consequence that may or may not come about. Entrepreneurship is even thought of in borderline-monastic terms, the sort of thing that can throw your whole life off balance in pursuit of, well, certainly not profits, like Keating. Instead, entrepreneurship is the pursuit of some other passion that doesn't fit into the logic of capitalism, even if every other aspect of it has to. Reflecting on a businessman who tanked his first company, the *Wall Street Journal* looked at James Lombardi, a man who burned himself out running his first business,

24. Leary, *Keywords*, 85.

only to start a second one while practicing a better work/life balance, "such as not working on Sundays"[25] among other things. This is, in Leary's words, "a story of a man who set off unprepared upon the lonely path of righteousness, was tested, and then redeemed."[26] The religious and spiritual language isn't Leary inserting language that isn't there; it's factual reporting, not a misleading interpretation. Business journals and books will use religious terms like 'zeal' and 'enthusiasm' to describe the individuals, who are even compared to religious figures at times. For example,

> In 2012, *CBS Evening News* profiled Richard Branson, the Virgin founder who has personified the entrepreneurship fantasy of artistic "vision" and moral zeal. Branson might be most accurately described as "investor," but "entrepreneur" is more than a mere professional function—it is Branson's personal *brand* and something like a code. Everything he does, from direct music sales to founding an airline, is an expression of his "values," not the mere desire to increase his capital. This moral sense lends itself easily to "social entrepreneurship," which the Charles Schwab Foundation for Social Entrepreneurship defines in part as the drive to "pursue poverty alleviation. . .with entrepreneurial zeal." A social entrepreneur is a "pragmatic visionary" who "innovates by finding a new product, a new service, or a new approach to a social problem." The final trait, however, is the real coup de grace: "Combines the characteristics represented by Richard Branson and Mother Teresa."[27]

The comparison between the worlds of business and religion isn't just the case at the individual level, the synthesis of public citizens, artists and religious believers into private entrepreneurs. It also works with larger economic systems as well, as was discovered by the theologian Harvey Cox in his *The Market as God*, the product of taking a strange suggestion from a friend.

> Some years ago, a friend advised me that if I wanted to know what was going on in the real world, I should skip the front page of the *New York Times* and turn immediately to the business section. Although my lifelong interest has been in the study of religion, I am always willing to expand my horizons, so I took

---

25. Quoted in Leary, *Keywords*, 86.
26. Leary, *Keywords*, pg. 86.
27. Leary, *Keywords*, 87.

the advice, vaguely fearful that I would have to cope with a new
and baffling vocabulary.[28]

He continues,

> I did not. Instead I was surprised to discover that most of the
> concepts I ran across were strangely familiar. Expecting a terra
> incognita, I found myself instead in a land of deja vu. The lexi-
> con of the *Wall Street Journal*, *Financial Times*, and *Economist*
> turned out to bear a striking resemblance to Genesis, the Epistle
> to the Romans, and Saint Augustine's City of God. Behind the
> descriptions of acquisitions and mergers, monetary policy, and
> the convolutions of the Dow and the NASDAQ, I gradually made
> out the pieces of a grand narrative about the inner meaning of
> human history, why things go wrong, and how to put them right.
> Theologians call these myths of origin, legends of the fall, and
> doctrines of sin and redemption. Here they were again, and in
> only thin disguise: chronicles about the creation of wealth, the
> seductive temptations of over-regulation, captivity to faceless
> business cycles, and, ultimately, salvation through the advent of
> free markets, with a small dose of ascetic belt-tightening along
> the way for those economies that fall into the sin of arrears. I
> realized then that my many years of studying religion and theol-
> ogy had prepared me to approach this mysterious thing called
> the economy more knowingly than I could have guessed.[29]

Concepts like the *invisible hand* serve a borderline spiritual mystification
process,[30] forcing us to put a blind faith in the markets infallibility[31] since
we mortals are ill-equipped to know any better. The spiritualization of markets fits right into Rand's novels, making labor-relations and material conditions insignificant or invisible when compared to the personal spiritual
visions of capitalism. This has arguably been going on for some time, with
Max Weber showing how certain orientations of capitalism tapping into a
personal or spiritual calling and arguing that it was for this that certain capitalist cultures were so successful,[32] or Bernard Mandeville in his *Fable of the*

---

28. Cox, *The Market as God*, 4-5.

29. Cox, *The Market as God*, 5.

30. Cox, *The Market as God*, 145.

31. Cox, *The Market as God*, 29.

32. Weber, *The Protestant Work Ethic and the Spirit of Capitalism*.

Bees.[33] In the same way that things like *avant-garde,*[34] *youth culture*[35] and *authenticity*[36] have functioned in various passive revolutions, spirituality has been commodified here, turned into a way of commodifying ones very self. One could reasonably ask whether Rand's perspective is fundamentally *new* or if it's simply a new coat of paint on an old idea, but the pervasiveness of its influence should be clear by now.

In closing, the key takeaway is that *Homo Economicus* was never the full picture; left behind were the politics of aspiration and affect, better encapsulated by a forgotten *Homo Economartist* and their corresponding aspirational and affective market, where work is the new worship service. So what happens when we investigate life in this new church? What happens when we try and see what sorts of lives these new believers are living? It's to this we now turn.

33. Meszaros, *Beyond Capital*, ch. 15.
34. Frank, "Monoculturalism."
35. Frank, "Rock n Roll is The Health of the State."
36. Frank, *What's the Matter With Kansas?*

Chapter 5—**Actually Existing Neoliberalism**

> I would be lying were I to claim that work suits me splendidly. Indeed it rather wears me down, I must say.
>
> —THOMAS MANN, *THE MAGIC MOUNTAIN*

So far, we started in the highly abstract theories of Heidegger, offering basic outlines of human subjectivity, and it's embeddedness in a particular way or understanding of its existence. We then narrowed things down by looking at a certain 'clearing' through the work of Ayn Rand to make explicit some of our own worlds values and ideals, to render certain implicit assumptions and practices explicit. Now we'll get even closer to the ground by looking at life under actually existing neoliberalism, and things are about to take a rather aggressive turn, as there's a rather intense disjoint between the ideas people often have about the world today and the reality of living in it. Peter Fleming has named this disjoint "the 'living gap' (*diastema* or purposeful disadjustment) between the pure abstraction of homo economicus and its systematic failure as a bearer of economic interests."[1] The world beyond unions and safety nets was supposed to galvanize a whole new way of living our lives, and reshape not just our world but the inhabitants as well; as Margaret Thatcher put it, "Economics are the method; the object is to change the heart and soul."

If one wants to understand the sort of soul shaped by neoliberal forces, the millennials generation is the place to start. Born in the years 1980-2000, millennials are the first generation to have lived their entire lives in the midst and wake of the neoliberal revolution brought about in the 1980's. Being born in 1993, I'm right in the middle of it, so to some degree this chapter will be a sort of sociological autobiography, although I hope to draw on others who've covered this territory better than I can. I'll be synthesizing here as well, using

1. Fleming, *The Death of Homo Economicus*, 99.

various sources to try and describe the situation as clearly as possible using various sets of data, but also borrowing from Heidegger and other thinkers to describe what it's like to *live* as one of the pieces of data.

Fortunately, a book-length biography of my generation has been written already, so I get to rely fairly heavily on Malcolm Harris' *Kids These Days* for this next chapter. Interestingly, early in the book Harris looks at a children's book from way back in the 1950's called *Danny Dunn and the Homework Machine*, a children's book about a kid named Danny who uses a machine to get his homework done extra quickly, leaving him time to play outside with his friends. When his teacher finds out, she doesn't ban him from using it, but does find a way to compensate for Danny's newfound homework efficiency: she simply gives him more homework.[2] It seems counterintuitive to think that more efficient technology would increase workload, but this is actually one of the laws of capital that were described over a century ago by Karl Marx himself. As the labor time required to produce a commodity is decreased and more can be made within a certain amount of time, the prices will go down. In order to maintain a certain level of profits, more have to be made, leading to an intensification of work and sometimes a lengthening of hours in order to increase the amount of time generating that ever-shrinking surplus value. This has come all the way back to kids in primary school, who are being prepared for this world of long hours and poor compensation from the beginning.

> Social scientist Sandra L. Hofferth studies how American children pass their days, using twenty-four-hour diaries completed by kids and their parents between 1981 and 2003. When it comes to school, technological advances haven't freed up any time for American kids. Between 1981 and 1997, elementary schoolers between the ages of six and eight recorded a whopping 146 percent gain in time spent studying, and another 32 percent between 1997 and 2003, making it a threefold increase over the time surveyed, in addition to a 19 percent increase in time at school. Kids age nine to twelve, like Danny, have sustained near 30 percent growth in homework, while their class time has increased by 14 percent.[3]

This increase in workload for young people is often explained by increased competition in a globalized economy; kids growing up in the United States now have to compete not just with the other kids of their local town, but for things like college admissions they have to compete with people from all

---

2. Harris, *Kids These Days*, 17-8.
3. Harris, *Kids These Days*, 20.

over the world. This has led to a host of strange phenomenon, perhaps most obviously in the form of a brand new economy of companies and organizations built around getting you into college. Scandal erupted in early 2019 with a number of high profile cases that showed just how far some parents were willing to go, with millions of dollars going into faked test scores and even athletic credentials. While the high profile celebrity cases captured headlines (and showed just how unloving and uncaring my parents were in comparison to Lori Loughlin and Felicity Huffman), they obscured a deeper trend that had been emerging, that of college admissions consultants, who had blossomed over the last couple decades, and was estimated to be a billion dollar industry in 2018.[4] Parents who are wealthy (or desperate) enough will throw down hundreds of thousands of dollars in order to give their kids a competitive edge in their quest to get into an ivy-league university. Interestingly, a lot of what these companies do isn't even help the kids get better test scores; instead, they'll puff out the students extracurricular section with a host of additions to help them stand out. Take the case of Christopher Rim, a Yale graduate who charges $1,500 an hour for his services of giving prospective ivy-students a 'hook';

> Working with kids plotting out their admissions stratagems as early as seventh grade, Rim sharpens that hook. A high-school client in Seattle had an idea to collect sneakers for poor kids who lacked running shoes. Enter Rim. "I helped draft email for the student and worked with him to figure out which executives to contact: Nike, Adidas, Asics," Rim said. Within a few days, one of the megabrands shipped four hundred pairs. Like other socially conscious consultants, Rim also takes on some pro bono cases. One of them, a formerly homeless student, wanted to send hygiene packages to homeless shelters. "We helped him connect with a huge corporation who funded everything, and he's sent fifty thousand homeless packages," Rim told me. "We helped him create that, helped him get press on it, helped him really take it to the next level."[5]

While the work being done here is obviously commendable, it is for the most part only available to a select few people, but also noteworthy is the way in which the college admission process is being inflated well beyond its original scope. "The old mission-trip-to-Guatemala essay has become passe. Now, ultrawealthy parents swap tales of launching charities just to give their kids interesting nonprofit work; one family reportedly bought a Botswanan

4. Davis, "Class Warfare," 97.
5. Davis, "Class Warfare," 99.

orphanage as grist for a college essay."[6] These are extreme cases, but it points to the larger trend Harris has pointed to; an increase in work is now required just to keep up. Getting ahead itself costs quite a bit extra.

Getting to college is the goal, but it's less a finish line and more a turn into an uphill trail. Stereotypes of college students tend to have them partying by night and taking useless humanities courses by day. I only did the latter as a student, but most kids today fit that stereotype even less.

> The average college student does not live on campus—only around 15 percent of undergraduates do. Most do not attend selective institutions that accept fewer than half of their applicants. Only 19 percent of full-time undergraduates in four-year public degree programs graduate on time, and it's 5 percent for two-year programs. Students from poor families who go to college will probably remain working-class—38 percent of people from low-income families will remain in the bottom two deciles regardless of their educational accomplishment.[7]

A lot of factors feed into this rather scattered approach to education. Part of it is the rise in cost: "Between 1979 and 2014, the price of tuition and fees at four-year nonprofit US colleges, adjusted for inflation, has jumped 197 percent at private schools and 280 percent at public ones . . . "[8] 'Why?' is an interesting question. Harris points out that the increased cost isn't actually going to the *education* part of your college education, since 75% of all courses are now taught by TA's and adjuncts,[9] and there's been a steady increase in part-time faculty as a way of cutting costs.[10] So where is all the money going? In a word: administration. Administrators, who often pull in six- and even seven-figure salaries,[11] are now required for colleges. Why? They need to help manage and maintain various side-projects for the college or university which are intended to attract the wealthy students who already had the expensive consultation to help them get into the school in the first place. Those students are more likely to become wealthy alumni (and big future donors), so a vicious cycle is generated of trying to attract the donor class with new gyms athletic facilities, with more students paying higher tuition rates.[12]

6. David, "Class Warfare," 100.
7. Harris, *Kids These Days*, 44.
8. Harris, *Kids These Days*, 42.
9. Harris, *Kids These Days*, 50.
10. Harris, *Kids These Days*, 51.
11. Harris, *Kids These Days*, 51.
12. Harris, *Kids These Days*, 52.

One shouldn't look at this transition as a natural development, either. Public universities were once seen as public goods, which is why they were so easily affordable in the mid-20th century. The gutting of their financial resources started in the wake of the protests and revolts of the 1960's which horrified many far-right conservatives to the point where it was decided they should no longer be a public good.[13] The result is a student body where the number of business majors has recently doubled,[14] while the more "radical" humanities programs have struggled to justify themselves in a financially austere market. But beyond the makeup of majors is the actual student experience. Between attendance of classes that is much more scattered and spread over time, there's also the number of students who work on top of classes tripling,[15] with around a quarter of those students working between 10pm and 8am. Students are also more likely to struggle to get all their meals.[16] And this is just the overworked day-to-day reality, before we consider the big picture and the big spectre of debt.

The rising price of college might've decreased its popularity, but with increasing specialization requirement for the workforce, college remains a necessity for many people. This might have been a problem, especially for middle- and working-class families trying to give their children a chance to climb the ladder. Fortunately, capital has been rather innovative in giving everyone a chance with a new way of paying: student loans! The student debt crisis has made a fair share of headlines lately, but the sheer size (almost 1.5 trillion dollars at the time of this writing) isn't the only reason it can be so horrifying to contemplate. Stories have surfaced about 'missed' payments where checks are cashed but the organization managing the loan doesn't take notice. Interest rates are so high at times that years of paying the required amoung makes almost no dent in the amount of debt. Companies managing loans get bought and sold, and the people trying to put their lives together have to figure out new interest rates and processes each time.[17] One company even tried to build a community around indebtedness, staging local dinners for its clients.[18] This hints not just at debt as a financial matter but one that is increasingly pervasive in the lives of the indebted. Unlike people who fold on a house they can no longer

13. MacLean, *Democracy in Chains*, ch. 7.

14. Harris, *Kids These Days*, 52.

15. Harris, *Kids These Days*, 44.

16. Harris, *Kids These Days*, 45.

17. Liebenthal, "The Incredible, Rage-Inducing Inside Story of America's Student Debt Machine."

18. Miller, "Been Down So Long It Looks Like Debt to Me," 89-90.

afford, one cannot simply walk away from their student debt. Meanwhile, a variety of tools have been developed to collect, even against people who can't make it. "Today, student debt is an exceptionally punishing kind of debt to have. Not only is it very hard to escape through bankruptcy, but student loans have no expiration date and collectors can garnish wages, Social Security payments, and even unemployment benefits."[19] Harris then summarizes the overall situation:

> Here's where we are now: All American children are told to ex-ercise self-discipline and spend the only things they have (their time and effort) working and competing for a spot in a college freshman class. If they're lucky enough to achieve this goal, they'll borrow on average tens of thousands of dollars from the government for an increasingly diluted education. Schools take this $100+ billion a year in government money, backed by their students' ability to do work in the future, and spend it like their job is to produce more spending. Colleges have dug themselves so deep into their shining marble pit that not even the vultures in the bond market want much to do with them. Meanwhile, debtors can't walk away from student loans unless they can walk away from themselves.[20]

That last comment should also be clarified; walking away from oneself in this scenario refers to either disappearing off the grid or suicide, the latter of which usually means your debt is passed on to your family.

All this debt is, in theory, worth it because once one graduates (in the face of an increasingly fractured and extended college-schedule), then one gets a new job and can pay off the loans.

Sadly, things don't get better from here for most people. Hourly wages have actually been stagnant for several decades, even as productivity and inflation continued to rise. Young people are often stereotyped as being lazy and unproductive, but that seems more an attempt to justify their financial precarity, while covering up an increasing gap.

> In fact, nonsupervisory workers' productivity increased rap-idly between 1972 and 2009, while real wages dipped. Until the 1970s, both metrics grew together; their disjuncture is perhaps the single phenomenon that defines Millennials thus far. Since young workers represent both a jump in productivity and a de-crease in labor costs, this means we're generating novel levels

19. Harris, *Kids These Days*, 62.
20. Harris, *Kids These Days*, 63-4.

of 'surplus value'—productivity beyond what workers receive in compensation.[21]

That wages are stagnant is fairly easy and straightforward to understand. Increases in productivity aren't always so clear, and point to a variety of changes in the nature of work that Harris breaks down.

One of the most significant changes in work over the last few decades is along gendered lines. Male education rates have slowed to some degree, while women's education has increased, which has to some degree translated into increases in wages for some women while many men have found their wages stagnant. The 'feminization' of the labor force then is, while at times overstated, definitely a thing, although Harris qualifies how this works as a victory for women: "Instead of the optimistic portrait of female empowerment that commentators like Rosin and Sheryl Sandberg paint, feminization reflects employers' successful attempts to reduce labor costs. Women's labor market participation has grown just as job demands intensify and wages stagnate."[22] The intensification of work can be hard to understand, since it would seem to eliminate a lot of rote tasks that women used to do; typing before the invention of copy-machines, managing and connecting phone-lines, bookkeeping and all sorts of other tasks once passed off to women have been replaced by computers. What work remains is increasingly the stuff that computers can't do (for now); manual tasks like cleaning and food preparation, as well as abstract tasks that involve certain sorts of problem-solving.

> On both the high and low ends, more work requires the communication and understanding of emotions and ideas. This humanization of work is one of the results of firms automating mechanizable jobs in the middle of the income distribution. It also spells more work for workers; 'Service with a smile' is harder than 'Service with whatever face you feel like making.' What this means intergenerationally is that, as job training has become a bigger part of childhood, kids are being prepared to work with their feelings and ideas. Or, if they're on the wrong side of polariarization, other people's feelings and ideas. They're being managed to work with their emotions, and to do it fast, with attention to detail, and well.[23]

21. Harris, *Kids These Days*, 75.
22. Harris, *Kids These Days*, 80.
23. Harris, *Kids These Days*, 77-8.

A disturbing example of this was provided by Emily Guendelsberger in her book *On the Clock*, where she worked a few low-wage jobs and reported her experience. One of the jobs she worked was at a call-center, a growing field given the 'human face' element is incredibly important to maintain for a number of corporations, and computers aren't quite able to help people navigate corporate bureaucracies (yet). 'Service with a smile' is compulsory, but it's also required alongside a dozen other types of jobs, leading to a fractured psyche that tries to balance half a dozen jobs all at once.

> Helper Emily wants to figure out the caller's problem and find a solution.

> Sales Emily wants to gather information about the customer and use it to formulate and deliver a personalized sales offer.

> Protocol Emily remembers the details of Convergys's systems and preferred verbiage, including the launch sequence.[24]

> Scribe Emily types notes on the reasons for the call and actions taken in real time.

> Conversation Emily is *supposed* to be in charge of listening and talking like a normal human being.

> Short-Term Memory Emily can hold on to passwords, addresses, and other hard-to-remember things until they're needed.

> Awareness Emily keeps an eye on the real world—whether a walker or manager is nearby, whether it's lunchtime, what's on the class group chat, how this call is affecting her metrics.

> Journalist Emily notes when something might be relevant to the book and tries to remember it until her next break—though, frankly, Journalist Emily rarely breaks through the others, who are extremely busy.

> And poor Boss Emily is stuck trying to keep everybody working in harmony.[25]

It's hard for me to imagine being in her position, not just because I've never worked in a call-center, but also because the actual task she's describing, that of holding a conversation with someone, keeping several numerical passwords

---

24. The sequence of uploading customer information and logging into their accounts, which Guendelsberger explains is surprisingly difficult because of how poorly designed the computer system they use is designed.

25. Guendelsberger, *On The Clock*, 170.

in your memory, reading and typing notes and trying to solve the customers problem is borderline impossible, and even unhealthy to attempt.

> . . .though 'multitasking' is a common job requirement, the last half century of cognitive science has been very clear that it's just not something humans are any good at. We may *think* we can do two things at once—Lord knows I used to. But we're actually just switching back and forth between tasks really fast, never fully concentrating on either and losing energy with every switch. We end up slower and less competent at both tasks than if we'd just focused on each one at a time. . .studies have linked attempts to multitask to a short-term increase in levels of cortisol and adrenaline—the 'stress hormones'—and long-term increases in depression and anxiety.[26]

Naturally, this need to manage a dozen tasks at once leads to Emily struggling to help the customer, since she's unable to even hear what the problem is, let alone work on actually solving it. This leads to a furious customer and an Emily exhausted from trying to juggle passwords, customer information, a couple different computer programs and a conversation all at once. Nobody wins.

The added complexity is also in jobs you wouldn't *think* have grown more complicated over the last several decades, but increasingly 'the customer is always right' attitudes have pushed companies to push their employees to manage added complications. Take the case of fast-food preparation: when McDonalds first debuted in 1955, the menu was pretty basic. Burgers, fries and soda, all made in the same standard way. This allowed employees to produce a large quantity of food fairly efficiently. It was boring, but at least it was just a matter of simple numbers (of burgers, fries and sodas). The real shift would eventually be forced by a competitor. "Burger King countered with 'Have it your way' in the '80's, and to compete, McDonald's started broadening its menu and allowing for special orders. Today, the average McDonald's menu has more than a hundred items, and special orders are commonplace."[27] This means employees are expected to maintain the same speed they always did, but with a larger number of menu items, and with customers adding their own special twists to complicate things.

These particular jobs are extreme cases, but they highlight how intensification works; it's not just that workers today are often doing many more things at once, but a lot of that has to be done now while being sensitive to the needs of a customer or supervisor who expect you to do it while maintaining

26. Guendelsberger, *On The Clock*, 170-1.
27. Guendelsberger, *On The Clock*, 269.

a certain attitude. This affective labor is suspected to be better suited for women, who are often raised to be sensitive to the emotional needs of others in ways that men aren't.[28] This has led to certain gains being made by women, while certain men are feeling left out. Some men have reacted with hostility to these changes, and have started to encourage we return to a previous period of time, with male breadwinners working while women manage the housework, but it's a bit more complicated than that. Women are making gains in the workplace and men are losing ground, but that doesn't mean women are simply *replacing* men, because with wages having been stagnant for so long, women aren't able to replace men in most cases. Instead, where one family member could support a family on a single job several decades ago, both are now required to keep a family financially afloat.

> Women are working more overall, men are doing more housework, and yet there's less getting done and less financial stability. This is what happens when all work becomes more like women's work: workers working more for less pay. We can see why corporations have adapted to the idea of women in the labor force. Plus, the ownership class can redirect popular blame for lousy work relations toward feminists. Millennial gender relations have been shaped by these changes in labor dynamics, and we can't understand the phenomenon of young misogyny without understanding the workplace. Just because some men's work tended to be better at a time when single-worker families were more common doesn't mean we can return to the former by returning to the latter. But that's the narrative misogynists use to interpret what's going on and how it could be fixed, and they've attracted a lot of angry and confused men who aren't sure about their place in the world. One antidote to this kind of thinking is an alternative framework for why and how workers (of all genders) came to be in such a precarious position.[29]

This brings us to the next key element of work today: precarity! This term cuts a couple ways; the main way people often think of it, precarity means that you can lose your work and wages without much of a warning. Deunionization means workers have fewer rights or guarantees, and fewer ways to defend themselves when the company hits a rough patch and starts shedding employees to save itself. However, this cuts the other way as well. Precarious work is also often flexible work, needed in shorter

---

28. Harris, *Kids These Days*, 78. It should be noted that this doesn't necessarily imply an essentialist view of gender. Instead, assumptions and expectations we have of children can shape them to be sensitive to different sorts of problems.

29. Harris, *Kids These Days*, 81.

bursts rather than longer, more steady periods of time. Many employees now work zero-hour contracts, where they don't get any guaranteed hours or pay, but have to be available via phone to come in whenever needed.[30] Many other employees get a schedule, but that can be a limited success for a lot of people: "part-time retail workers (for example) still can't draw a clear line between work-time and the rest of their lives, because they never know when the boss might need them. According to the National Longitudinal Study of Youth data, nearly 40 percent of early-career workers receive their work schedules a week or less in advance. That's not a lot of time to plan your life."[31] Increasingly, a lot of workers schedules, especially in the case of retail and fast-food workers, are determined by algorithms that try to calculate the precise number of workers that will be needed for a certain period of time. This keeps expenses at the bare minimum, but pushes workers that much harder to keep up. Combine this with the increasing multi-tasking demands workers have to keep up with, and jobs are becoming increasingly stressful both *on* and *off* the clock, since a text message can suddenly interrupt a relaxing afternoon.

'Always on' sometimes is compensated though, especially among more professional positions picked up by college graduates, although this has its own downsides.

> On the professional side of polarization, the proportion of men and women working more than fifty hours a week has grown significantly. Innovations in productive technology make it possible for these high-skill employees to be effectively at work wherever or whenever they happen to be in space and time. There have always been people who spend all their time working—some of them better compensated than others—but at least in professional jobs, this condition has generalized. No longer are a good education and a good career dependable precursors to a life with lots of leisure time. For young people who are working hard to put themselves on the successful side, they're setting themselves up for more of the same.[32]

So if you're lucky enough to get through college and land yourself a professional job, it's only a partial victory. You do get to work in the comfort of your home or favorite coffee shop, but you're also working more hours. Beyond the increased amount of time employees put in, this also starts to blur their professional and private lives together. Vacations now involve

---

30. Antunes, "The New Service Proletariat."
31. Harris, *Kids These Days*, 84.
32. Harris, *Kids These Days*, 84.

time spent answering emails, and a relaxing evening or weekend can often be interrupted by a phone call. If you don't answer, someone else down the line will. If you're lucky enough that you feel comfortable letting it ring and go to voicemail, you're extremely lucky. This slow invasion of private life by work got so bad that France even introduced laws in 2017 that disallowed employers from calling employees once they'd clocked out.[33]

Millennials however, having gone deep into debt to get the education that qualified them for the job, aren't exactly in a good place to negotiate for better working conditions. They paid to get themselves a couple steps up the ladder only to find out that the only way to keep their spot is to keep moving and never stop.

Combine all this with the increase in part-time work, longer periods of unemployment between jobs, an increase in the use of unpaid interns which depresses wages for everyone, decreases in union membership and strike participation, and you have a perfect storm that is hitting millennials (and zoomers as they start to enter college and the workforce) with endless demands that have no real payoff beyond keeping the debt collector away for a couple more days.

Even people 'at the top' have it rough, in their own way. Young people working in the financial sector can be pushed especially hard, often putting in so much overtime that one young J.P. Morgan analyst calculated that his post-tax hourly salary was around $16/hr because of the brutal hours they worked.[34] The schedule itself demands olympic feats on the part of the employees, with '9-to-5' often referring to a working schedule of 9am to 5am the next morning. In some cities, cab drivers even know when they take a young financial intern home in the wee hours of the morning that they can just wait outside their house; once they've showered and changed, they'll come right back out and need a ride back to the office. I imagine a combination of energy drinks and other substances help make this possible, but occasionally someone just can't take the heat. Such was the case of Moritz Erhardt, who literally collapsed dead from exhaustion one morning after working until 6am three days in a row.[35]

Naturally it's hard for most people to feel sympathy for people working in the high-powered financial sector which is often responsible for their own various forms of precarity, but the key takeaway here is that things suck on all rungs of the ladder, not just the bottom. Call-center employees and

33. Petroff and Cornevin, "France gives workers 'right to disconnect' from office email."

34. Harris, *Kids These Days*, 102.

35. Harris, *Kids These Days*, 103.

McDonald's workers are getting pushed harder and harder for lame wages that keep them on the edge of financial ruin. Those at the top are literally getting worked to death (if not something closely resembling it) and many of their wages aren't *that* much better all things considered. Everyone in the middle experiences the squeeze from both directions, with stagnant wages making debt hard to pay off, and with increased work hours and side-gigs as the only real option many have.

This is to say nothing of the ways in which markets and market-ideology have, for quite some time, come down even harder on what we might describe as *others*, groups of people who didn't fit the typical expectation for what a person (or their family unit) should look and behave like. This was detailed excellently by Melinda Cooper in her *Family Values*, which looked at the way many policies that were supposedly neutral hurt specific groups of people. For example, with the inflation of asset values combined with stagnant wages, families that already owned a lot were able to coast and even thrive without having to work as much, while those who actually depended on the wages provided for their labor (the theoretical basis of capitalism) struggled.[36] More disturbingly is the way in which the rhetoric of 'human capital' was used to legitimate a lack of intervention in the AIDS crisis of the 1990's, since the communities that struggled the most (mostly people of color and LGBTQ+ communities) were seen, from the point of view of capital, as 'bad investments.'[37] One could add discrimination in the housing market,[38] or the way in which anti-union rhetoric has often been connected with antiblack racism in the US[39] and a picture slowly emerges about the way in which the values of market logic and financial common-sense have often been a cover for the ways in which certain groups have always been kept on the margins, albeit under the guise of allegedly 'neutral' ideas about 'productivity' or 'efficiency'. Put in the policy jargon of legalese, or to borrow Robert Knox's term *law-sterity*,[40] the ways of shaping behavior are even made to disappear.

All this doesn't take away the analysis we've been developing in this chapter; instead it should clarify a couple things, mainly that while the struggles of white cisgendered heterosexual men with student debt and shitty wages aren't fake or less real or worth taking seriously, the 'squeeze' many people at our cultural center are starting to feel has been present in

---

36. Cooper, *Family Values*, ch. 4.

37. Cooper, *Family Values*, ch. 5.

38. Taylor, *Race for Profit*.

39. Hosang and Lowndes, *Producers, Parasites, Patriots*, ch. 1.

40. Knox, "Against Law-Sterity."

marginalized groups for quite some time. The precarity isn't just increasing in intensity, but reaching new communities, leaving fewer and fewer people on stable ground. To the degree that there ever was a 'good old days' that we might consider going back to, it only appears that way for people who weren't near the noise and clutter at the margins. As Robin James eloquently put it rather recently: "Though harmony is aesthetically pleasurable, it is only possible because cultural practices subordinate some frequencies (dissonant ones) to others (consonant ones). A harmonious society is one structured by a relation of subordination."[41] This should also make us wary of any calls to return to 'the good ol' days,' since it brings up a question of *who* they were good for and *what* would be needed to make such a return, and if such a return is desirable or even possible.

All-in-all, the key lesson here is that while there are specific ways in which different groups of people are feeling pushed and pulled, the entrepreneurial lifestyle of *Home Economartist* is starting to look like a bad investment.

41. James, *The Sonic Episteme*, 167.

Chapter 6—**Collapse of a Model**

No one has the right to regard the fear of famine which is so striking in underdeveloped societies, or the Great Fears of peasants under feudalism confronting the spectre of starvation, as mere subjective feelings. On the contrary, they represent the interiorisation of objective conditions and are themselves an origin of praxis.

—JEAN PAUL SARTRE, *CRITIQUE OF DIALECTICAL REASON*

Heidegger's thought has helped us understand certain cultural developments in the last several decades, particularly around our ways of understanding our own subjectivity, and its relation to things like work. However, the frameworks he provides remain limited, although in some telling ways. Jason Read, in dialogue of Etienne Balibar's theory of the 'other scene,' writes

> politics and the economy each short-circuit the other. The effects of the economy are always displaced onto politics, and vice versa. . .This logic of displacement, of the absent cause, can alternately be understood as a logic of individuation: the economy can only have effects if it is individuated in comportments, ways of being and thinking; conversely, ways of being and thinking, what Balibar calls symbolic or subjection, can only truly have any efficacy if they effect positions with respect to distribution and production of resources and power within society, having economic effects.[1]

So any proper understanding of a particular *epoch* (to use Heidegger's term) means both understanding the material conditions and the way those conditions were understood by those living in them. Heidegger's philosophy offers us ways of understanding the latter, but not so much the former. For

1. Read, *The Politics of Transindividuality*, 89.

that, we'll need to supplement his thinking, so we'll briefly turn to Marx. This will not be a summary of all his thought, only a supplemental borrowing of a few key elements.

It's worth starting with the way Marx splits commodities up. Commodities are valuable, but under capitalism, that value has two types; *use* and *exchange*, the former being "the usefulness of a thing"[2] and the latter being the "mode of expression, or form of appearance, of value"[3] which is determined by the socially necessary labor time for a thing's production.[4] It's generally assumed that things are produced to satisfy needs, but in the case of commodities, that ceases to be the case. Instead, things are produced to satisfy exchange, rather than use values.[5] A couple things result from this.

The first is a new equation is needed to account for this difference. Following Marx, we'll use the letter M for money, and C for commodities. In a pre-capitalist bartering system, for example, the equation C-M-C described most interactions, where a commodity was exchanged for some money that would eventually be exchanged for a different commodity. In this way, a pig farmer would sell a couple pigs for some money that could then be used to purchase corn for his remaining pigs. The money here is intended merely as a placeholder while the farmer goes to find corn. In other words, it's still simply a means to an end, the end being satisfying certain needs via certain use values. This changes under capitalism, where the equation gets inverted to M-C-M. Here things get a bit more complicated, because the equation here is actually M-C-M'. The final M' can then be broken down to M+MΔ, which represents the original sum of money put forward in the beginning, *plus* the change in money withdrawn at the end. So here instead of our farmer, we have an investor who puts forward \$100 for some pigs, only to later resell them for \$110. This extra \$10 is called *surplus-value*.[6]

The second result is derived from the first; this equation systematizes an inability to be satisfied. The farmer, for example, can only handle so many pigs, and only need so much corn. However, the need for more money can never be satiated in the same way, since it was never intended to satisfy use-values in the first place. It was always a placeholder, so turning it into an end in itself opens us up to chase satiation down a never-ending rabbithole, as Marx writes:

2. Marx, *Capital* Vol 1, 126.
3. Marx, *Capital* Vol 1, 128.
4. Marx, *Capital* Vol 1, 129.
5. Marx, *Capital* Vol 1, 250.
6. Marx, *Capital* Vol 1, 251.

> The simple circulation of commodities—selling in order to buy—is a means to a final goal which lies outside circulation, namely the appropriation of use-values, the satisfaction of needs. As against this, the circulation of money as capital is an end in itself, for the valorization of value takes place only within this constantly renewed movement. The movement of capital is therefore limitless.[7]

Already we can see how Marx's prediction that these forms harbor the possibility of crises[8] may bear itself out. A system forced to constantly grow with indifference to whether it's satisfying actual needs with use-values is shaky ground to begin with. Further complicating matters, however, is the tendency of rates of profit to fall as time goes on and technology gets better. How does this happen? Remember that a things exchange value is determined by the socially necessary labour time required to produce the commodity, as we said above. Socially necessary labour time is the average required time to produce a commodity. Things like technological improvements (or driving workers harder within a particular amount of time, or for a longer period of time) thus decrease the value of the commodity, leading to the amount of surplus value produced per commodity going down. One can try and amp up production to make up for the difference, such as driving workers for either longer or more intense hours, or lowering wages, but these don't overcome the antagonism; they simply reproduce more intense versions of it.[9] However, this antagonistic relationship, one where the very dynamics of capital itself demand more and more labor to make up for lowered profit-rates, gives us a different way of thinking about the question of why neoliberal formations of labor and subjectivity emerged in the wake of the economic stagnation of the 1960's and 70's.

'What happened?' is a difficult question to answer, although there are a few things we can point to. Starting in the late 60's and early 70's, the economy began to struggle. Edward Berkowitz summarizes:

> Between 1970 and 1973, the unemployment rate never rose above 6 percent, and the inflation rate peaked at 6.2 percent. Between 1974 and 1981, the unemployment rate never went below 5 percent, and the inflation rate reached 7 percent or higher in 1974, 1975, and every year between 1978 and 1981. What economists call stagflation—the simultaneous appearance of high prices and high unemployment—had become a

7. Marx, *Capital* Vol 1, 253.
8. Marx, *Capital* Vol 1, 209.
9. Marx, *Capital* Vol 1, 656-60.

fact of American life. Professional economists, who had been summoned to Washington after the Second World War and put in charge of advising the president on the management of the economy, emerged as heroes in the sixties. Their professional tools gave them the ability to fine-tune the economy so that growth became the norm and the fear of depression receded. After 1973, however, the economy developed an immunity to the economists' medicine. The prevailing theories no longer predicted economic performance.[10]

There were a number of individual components to the economic disarray. The oil shocks of the 70's, where Arab countries briefly stopped selling the US oil, not only jacked up the price of oil but of production in all industries.[11] Declining rates of productivity-increase was also an issue.[12] There was also the fact that the 70's were inheriting many of the problems of the 60's, a period of enormous expenses. President Johnson had attempted to fund a variety of enormous social programs while simultaneously waging a war in Vietnam, all the while refusing to raise taxes to fund either, alongside a number of formerly colonized nations achieving independence, which raised the price of certain imports[13] and deflated the value of certain assets.[14] Add on to all this was the way in which structural unemployment led to declining consumption and profits.[15] On top of this, many areas of production, to compensate for the falling profits, started investing in the increasingly deregulated financial sector in hopes of catching some of the runaway inflation on a good investment, often at the expense of the wages and stability of their actual workers.[16]

All this, however, doesn't quite explain the underlying issue that the dynamics of capital themselves are bound to create when left to run for too long, which is to slowly generate decreased rates of profit. Antunes summarizes:

> Indeed, the so-called crisis of Fordism and Keynesianism was the phenomenal expression of a more complex crisis. Its deepest significance lay in a *structural crisis of capital*, with a clear tendency of the rate of profit to fall, as a result of the factors

10. Berkowitz, *Something Happened*, 1-2.
11. Berkowitz, *Something Happened*, 55.
12. Berkowitz, *Something Happened*, 66.
13. Cooper, *Family Values*, 26.
14. Piketty, *Capital in the Twenty-First Century*, 121-2.
15. Antunes, *The Meanings of Work*, 15.
16. Antunes, *The Meanings of Work*, 15; Berkowitz, *Something Happened*, 54.

above. It was also the manifestation of both the *destructive logic* of capitalism—present in the intensification of the *law of the tendency of the use-value* of commodities *to fall*—and the *uncontrollability* of capital's social-metabolic order. As its structural crisis was unleashed, the mechanism of 'regulation' that was in place in various advanced-capitalist countries, especially in Europe, began to collapse along with it.

He continues:

As a response to its crisis, a process of reorganisation began, of capital and its ideological and political system of domination. The most prominent features of this process included the advent of neoliberalism, with the privatisation of the state, the deregulation of labour-rights and the dismantling of the state-productive sector, of which the Thatcher-Reagan era is the strongest expression. To this was added an intense process of production- and labour-restructuring, with a view to providing capital with the necessary tools with which to try to re-establish earlier patterns of expression.[17]

In this way, *Homo Economartist* can be seen as a sort of 'passive revolution,' a method of re-subalternization.[18]

It's also worth noting that this view doesn't necessarily entail visions of the individuals within the system. It's usually assumed that Marx believed all rich people were evil, and the poor and disadvantaged are generally innocent. This itself was always a gross caricature of his views, but the important element I'm getting at here is that the dynamics of capital have a tendency to produce contradictory and problematic situations *regardless* of how kind and generous the bourgeoise might be. Constant expansion is bound to run into limitations and cause social problems, many of which would be analyzed in Marx's later works.[19] Similar to this assumption about Marx is his supposed obsession with class, which is certainly central to his analysis[20] but is also incomplete without understanding the contradictory dynamics of capital itself, which exacerbate the tensions between owners

---

17. Antunes, *The Meanings of Work*, 17.

18. Modonesi, *The Antagonistic Principle*, ch. 5

19. See *Capital* Vol 3, as well as Istvan Meszaros' *Beyond Capital*, part 3 for a look at the way this would play out in the 20th century, including the failure of the Soviet experiment

20. Those looking for a focus on Marx's theory of class should read Das' *Marxist Class Theory for a Skeptical Audience*.

and producers. For Marx, the people at the top do not have to be evil to create a horrific situation; capital does that for them.

We've been examining things through a cultural and affective lens using Heidegger's hermeneutic ontology, but that has its limits and could never get us the sort of analysis that Marxist theory gives us. While this shouldn't be used to bash Heidegger, as he simply had other things he preferred to focus on, if *we* wish to get a fuller picture of our current state of affairs, we inevitably have to supplement him. The result if we don't give his ontology any sort of materialist supplement is it becomes too abstract to be capable of helping us understand our current crisis. The result is that we can only think in affective and cultural terms if we limit ourselves to his work alone. To quote Richard Wolin at length:

> Insofar as 'modern technology as an ordering revealing is no merely human doing,' its triumph must be mythologically traced back to the 'destining of Being' itself: its primordial source is 'enframing,' rather than, say, a concrete historical social formation—capitalism—that has over the course of time assumed an independent logic. And thus, insofar as the dominion of 'enframing' is a 'destiny' wholly independent of the powers of human action or will, those powers can play no role in reversing this condition. Thus, *Seinsgeschick is a fate humanity is condemned passively to endure.* Or as Heidegger himself observes, all depends on whether 'Being itself reaches its culmination and reverses the oblivion which derives from Being itself.'[21]

Our turn to Marx's analytic shouldn't deter us, however, from studying the affective results. Instead, it should help us understand anew the affective result when people have a way of thinking critically about their situation (as well as possibilities for change) closed off and covered up.

---

21. Wolin, *The Politics of Being*, 164.

Chapter 7—**Mood**

Visceral response is a trained thing, not just autonomic activity. Intuition is where affect meets history, in all of its chaos, normative ideology, and embodied practices of discipline and invention.

—Lauren Berlant, *Cruel Optimism*

We've drawn attention to the difference between the ideals of a neoliberal society and life as it's actually lived, but have yet to examine what this will do to the subject. Reading Heidegger's work on technology, one will likely feel a strong feeling of malaise or melancholy as technological approaches to life started to shape us into uncomfortable positions. The switch from citizens to entrepreneurs has forced kids to turn themselves into investment portfolios, to treat every second as a chance to 'improve' their returns on the 'investments' their parents make on them. People are now human capital, given the chance to produce a good return or be considered a failure.

A number of writers have stepped in to attempt to make sense of the sort of subject that is bound to emerge from the conditions of late capitalism; what sort of person results when people are expected to be 'always on', to turn everything they do into either a possible work opportunity or something they can put on a college application or resume? And what happens when they have to do all of it with a smile? And remember, the smile isn't just because the supervisor and customers now expect it, but because in expressing your entrepreneurship, you're expressing the deepest and most foundational elements of you humanity. You're smiling because you love doing this. Right?

It turns out, many people are struggling to keep up with the pace set by late capitalism. A particular sort of mood has set in. Mood is a term that has a special sense in *Being and Time*, and is worth revisiting. The German phrase where Heidegger introduces the term, *die Stimmung, das Gestimmstein*, "our mood, our being-attuned"[1] is a major hint. He even draws attention to the similarity of *Stimmung* to its relation to attunement, and the German word can refer to the tuning of an instrument, among other things.[2] People always have moods, and as with the strife instigated by art, they both open up the world in such-and-such a way, while also closing other possibilities off; "The 'bare mood' discloses the 'there' more primordially, but correspondingly it *closes* it *off* more stubbornly than any *not*-perceiving."[3] The mood itself is the possibility of having a world disclosed at all; "*The mood has already disclosed, in every case, Being-in-the-world as a whole, and makes it possible first of all to direct oneself towards something.*"[4] Being in different moods causes different things to show up in different ways. A doll, for example, can be encountered in different ways based on the surroundings, as well as the person encountering it. When we watch *Toy Story* and see Miss Bo Peep, one might experience a sense of warmth or elation, since she 'occurs' for us in the context of some of our favorite toys and characters growing up. A very different mood will likely be experienced if you happen to see Chucky from *Child's Play*, especially if you caught it when you were still a bit too young. The point is that 'encountering' either of these characters involves not just some basic sensation and acknowledgment that they're there, but always involves a much richer personal dynamic that helps make up what they are. One doesn't encounter Bo Peep as being threatening unless one is being subversive, and even then you've only introduced a new take on Bo Peep "by way of a counter-mood; we are never free of moods."[5]

Moods are actually, in Heidegger's view, a more basic version of what he calls state-of-mind, or *Befindlichkeit*. States-of-mind and moods are what help us encounter the world in the ways that we do; the world is made available to us because we are open to it in particular ways and particular angles. As we've already seen with things like language and descriptions, our encountering of the world is never neutral; it's mediated by certain terms and phrases, and now we have another mental apparatus that helps determine and disclose the world in a particular way for us.

> This prior disclosedness of the world belongs to Being-in and is partly constituted by one's state-of-mind. Letting something be encountered is primarily *circumspective*; it is not just sensing something, or staring at it. It implies circumspective concern,

1. Heidegger, *Being and Time*, 134.
2. Heidegger, *Being and Time*, 134, note 3.
3. Heidegger, *Being and Time*, 136.
4. Heidegger, *Being and Time*, 137.
5. Heidegger, *Being and Time*, 136.

and has the character of becoming affected in some way; we can see this more precisely from the standpoint of state-of-mind. But to be affected by the unserviceable, resistant, or threatening character of that which is ready-to-hand, becomes ontologically possible only in so far as Being-in as such has been determined existentially beforehand in such a manner that what it encounters within-the-world can *"matter to"* it is grounded in this way. The fact that this sort of thing can "matter" to it is grounded in one's state-of-mind; and as a state-of-mind it has already disclosed the world—as something by which it can be threatened, for instance. Only something which is in the state-of-mind of fearing (or fearlessness) can discover that what is environmentally ready-to-hand is threatening. Dasein's openness to the world is constituted existentially by the attunement of a state-of-mind.[6]

So if mood discloses the world in a particular way, what would be the mood of actually existing *Homo Economartist*?

Mark Fisher's work is worth looking at, not just because he offers analysis of the pervasive moods and attitudes we carry with us today, but because his writing style itself seems to reflect it. His best known work, *Capitalist Realism*, is barely 80 pages long, and jumps from a variety of topics in history, pop culture and politics to describe the ways people are attuned to their surroundings today, even using terms like 'atmosphere' and 'ideological climate'[7] to unpack what he calls *capitalist realism*, a mood that emerges when "it is easier to imagine the end of the world than it is to imagine the end of capitalism."[8] Using the film *Children of Men* as an example, he writes of a time where a disaster hasn't quite occurred, but seems to be being dragged out over a long period of time. The film occurs in the wake of massive infertility in women, where none are capable of bearing children anymore. Naturally, this leads to large-scale social breakdown, but interestingly, it occurs in pockets and cracks; many parts of society manage to continue selling coffee or weapons, religion continues to be a major force in a variety of directions, and the police and military either put people in cages or kill them in order to keep the 'peace'. This is not total dystopia; it's in many ways our current reality, just dialed ahead a couple decades.

The main character, Theo, suffers from intense depression, but he continues with his day. He wanders around in a state of vague indifference to the violence, protests and decay that is taking over his world. The world no

6. Heidegger, *Being and Time*, 137.
7. Fisher, *Capitalist Realism*, 16 and 29.
8. Fisher, *Capitalist Realism*, 2.

longer *lights up* for him to be disclosed in any meaningful way. Heidegger's term for this was *unheimlich*, literally *unhomelike*. Bear in mind the German terms for uncanniness and state-of-mind, *unheimlich* and *Befindlichkeit*, both contain the word for light, *licht*, which we've seen plays a particular role in Heidegger's conception of the subject. Normally the world lights up in a certain way, but when we experience uncanniness, the normal process of illumination fails. This imaginative failure is what interests Fisher.

Capitalism under *capitalist realism* isn't often sold to us as *good* or *desirable*. Instead, it is presented as *realistic*, as a form of safety. "Capitalist realism presents itself as a shield protecting us from the perils posed by belief itself. The attitude of ironic distance proper to postmodern capitalism is supposed to immunize us against the seductions of fanaticism. Lowering our expectations, we are told, is a small price to pay for being protected from terror and totalitarianism."[9] This creates a strange form of stockholm syndrome, where we refuse to consider a world that could be better in any way. The result is a sort of affective and ideological schizophrenia, where several ideas, moods and affects all mix together as people, particularly the young, try to cope and make sense of the world around them.

One effect of this is the *precorporation* of subversion and dissent. Since actual political dissent isn't really an option, rebellion has to be curated by "the establishment of settled 'alternative' or 'independent' cultural zones, which endlessly repeat older gestures of rebellion and contestation as if for the first time. 'Alternative' and 'independent' don't designate something outside mainstream culture; rather, they are styles, in fact *the* dominant styles, within the mainstream."[10] Early examples of this were places like MTV, corporate-funded zones of "dissent" that expressed the anger, frustration and anxiety produced by an increasingly deregulated and unpredictable world, but never turned it into effort to actually change it. This wasn't *failure*, however; the point was to incorporate dissent into the very mechanisms that drive capital itself, a subversion of subversion itself. Kurt Cobaine seemed to wrestle with this tension, that his success as a subversive rockstar meant he'd been incorporated into the system itself. However, his musical heirs managed to remove the angst that drove his music and instead gave us a certain pastiche rock, although it hardly mattered because by that time "rock was already being eclipsed by hip hop, whose global success has presupposed just the kind of precorporation by capital which I alluded to above. For much hip hop, any 'naive' hope that youth culture

9. Fisher, *Capitalist Realism*, 5.

10. Fisher, *Capitalist Realism*, 9.

could change anything has been replaced by the hard-headed embracing of a brutally reductive version of 'reality.'"[11]

The subversion of dissent also tends to produce ironic detachment and cynicism. For an example of how cynicism actually works in practice, one can look at the show that showed neoliberal warfare up close, HBO's *Generation Kill*, a 7-part miniseries that followed some reconnaissance Marines in the 2003 invasion of Iraq. The Marines in the show are elite, all highly trained and equipped. . .Sort of. They actually spend most of the first episode and much of the rest of the series scrounging around for supplies and equipment. They even get an embedded reporter to order various things for them, because military personnel aren't allowed to order things like potato chips and baby wipes in bulk. They also reveal they had to spend much of their own money patching up their humvee's. The first episode has Marines spending 10 hour days in the hot sun fixing vehicles up without the pieces to do so. They don't even have enough batteries for their night-vision, and perhaps most pathetic of all is the shortage of maps of their area of operation. Printed pieces of paper they need to navigate the combat zone, and the higher ups didn't print enough. Naturally, with all these problems, as well as the fact that many of the higher-ups are clearly incompetent, the Marines refuse to go into combat, staging a large-scale rebellion and refusing to charge ahead.

Just kidding! Obviously they go ahead, and at first they're even excited, since they've been waiting several weeks in a desert with nothing to do. Semi-adequately equipped, they head on to their objective, a bridge that needs taking. Until their mission changes, that is. This becomes a running theme throughout the series, as various units all get shifted around from one mission to the other, with no consistent overarching strategy being apparent to the men on the ground as they're constantly thrown as bait into ambushes they're not properly equipped for, all for the sake of getting to Baghdad as quickly as possible. Even when they arrive in the city, they're moved from one neighborhood to the next, rendering them incapable of forming long-lasting relationships with the community that allow for the sort of nation-building that was ostensibly what they were there for. Eventually they're encouraged to decrease violence and "ramp up the aggressiveness", but that's as specific as the instructions get; go into a killzone in the middle of the night and 'secure the area.'

Lack of supplies is paired with a lack of sleep, something they make up for by literally chugging Rip Fuel, weight loss pills that give them an energy boost to get through 30- and 40-hour stretches of no sleep. That only works so

11. Fisher, *Capitalist Realism*, 10.

long, and eventually the fatigue takes its toll, with one of the Marines feeling a bit jumpy and shooting a civilian. The scene, at the end of episode 5, is made more disturbing by the fact that the Marine in question seems confused about what just happened. His sergeant has to pull him aside and try and reassure him "We're just doing our jobs," although the Marine has a vague awareness that penetrates his exhaustion that he's done something wrong.

So how do the Marines cope with these conditions? The immediate answer is humor; they constantly make jokes about killing civilians, fucking the local women (and each other, since the only way for men to deal with the close-quarter intimacy war involves is by joking it off), and enjoying the spectacle that they are very clearly *not* enjoying. But underlying the humor are more complicated mechanisms or cynicism and ironic detachment. The goal of the jokes isn't just to blow off steam in a stressful situation; it's a refusal to take it seriously, to be burdened by it. When they're ordered out of their MOPP suits (suits that would protect them from an anticipated attack from Saddam's chemical weapons), the reporter says this proves the reports of chemical weapons was fabricated, and so the whole war was built on a lie. "Isn't that the whole reason why we're here?"

"Hey reporter," one Marine responds. "The point is we get to kill people."

The whole reason for their being there has shifted, but they roll with it. That's life under late capitalism, not just in the warzones that it creates (yes, *creates*[12]) but in the everydayness in the homeland. This is Fisher's analysis of events like the Olympics, events that are supposed to depict athletic prowess and international solidarity, and which echo to a variety of ancient traditions, but at the same time are now sponsored by major corporations, many of which ironically now sell us various forms of poison.

> Cynicism is just about the only rational response to the double-think of the McDonalds and Coca-Cola sponsorship (one of the most prominent things you see as you pass the Olympic site on the train line up from Liverpool Street is the McDonalds logo). As Paolo Virno argues, cynicism is now an attitude that is simply a requirement for late-capitalist subjectivity, a way of navigating a world governed by rules that are groundless and arbitrary.[13]

Cynicism is a coping mechanism for dealing with something that is simultaneously supposed to bear a lot of emotional and cultural weight, but is also blatantly a product in both the literal and figurative sense. When everything

---

12. Klein, *The Shock Doctrine*, ch. 5-6.
13. Fisher, "The London Hunger Games," 512.

is a product, it becomes hard to really get invested in it, so alternative routes for our emotions become necessary.

Running parallel to the cynicism is increasing rates of depression, but Fisher is interested in the context *around* the increased diagnosis'. Like the underequipped Marines being flung across a nation in a matter of a couple weeks, workers today are expected to pick up and drop assignments at a whim, and they always have to be on-call;

> Labourers are expected to be waiting outside the metaphorical factory gates with their boots on, every morning without fail. . .It is hardly surprising that people who live in such conditions— where their hours and pay can always be increased or decreased, and their terms of employment are extremely tenuous—should experience anxiety, depression and hopelessness. And it may at first seem remarkable that so many workers have been persuaded to accept such deteriorating conditions as "natural", and to look inward—into their brain chemistry or into their personal history—for the sources of any stress they may be feeling. . .this privatization of stress has become just one more taken-for-granted dimension of a seemingly depoliticized world.[14]

What's worth noting is the way in which our everyday understanding in the highly individualized late-capitalist world doesn't push us to think about the context which produce higher rates of depression; mirroring Heidegger's increasing concern about the over-systematization of knowledge, depression and other mental health issues are taken to be chemical imbalances that can be addressed with medication that gets people back to their more productive selves. These pills don't actually produce happiness, as stereotypes often push one to believe; instead many patients instead describe them as putting them in a much more bearable fog, one that allows people to function and go about their lives, but in a more numb fashion than usual.

The fact that the Marines were experiencing the precarity that would later be shifted to the homefront is also telling as an example of what Jonathon Crary has described as the militarization of everyday life. Military research has been conducted on sleepless periods of animals to see if it's possible to produce sleepless *people*, and "As history has shown, war-related innovations are inevitably assimilated into a broader social sphere, and the sleepless soldier would be the forerunner of the sleepless worker or consumer. Non-sleep products, when aggressively promoted by pharmaceutical companies, would become first a lifestyle option, and eventually, for many,

---

14. Fisher, "The Privatisation of Stress," 461.

a necessity."[15] The Marines of *Generation Kill* would eventually become the millennial banking interns of *Kids These Days*.

That depression, anxiety, ADHD and other mental issues are increasing, especially among young people, should be uncontroversial. Every week a new headline comes out about how kids are struggling to focus in school, or reporting higher levels of anxiety than previous generations. However, the normal way of thinking about these issues is in personal terms, often in terms of brain chemistry. To the extent that social factors play a role, they're only seen as the catalyst for the real problem, rather than being the problem itself, which leads to solutions being put on offer that tend to think in incredibly personal terms. Andrew Solomon, author of *The Noonday Demon*, an enormous work on depression, carries this attitude in his introduction. While Solomon's work is admirably well-researched and involves chapters on a whole host of issues related to depression, his vision of it is surprisingly narrow. Even when he recognizes that depression is a uniquely historical phenomena that we are experiencing in a unique fashion, his solutions are also stuck in modernity's epistemological scaffolding as well.

> The climbing rates of depression are without question the consequences of modernity. The pace of life, the technological chaos of it, the alienation of people from one another, the breakdown of traditional family structures, the loneliness that is endemic, the failure of systems of belief (religious, moral, political, social—anything that seemed once to give life meaning and direction to life) have been catastrophic. Fortunately, we have developed systems for coping with the problem. We have medications that address the organic disturbances, and therapies that address the emotional upheavals of chronic disease. Depression is an increasing cost for our society, but it is not ruinous. We have the psychological equivalents of sunscreens and baseball hats and shade.[16]

But the problems Solomon here gives are social, political and economic in nature. Why does he double down in personal solutions to systemic problems? Fisher's contention was that part of the way capitalism works is that it has slowly but surely narrowed our vision, so that we can only think in narrow, individualistic terms, and this goes for both our problems and the solutions to said problems. While Solomon does see current rates of depression as being related to social issues, he doesn't see social solutions as worth pursuing due to either the impossibility of overcoming them, or the inability

15. Crary, 24/7, 3.
16. Solomon, *The Noonday Demon*, 31-2.

to see any alternatives, which is exactly what Mark Fisher designates as the ultimate malaise of our time; to repeat him from earlier, "it is easier to imagine the end of the world than it is to imagine the end of capitalism." The inability to imagine alternatives is blatantly visible in Solomon's passage as well. Systemic causes are acknowledged, but the solutions fall back on individual changes in personal behavior, and even come in the form of products such as 'sunblock' and 'shade'. Fisher is worth quoting at length:

> The current ruling ontology denies any possibility of a social causation of mental illness. The chemico-biologization of mental illness is of course strictly commensurate with its depoliticization. Considering mental illness an individual chemico-biologization problem has enormous benefits for capitalism. First, it reinforces Capital's drive towards atomistic individualization (you are sick because of your brain chemistry). Second, it provides an enormously lucrative market in which multinational pharmaceutical companies can peddle their pharmaceuticals (we can cure with our SSRIs). It goes without saying that all mental illnesses are neurologically instantiated, but this says nothing about their causation.[17]

Solomon points at the problem, but fails to see that the issue at hand is being driven by relentless capital accumulation (which then sells the peace and stability it stole from you for the price of a bottle of pills). This weird contradiction is summed up nicely by Miya Tokumitsu:

> here's the truly wonderful thing about neoliberalism—as it turns us all into paranoid, jealous schemers, it offers to sell us bromides to ameliorate the very bad feelings of self-doubt and alienation it conjures in our dark nights of the soul. Neoliberalism has not only given us crippling anxiety, but also its apparent remedy. It is no coincidence that as we become more nervous, 'wellness' and 'self-care' have become mainstream industries. Over the last few decades, workplaces have become ever more oppressive, intensely tracking workers' bodies, demanding longer hours, and weakening workers' bargaining rights while also instituting wellness and mentoring programs on an ever greater scale.[18]

She brings up the example of striking teachers who experienced a simultaneous decrease in school funding with a new requirement to wear fitbits to keep track of their movement and encourage healthier lifestyles. "Capitalism will deplete you," she concludes, "while letting you think you have the means

17. Fisher, *Capitalist Realism*, 37.
18. Tokomitsu, "Tell Me It's Going to be OK," 9.

to improve your lot. Indeed, it will attempt to force its therapy on you."[19] This is but one more example of Fisher's conclusion that we're being sold remedies by a system that itself is the issue.

What Fisher and others show us is a particular expression of Heidegger's critique of everydayness, that it is something we 'fall' into and find ourselves trapped in and alienated by. The everyday idle chatter about empowerment and autonomy allows increasingly aggressive demands to be imposed on individuals, demands that come from systemic changes that sell us individual solutions. This obscuring of the actual problems is not only a part of fallen everydayness, but it also fits in with Heidegger's conception of truth as unconcealment, the burying-over of certain phenomena, which is often partial.[20] The prevailing ideology of capitalist individualism cannot deny that there are issues, but it can try and filter them through particular lenses that may prevent proper action being taken. This develops into a sort of cultural schizophrenia where we learn to blame ourselves for things well beyond our control, as Adam Kotsko summarizes: "our lives are increasingly hemmed in by a logic of entrapment and victim-blaming. The psychic life of neoliberalism, as so memorably characterized by Mark Fisher in *Capitalist Realism*, is shot through with anxiety and shame. We have to be in a constant state of high alert, always 'hustling' for opportunities and connections, always planning for every contingency (including the inherently unpredictable vagaries of health and longevity)."[21]

The constant pressure to keep up with impossible expectations leads to eventual breakdown, but this breakdown, in our current world, leads to individualized solutions that are a distinct way of doubling down on the initial mindset while ignoring the broader issues. Combine the decreased wages and increased workload, intensification of indebtedness, personalized 'decision-making' that reduces all aspects of life to various examples of consumer choice and the growing spectre of climate change, and you have a recipe for a subject that will eventually tune out, since their whole subjectivity is now wired around a philosophical indebtedness to a tradition of now-literal debt.[22]

This *tuning out* can actually be found throughout Heidegger's work, but it comes in a variety of ways. His writings on technology, for example, while helpful, can also give way to a couple different feelings that might give way to depression. One is the implicit nostalgia in the background

---

19. Tokomitsu, "Tell Me It's Going to be OK," 9.

20. Heidegger, *Being and Time*, 36.

21. Kotsko, *Neoliberalism's Demons*, 95.

22. See Lazzarato, *The Making of Indebted Man*.

of much of his writings, the sense that there was some organic past where all was in some sort of harmony, but which is now being corrupted by a particular force. While Heidegger doesn't come out with this explicitly, it's hard not to have a feeling that things were somehow *better* back then. While I've argued things have gotten worse in certain ways, the difference lies in the second source of Heidegger's increasingly depressive tone, and that is his fatalistic anonymity.

Technology, as I've argued, is related to a way of thinking about and interpreting the world, seeing it all as resources on-call for whenever happens to be convenient. However, Heidegger's own descriptions of technology has a profound practical effect, psychologizing it to the point where "Human activity can never directly counter this danger."[23] Instead, we are left to "ponder the fact that all saving power must be of a higher essence than what is endangered . . . "[24] This analysis leaves us with a deep sense of where we are, but with little ability to actually address it. To repeat a passage cited earlier:

> Insofar as 'modern technology as an ordering revealing is no merely human doing,' its triumph must be mythologically traced back to the 'destining of Being' itself: its primordial source is 'enframing' rather than, say, a concrete historical social formation—capitalism—that has over the course of time assumed an independent logic. And thus, insofar as the dominion of 'enframing' is a 'destiny' wholly independent of the powers of human action or will, those powers can play no role in reversing this condition. Thus, *Seinsgeschick is a fate humanity is condemned to passively endure.* Or as Heidegger himself observes, all depends on whether 'Being itself reaches its culmination and reverses the oblivion which derives from Being itself.[25]

This is, in my opinion, one of the most valuable insights we can glean from Heidegger's work; not in what it pulls off successfully, but where it falls short. In this case, the contrast between Heidegger's success in giving us a careful hermeneutics of the first-person perspective and his failure to go beyond it then leads to a pessimism and political quietism that is left waiting for some future transition to a new understanding of being.

I would argue this is the most depressing thing in Heidegger's work, but it's also very telling. In his work on technology, he sees *techne* as having a sort of inevitability, an inertia too great for us to do anything about other

23. Heidegger, "The Question Concerning Technology," 33.
24. Heidegger, "The Question Concerning Technology," 33-4.
25. Woli, *The Politics of Being*, 164.

than wait. This leaves us stuck standing in a neverending now, something Heidegger explored shortly after *Being and Time* was published:

> Nothing can come because the *horizon of the future* has been unbound. *Sealing off* the past and *unbinding* the future do not eliminate the 'now', but they take away its possibility of a transition from not-yet to no-longer, its flowing. Sealed off and unbound on both sides, it becomes stuck in its abiding standing, and in its being stuck *it stretches itself.* Without the possibility of transition, only persisting remains for it—it must remain *standing.*[26]

This sense of a lack of agency is paired with a loss of temporality, a sense that there is no future for us to act upon, just an ever-recurring *now* in which we're stuck. Heidegger's 'standing now' is different than the one I've been describing, however. Heidegger' describes the "phenomenal signature of profound boredom. . .a wasteland of lost meaning, a desert of senseless existence that has totally transformed all of the temporal dimensions, past, present, and future."[27] Meanwhile, Fisher and Harris' contemporary vision is much more fast-paced; it's the inability to pause, the constant need to sell or advertise ourselves, pursue side-hustles and develop ourselves as human capital that drives their sense of increasing rates of mental health issues, but the overlap between them is the increased sense that there is nothing to be done, that there's nothing new that can be tried. There's also, to be added to all this, the psychological weight of trying to balance what might be one's own personal commitments and aspirations with a situation that doesn't allow for such a commitment, such as when the demands of climate change come up against an apparent financial impossibility. This induces both a personal and sociological schizophrenia, where one is forced to assimilate "society's antagonisms into the emotional world of the subject,"[28] repressing certain needs and desires so as to serve others, and when your ability to pay next month's rent is on the line, it's hard to say it's a serious choice in a lot of cases.

But is there nothing Heidegger had to offer his own subject, the depressed Dasein of *Being and Time*?

---

26. Heidegger, *The Fundamental Concepts of Metaphysics*, 125.

27. Slaby, Paskaleva and Stephan, "Enactive Emotion and Impaired Agency in Depression," 33.

28. Finkeld, *Excessive Subjectivity*, 145.

Chapter 8—**Getting Lost**

And in that moment it comes over you—you don't know why or how, but you feel dizzy watching them bring in the soup. The tenses of verbs become confused, they blend and what is now revealed to you as the true tense of all existence is the "inelastic present," the tense in which they bring you soup for all eternity.

—THOMAS MANN, *THE MAGIC MOUNTAIN*

We can, given the path we've been walking, make two broad claims about young people today 1) they're fucked, and 2) they've been deprived of the language to say express their fuckedness. Faced with an impossible situation and unable to make clear sense of it, a particular sort of subject is bound to arrive.

Before unpacking *anxiety*, it's worth understanding from an existential point-of-view how capitalism has entrenched itself today. We've talked about the dynamics of capital, and their inherent contradictions. So why do we continue down this path? There are a couple things that need to be pulled together at this point.

First, let us recall the common understanding of capitalism exemplified by Ayn Rand; capitalism is a system of personal expression, not a method of production and distribution. Her work highlights a way of understanding ourselves and our world that does as much to conceal as it does to reveal. This obviously brings us back to the artistic clearing we discussed earlier, but also calls attention to another element of Heidegger's thought. The best place to start with this is in Heidegger's discussion of 'The everyday Being of the "there", and the falling of Dasein'. This occurs a few sections after his introduction of the They, the Others who Dasein finds itself subjected to, surrendered and dominated by. In the sections at hand, we see a number of ways this dictatorship operates.

Heidegger starts with idle talk (*Gerede*), "a positive phenomenon which constitutes the kind of Being of everyday Dasein's understanding and interpreting."[1] This phenomenon fits in with his methodical deconstruction of language and subjectivity, his constant pushing against the idea that we stand outside our world and look in, instead emphasizing that we are immersed in and constituted by our world, and a central element of this is language. "In the language which is spoken when one expresses oneself, there lies an average intelligibility . . . "[2] This 'average intelligibility' should be thought of as a shared realm that's already co-disclosed between you and those around you before you even begin sharing information with one another. This shared communication doesn't convey as much information as we typically imagine, although that doesn't mean nothing is happening; instead, connections that are already there are made more explicit, and shared knowledge is allowed to stand out a bit more sharply against the background, as Heidegger writes "What is said-in-the-talk gets understood; but what the talk is about is understood only approximately and superficially. We have the same thing in view, because it is in the same averageness that we have a common understanding of what is said."[3] This shared communication doesn't offer up a series of propositions about reality, but instead works to create a shared mood. For example, shortly before writing this passage, I sat down for a coffee chat with a friend. Greetings were exchanged, followed by catching up, during which we talked about various events, and then we started to talk about our feelings regarding mutual acquaintances, politics, what we were reading, and so on. In all this, some information is conveyed, but in many instances, even while we are constantly talking, information is not being conveyed in a direct manner. When we gripe about our issues with current political shenanigans, or a friend we've both turned sour on, the information we convey isn't really new to either of us. Sure, we might not have heard about this specific thing, but we know the general gist of it. Instead, "this discoursing . . . does not communicate in such a way as to let this entity be appropriated in a primordial manner, but communicates rather by following the route of gossiping and passing the word along. What is said-in-the-talk as such spreads in wider circles and takes on an authoritative character."[4] The language he uses here can sound somewhat deprecatory, especially when he says that "Idle talk is the possibility of understanding everything without previously making the thing one's own"[5],

---

1. Heidegger, *Being and Time*, 167.
2. Heidegger, *Being and Time*, 168.
3. Heidegger, *Being and Time*, 168.
4. Heidegger, *Being and Time*, 168.
5. Heidegger, *Being and Time*, 169.

which will receive an imperative in the opposite direction when he talks about *authenticity* as *ownedness*, but it's important to remember that there is a positive element to this. As with me and my friend talking over coffee, idle chatter allows us to blow off steam and air grievances, to connect emotionally and laugh a little. Our connecting to one another is always mediated by language, but it's not just language as information-conveyance; it's much broader and more diverse than that. It also helps us navigate the world, since it means we don't need to investigate every little thing. Instead, 'idle knowledge', what is more commonly referred to as 'common sense', is allowed to guide us. This common sense is established by the Others, and They become the They in 'you know what they say . . . ' This can prevent us from wasting time investigating every possible question, instead allowing us to focus on what's really important. Another benefit is that basic social protocols wouldn't happen without this sort of idle chatter, and we often don't notice these basic protocols until someone breaks them, either out of rudeness or a simple unawareness, which can often be either hilarious or humiliating, depending on the context. But this idle chatter, so essential to our navigating of daily life, can also come to cover our daily life over. Idle talk helps constitute us in our world, but it also can disconnect us from it, as Heidegger writes "when Dasein maintains itself in idle talk, it is—as genuine Being-in-the-world—cut off from its primary and primordially genuine relationships-of-Being towards the world, towards Dasein-with, and towards its very Being-in."[6] This idle existence never gets to the bottom of things, instead picking up the dialogue it's surrounded by and passes it on in whatever way is most expedient and easiest. One can think of a number of churches (especially larger ones) for a great example. While much of the rhetoric and terminology in church communities has incredibly deep roots going back centuries, with vast amount of commentary available unpacking it's hidden layers, most people today, churchgoing or not, are generally unaware of this hidden depth. Instead they might use words like salvation, redemption, forgiveness, sacrifice, indebtedness and so on without having a deeper understanding of what you're standing on. You might not know what it means to have your sins forgiven, or to follow Christ, but you know that it's happened and that you're doing it. Again, this is a double-edged sword. On the one hand, younger believers and new converts need a place to start, but the trouble is when one finds oneself unable to interrogate the very language they're stuck with, unable to formulate questions about it. One will eventually come across doubts, and a superficial faith will simultaneously not quench the doubts while also not allowing serious questions to be properly formulated, leading one to be stuck in an alienated life. As Heidegger puts it:

6. Heidegger, *Being and Time*, 170.

The average understanding of the reader will never be able to decide what has been drawn from primordial sources with a struggle and how much is just gossip. The average understanding, moreover, will not want any such distinction, and does not need it, because, of course, it understands everything . . . The dominance of the public way in which thing have been interpreted has already been decisive even for the possibilities of having a mood—that is, for the basic way in which Dasein lets the world matter to it. The 'they'; prescribes one's state-of-mind, and determines what and how one 'sees' . . . Such a Dasein keeps floating unattached; yet in so doing, it is always alongside the world, with Others, and towards itself.[7]

The next mode of domination by Others Heidegger gives us is curiosity (Neugier), which he indirectly gets from the first words of Aristotle's treatise *The Metaphysics*, which read "All men by nature desire to know" although Heidegger renders it as "The care for seeing is essential to man's being."[8] This emphasis on knowing as a form of perception leads Heidegger to connect the word in the first sentence, usually translated as to know, with its root meaning, to see.[9] Thus, seeing has a sort of cognitive connection, one he finds in Augustine's Confessions, where it's written that "Seeing belongs properly to the eyes. . .But we even use this word 'seeing' for the other senses when we devote them to cognizing."[10] But as with our communication, there is a sort of 'idle seeing' available that we often fall into. "When curiosity has become free, however, it concerns itself with seeing, not in order to understand what is seen (that is, to come into a Being towards it) but just in order to see. It seeks novelty only in order to leap from it anew to another novelty."[11] One experiences this in places such as art museums, where one is suddenly confronted with an enormous array of 'must-see' classics by the greats, and with only a few hours to see it all, so rather than spending a large amount of time in front of any particular piece, you run along and try and see all of them. As soon as one has 'seen' one painting, one moves along to the next, because it would be a waste if you spent all your time studying Da Vinci's Mona Lisa during your visit to the Louvre while missing out on The Virgin on the Rocks (especially given the obvious superiority of the latter). But this goes beyond the classics; this superficial curiosity also wants to see

7. Heidegger, *Being and Time*, 169-70.
8. Heidegger, *Being and Time*, 170-1.
9. Heidegger, *Being and Time*, 171 note 2.
10. Heidegger, *Being and Time*, 171.
11. Heidegger, *Being and Time*, 172.

all the biggest movies, hear the best music and see all the world has to offer, and all as quickly as possible. This might sound like one is simply living life to the fullest, but the tragedy is that the opposite is the case; instead "curiosity is characterized by a specific way of not tarrying alongside what is closest."[12] One might 'see' all the world has to offer, but one never takes the time to understand why it's worth seeing in the first place. "Curiosity has nothing to do with observing entities and marveling at them . . . To be amazed to the point of not understanding is something in which it has no interest. Rather it concerns itself with a kind of knowing, but just in order to have known."[13] Here, one isn't looking to learn, but to have information ready to offer when one is asked. One is simply trying to escape boredom, simply being "concerned with the possibility of distraction."[14] One hops from one church to the next, one book or author to the next, and sees this and that movie, but if asked more than a couple questions about any of them, would come up blank. "Curiosity is everywhere and nowhere. This mode of Being-in-the-world reveals a new kind of Being of everyday Dasein—a kind in which Dasein is constantly uprooting itself."[15]

And curiosity connects with idle talk; the two are not isolated phenomenon, but part of a larger way of living our lives that Heidegger is trying to work out. "Idle talk controls even the ways in which one may be curious. It says what one 'must' have read and seen. In being everywhere and nowhere, curiosity is delivered over to idle talk. These two everyday modes of Being for discourse and sight are not just present-at-hand side by side in their tendency to uproot, but either of these ways-to-be drags the other one with it."[16] So if we remember our person at the Louvre, their curiosity prevents them from staying for long in front of any single image or work, but idle chatter also determines which works they bother to see. One must see the Mona Lisa, due to its being perhaps the most famous image in the world, but few people could tell you why it's so famous. Any film student must see *Citizen Kane*, and literature students must have read Shakespeare, since their status is taken for granted, although few could tell you why any of these are such important works to have absorbed. Notice that this isn't to denigrate the works in question, but only to point out that we don't survey everything for ourselves and decide on our favorites, but are born into a world that has already done some curation for us, with established high and low points, and

12. Heidegger, *Being and Time*, 172.
13. Heidegger, *Being and Time*, 172.
14. Heidegger, *Being and Time*, 172.
15. Heidegger, *Being and Time*, 173.
16. Heidegger, *Being and Time*, 173.

there is a positive side to all this. Reading everything is impossible, and having a vague sense of what is especially worth your limited time isn't in itself bad, but one can easily find themselves simply reading the classics because they are classics according to idle chatter's 'common sense', and curiosity can push one to simply jump from one work to another without stopping to 'tarry alongside' a work and study what makes it a classic. Any student of the humanities knows the feeling of feeling you need to have read everything in one's respective field since it can often seem that everyone else has, but if you inquire into anyone's understanding of many of the key works, their understanding will rarely go all that far.

These twin phenomenon overlap to create a superficial structure of what is and isn't important or true, while closing off one's ability to interrogate what it's structure actually is or whether or not it is true, seeming to know everything while letting you learn nothing: "Curiosity, for which nothing is closed off, and idle talk, for which there is nothing that is not understood, provide themselves (that is, the Dasein which is in this manner) with the guarantee of a 'life' which, supposedly, is genuinely 'lively'. But with this supposition a third phenomenon now shows itself, but which the disclosedness of everyday Dasein is characterized."[17] This third phenomenon is ambiguity, in which "Everything looks as if it were genuinely understood, genuinely taken hold of, genuinely spoken, though at bottom it is not; or else it does not look so, and yet at bottom it is."[18] In the former case here, one might think of literary classics which everyone can talk about, but not because of any in-depth study they've done on their own. Instead, they perhaps read Pierre Bayard's *How to Talk About Books You Haven't Read*, and skimmed the Wikipedia pages. One thinks of the numerous people who can tell you that James Joyce's *Ulysses* is modeled after Homer's *Odyssey*, even if they haven't read either of those works. The inverse is where something can appear to be nonsense, but to a trained eye it can be a masterpiece, something arguably true of James Joyce's *Finnegans Wake*, as well as a number of philosophical classics which can appear to be nonsense at first attempt, but repeated readings can reveal a much more rigorous structure underneath, Heidegger's work being an exemplary example of this. But this ambiguity goes beyond books; it pervades everything in our lives, everything we experience and discuss: "Everyone is acquainted with what is up for discussion and what occurs, and everyone discusses it; but everyone also knows already how to talk about what has to happen first—about what is not yet up for discussion but 'really' must be done. Already

17. Heidegger, *Being and Time*, 173.
18. Heidegger, *Being and Time*, 173.

everyone has surmised and scented out in advance what Others have also surmised and scented out."[19] To return to our example of Joyce's Ulysses, everyone is always already familiar with the book, and everyone has an opinion on it, regardless of what that opinion is. The book is always either a masterpiece, arguably the greatest novel ever written, or it is nonsensical junk, deeply perverted and the sort of book that is only read by people who want to claim to have read it, nothing more. This immediacy of opinions on the table actually works to close off genuine questioning; one can often find themselves at a loss when trying to form a well-thought opinion, since "This Being-on-the-scent is of course based upon hearsay, for if anyone is genuinely 'on the scent' of anything, he does not speak about it; and this is the most entangling way in which ambiguity present Dasein's possibilities so that they will already be stifled in their power."[20] But beyond having a series of pre-made scripts available on every topic, ambiguity also works by speeding reality up too fast for anyone to stop and give proper study. Twitter and other social media are obvious examples, with our political and news cycles always already out-of-date by time anyone encounters them, but even within supposedly more slowly paced academic environments there is a demand for being up-to-date and having read everything relevant to the topic at hand. While this can obviously be useful at times for helping a reader situate a work in a broader context and understand specifically what an author is trying to do, it can also hinder the sorts of work that can be written, since most books are forced into making very specific interventions into very specific debates. The common complaint that academics are out of touch or fail to respond to broader public needs is often hyperbolic (and also a complaint that the writing is too difficult for lazier readers) but even where it's true, blaming professors trying to secure increasingly precarious tenured positions misses that they are often forced to do the incredibly esoteric work they do. In all these cases, however, the central point is that public interest often covers up the serious things that are happening underneath; a (in)famous tweet, movie or scholarly work won't be studied or discussed with care so long as the public is obsessively playing out pre-made scripts about them: "Idle talk and curiosity take care in their ambiguity or ensure that what is genuinely and newly created is out of date as soon as it emerges before the public. Such a new creation can become free in its positive possibilities only if the idle talk which covers it up has become ineffective, and if the 'common' interest has died away."[21]

19. Heidegger, *Being and Time*, 173.
20. Heidegger, *Being and Time*, 173.
21. Heidegger, *Being and Time*, 174.

These three phenomenon being elucidated, we can move onto Heidegger's central concept here, which lays underneath all three of these. "Idle talk, curiosity and ambiguity characterize the way in which, in an everyday manner, Dasein is its 'there' . . . In these, and in the way they are interconnected in their Being, there is revealed a basic kind of Being which belongs to everydayness; we call this the 'falling' of Dasein."[22] 'Fallenness' is a basic function of the everydayness we all live, and is not intended to be pejorative. The fallenness of Dasein "does not express any negative evaluation, but is used to signify that Dasein is proximally and for the most part alongside the 'world' of its concern. This 'absorption in' . . . has mostly the character of Being-lost in the publicness of the 'they'. Dasein has, in the first instance, fallen away from itself as an authentic potentiality for Being its Self, and has fallen into the 'world'. 'Fallenness' into the 'world' means an absorption in Being-with-one-another, in so far as the latter is guided by idle talk, curiosity, and ambiguity."[23] So the three phenomenon we've just discussed drive one towards fallenness; they are ways in which "Dasein prepares for itself a constant temptation towards falling. Being-in-the-world is in itself tempting."[24] The use of the words 'fallenness' and 'temptation' are here intended to signify religiously-neutral aspects of our lives, although this was during Heidegger's 'protestant-period' where he was also immersed in the works of Saint Paul, Saint Augustine and Soren Kierkegaard, and theologians have gotten a lot out of this aspect of his work, and many people raised in church culture will hear a secularized version of being 'Not of This World'.[25] The difference is that the church will insist on an 'original you' above all the consumerism of the world that you need to return to, while for Heidegger we shouldn't "take the fallenness of Dasein as a 'fall' from a purer and higher 'primal status'."[26] Instead, his point is that people, primarily and for the most part, live inauthentically and fallen lives, and he is here trying to spell out exactly how this inauthenticity work. The word 'inauthenticity' (and it's corollary 'authenticity') themselves deserve some elucidation, since their translation can be misleading. "On no account," he writes, "do the terms 'inauthentic' and 'non-authentic' signify 'really not'"[27] as they might in the case of fool's gold or monopoly money, which replicate things of high monetary value but are 'really not' all that valuable. The word Heidegger uses for

22. Heidegger, *Being and Time*, 175.

23. Heidegger, *Being and Time*, 175.

24. Heidegger, *Being and Time*, 177.

25. See for example Marion, *God Without Being*.

26. Heidegger, *Being and Time*, 176.

27. Heidegger, *Being and Time*, 176.

authentic is *eigentlich*. The root *eigen* translates to *own*, as in ownership, and the German *Eigentum* refers to legal property or possession. So inauthentic living is not 'not really living' living, but not having possession over your life, letting things like idle talk and the 'others' determine how you lead your life. This leads to an existential 'tranquility', although "this tranquility in inauthentic Being does not seduce one into stagnation and inactivity, but drives one into uninhibited 'hustle'.[28] The word hustle, *Betrieb*, contains the root *trieb*, which will be familiar to anyone who's read any Freud, since the drive is a central concept in his own theories. For Heidegger, however, this drivenness, or hustle, is to keep up with the others and their expectations of you. The stereotypical example is of having as flashy a life as your neighbors, 'keeping up with the Joneses' being the common expression, having as big a house, as nice a yard, as many cars and kids as some hypothetical average family, although this hustle can take other forms as well. One thinks of the person who has read everything, but could tell you very little about it, or can only repeat the cliché bits, or the person who offers up clichés and stereo-types as if it were deep wisdom. "Versatile curiosity and restlessly 'knowing it all' masquerade as a universal understanding of Dasein. But at bottom it remains indefinite what is really to be understood, and the question has not even been asked . . . When Dasein, tranquillized, and 'understanding' everything, thus compares itself with everything, it drifts along towards an alienation in which its ownmost potentiality-for-Being is hidden from it. Falling Being-in-the-world is not only tempting and tranquillizing; it is at the same time alienating."[29]

So to summarize, we ordinarily live our lives in a superficial state, largely determined by our co-existence with others. We see and enjoy the movies they see and like, react to what they react to, and generally live our lives without investigating them too much. And while Heidegger will come to criticize elements of this way of existing, he also sees it as a fundamental, and at times acceptable, way to be. This everdayness helps us navigate huge amounts of information, allowing us to focus on particular tasks while drowning out existential 'background noise'. When deciding how to live our lives, starting from scratch would be overwhelming. Having a general sense of what I ought to do (get a job, make and save some money, move out of my parents basement, etc.) helps get the ball rolling. The trouble is that we can at times get lost in this superficial form of existence, simply following a preset path without ever asking why we do things this way, or if they could be done another, better way. As time goes on, certain patterns

28. Heidegger, *Being and Time*, 177-8.
29. Heidegger, *Being and Time*, 178.

that might've been helpful as we learned to navigate the world become so set in stone that we eventually lack the capacity to see them as contingent or designed, seeing them instead as natural or eternal. One might think of roads as being a very obvious preset path, but they were designed and planned at some point, and they could have been planned differently (or you can get a Jeep and just go offroading). This goes for other, more important things as well. Gender roles and family structures have a history of change and development, but the heteronormative image we have of a mother, father, 2.5 kids and a dog often appears as if it were some sort of everlasting standard, which is far from the case. What's more, this belief in a certain 'naturalness' can prevent us from pursuing a lifestyle that is more closely aligned with our own desires. Not wanting to have kids or get married, or pursuing non-heteronormative lifestyles, may not appear for one as a possible option for how to lead one's life, nevermind the condemnation of others who do pursue such paths. This is lostness in the they taken to an extreme that can be harmful if not checked, but the question then arises, if one is lost in the they, how does one find or rediscover oneself? How does one move from inauthentic to authentic existence?

We've developed a subject that understands itself in a very particular way, that is *attuned* to a particular sort of *sound*. In our current late capitalist moment, it's a cacophonous and jarring one, throwing us in a dozen directions at once as we try and keep up with the melody. More recently, we've developed a way in which we get lost in that sound, unable to conceptualize a different, more holistic and engaging harmony. How does one get out of that lostness and find a more authentic tune?

In his description of everyday being-towards-death, Heidegger sees many people describing death in a reductive way, simply as an event that will happen eventually, so as to avoid thinking about it. However, there is another way of thinking about it, and that is *anticipation*.

> Anticipation, however, unlike inauthentic being-towards-death, does not evade the fact that death is not to be outstripped; instead, anticipation frees itself *for* accepting this. When, by anticipation, one becomes free *for* one's own death, one is liberated from one's lostness in those possibilities which may accidentally thrust themselves upon one; and one is liberated in such a way that for the first time one can authentically understand and choose among the factical possibilities lying ahead of that possibility which is not to be outstripped. Anticipation discloses to existence that its uttermost possibility lies

in giving itself up, and thus it shatters all one's tenaciousness to
whatever existence one has reached.[30]

Further down, he adds that anticipation of death "demands Dasein itself in the
full authenticity of its existence."[31] What does Heidegger mean by 'authenticity' here? This returns us to the German term, *eigentlich*, which contains the
root *eigen*, meaning 'own' as in 'my own'. What does it mean to 'own' one's life
in an authentic sense? What does Heidegger mean to describe an individual
who breaks out of the They and becomes authentic?

There is, as with all of Heidegger's thought, some ambivalence from
which we're forced to wrestle with a plurality of possibilities. I'd argue that
this is to our benefit, since it allows us to maintain some consistency, allowing the single text to carry us down a couple potential paths. We're at
a fork in the road, and a decision has to be made on how we'll conduct
ourselves. Before turning to the final chapters, some preliminary remarks
ought to be made.

Late in *Being and Time*, Heidegger introduces *the call*, which we've
already seen discussed in our discussion of Weberian vocation and Rand-
ian spirituality (chapter 4). The German *Ruf* has parallels with a number of
other terms, such as *Anruf* (appeal) and *Aufruf* (summoning). By receiving a call of conscience, one experiences "an *appeal* to Dasein by calling it
to its ownmost potentiality-for-Being-its-Self; and this is done by way of
summoning it to its ownmost Being-guilty."[32] Guilt, *schuld*, could also be
rendered as *indebtedness* or *responsibility*, although the former is also telling, since it reminds us about *authenticity* being connected to *eigenschaft*
(ownership). When Heidegger says we are guilty or indebted, there are two
ways this can be understood. Along these lines, we've discussed how we
are always-already *indebted* to a certain understanding of ourselves, in our
case as *Homo Economartist*. We bear a debt, both philosophical and under
late capitalism often literal, that defines and shapes us. However, while idle
chatter closes off alternative possibilities, the call cuts through the idle noise,
and breaks us out of the stranglehold of the They-self.

An objection might be made that the call doesn't imply a particular
program or course of action, although to this Heidegger would likely shrug
and agree.

> We miss a 'positive' content in that which is called, *because we
> expect to be told something currently useful about assured pos-
> sibilities of 'taking action' which are available and calculable.*
> This expectation has its basis within the horizon of that way of

---

30. Heidegger, *Being and Time*, 264.
31. Heidegger, *Being and Time*, 265.
32. Heidegger, *Being and Time*, 269.

interpreting which belongs to common-sense concern—a way of interpreting which forces Dasein's existence to be subsumed under the idea of a business procedure that can be regulated. Such expectations (and in part these tacitly underlie even the demand for a *material* ethic of value as contrasted with on that is 'merely' formal) are of course disappointed by the conscience. The call of conscience fails to give any such 'practical injunctions, *solely because* it summons Dasein to existence, to its own-most potentiality-for-Being-its-Self.[33]

So if the call doesn't give us a plan, what *does* it give us? Heidegger's own description here is somewhat ambiguous and repeats itself across a number of chapters,[34] but essentially the call wrests us from the They, our inauthentic everydayness, and forces us to wrestle with not only the way we are *indebted* to a certain way of being, but the fact that in being such-and-such a way we are making a choice to be so. The call gives us a chance to move towards a more authentic, unalienated life, because it not only shows us how we are living out a particular set of decisions and choices, but also forces us to potentially take responsibility for them, for ourselves. Contra the idea that 'there is no alternative', Heideggerian authenticity forces us to recognize the way in which certain necessities are actually choices, decisions, developed orientations rather than neutral descriptions.

But what might *authenticity* look like for us today? We've been setting ourselves up with a more specifically anticapitalist perspective, looking at everyday life under late capitalism, the constant drive in the service of capital's own insatiability, and recent events would suggest many people, particularly young ones, are picking this up. In the Democratic presidential primaries in both 2016 and 2020, the democratic socialist Bernie Sanders led an electoral insurrection of sorts, winning enormous amounts of the youth vote, barely being stopped by a series of last-minute decisions and 'coalitions' that were thrown together. Kids these days are picking up on a call (rather than a Weberian 'vocation'), something that has broken capital's ideological stranglehold, and are demanding the chance to *be* something other than an investment portfolio. The question is, *can* we take responsibility for the shape of our personal and social structures? Can we *be* anything other than an investment option?

---

33. Heidegger, *Being and Time*, 294

34. Most of his discussion of this topic comes from division II, chapter 2, which does explain the ambiguity to some degree. The first division of *Being and Time* was developed with patience and care over several years; the second was written in a much more rushed fashion as he tried to meet some publishing deadlines, since he was up for an academic promotion and had to publish something in order to qualify, an interesting reminder that even the most abstract of theories were developed in and shaped by particular conditions.

Chapter 9—**Peterson**

The conflict between what we know and what we don't know is played out in all art, that is what has driven it over the centuries, and that situation is never fixed, never stable, because the moment we find out something new, something else new appears of which we know nothing.

—KARL OVE KNAUSGAARD, *MY STRUGGLE VOL VI*

And so, we now finally get to Jordan Peterson. Like Ayn Rand, Peterson's work has been deeply divisive in the last few years, infuriating some while gaining deep admiration from others. This comes from a number of places that go beyond the usual polarized nature of our media landscape today. For one, there are actually several different Petersons. The one most people know and love/hate comes in the form of interviews on podcasts or clips of talks scattered around YouTube either on his own channel or under channels with names like 'Hidden Wisdom' where he discusses everything from the horrors of the Stalinist purges to the mythological significance of Disney films. These clips can range from a couple minutes to a couple hours. Beyond that, but still slightly connected, is Peterson the author, first of the 500-page tome *Maps of Meaning*, following it up almost 20 years later with the semi-connected self-help book *12 Rules for Life*, which he says was intended to carry the same main themes to a more general audience.[1] This Peterson is concerned with using the theories of psychoanalysis and comparative mythology to extract key themes of the human condition, and apply them to larger philosophical and political questions. This Peterson is at times more similar to the YouTube and podcasting personality, offering anecdotes on the meaning of life to curious listeners, and at times more scholarly, investigating theoretical texts and trying to put together a systematic worldview or ontology. And then there's a third Peterson, the professor

---

1. Peterson, *12 Rules for Life*, xxvii-xxix.

of psychology, with his main interests being theories of personality, as well as addiction, particularly with alcohol, his dissertation even focusing on dispositions for alcoholism.

I bring all this up to clarify my own approach to Peterson, which will be to focus on the middle one that writes books. Occasional reference may be made to some of his essays, interviews or video-clips, but my focus will be on the theories put forth in his written work. There are several reasons for this. The first is admittedly a quirk in my own personality; I just prefer reading and taking notes on books rather than scouring through podcasts or videos. I personally have no problem with academics who choose to take their ideas online (I actually wish more would put forth the effort Peterson has to make their content more accessible to the general public), but I'm old-fashioned here. I'll not be addressing his academic essays for the most part, partly because most of it isn't accessible to me (either being behind a paywall, beyond my own expertise, or both), and also because this isn't the Peterson most people know or care about. Most found him on the internet, and if they felt so inclined tried out his books. On top of all this, focusing on his books allows for us to really dig into his core ideas without having to reference and draw from dozens of different sources, taking random quotes out of context and piecing together a worldview from across all those different sources. An exploration of *Maps of Meaning* (and *12 Rules* to a lesser extent) allows us to explore a host of themes without needing to stitch them together; he's done that for us.

This move to focus on his written work may raise the objection that I'm 'picking my Peterson,' focusing on the work of his that suits *me* while ignoring the output that has resonated with so many others. However, the alternative is to engage with a collection of interviews and YouTube videos scattered across the web, which some people have done. However, this sort of critique often meets the objection that those are just meant to be introductions to his main ideas expressed in his academic work. In going to his books, I'm skipping this step and going to the source. It might be objected that I'm focusing on a single snapshot of an evolving worldview, which is again true, but if this is held as an objection then no criticism is possible at all. *Maps of Meaning* itself is itself the product of spending 3 hours a day for almost 15 years, followed by lecturing on the material for decades afterward.[2] It's 500 pages long, and attempts to build a whole philosophical system from the ground up. There's little reason to think he has changed his views in any substantial way since its publication. It seems if there were ever a book that was 'fair game' for criticism, this would be it.

---

2. Peterson, *12 Rules for Life*, xxvii.

Meanwhile, this move may also draw complaints from his detractors, complaining that I'm insufficient in addressing his problematic forays into the contemporary culture wars and politics. In focusing on his theories of psychology and ignoring his political interventions, I may be accused of giving him too much credit and buying into his own claim in an interview that "what I'm doing is not political. It's psychological . . . "[3] This quote-turned-headline for an interview with Peterson drew laughs from a number of Peterson's critics, since his entry into the public spotlight was criticism of political legislation, but it's also questionable given how much of his written work is inspired by politics, the preface to *Maps of Meaning* even detailing how he was inspired to study psychology as a way of understanding various political atrocities. It seems obvious that a significant portion of his output is political in nature.

In the face of this apparently common-sense objection, I actually want to take Peterson completely seriously here. As will hopefully become clear, Petersons politics emerge out of a particular theory of the subject, a particular way of imagining how we navigate and interpret our world, and the implications it has for politics. To put my views up front, I do not agree with Peterson on much; I think he is poorly informed on a number of issues he discusses, and his political orientation borders on reactionary at times. However, the only way beyond here is through, and so to do so, we'll be going through his work, reading *Maps of Meaning* alongside *Being and Time*,[4] trying to use both to learn how to navigate these times out of joint.[5]

Maps of Meaning is not an ordinary or easy book, and like Heidegger's *Being and Time*, has drawn accusations of being nonsensical and unverifiable. If you've made it this far into *this book* however, these sorts of accusations probably won't dissuade you too much. Upon first reading it, I was actually struck by how similar the two books were in some of their themes and approaches, although I've found little evidence that Peterson has read much Heidegger. The only point where he actually mentions Heidegger directly, aside from occasional brief mentions in a couple of his online

3. Peterson and Robertson, "What I'm Doing is Not Political . . . "

4. Much of the comparative work here will be adapted from a presentation I gave shortly before deciding to try writing the present volume. See Dozeman, "Mythic Individualism."

5. Those understandably looking for an engagement with his political orientations should read see the sources mentioned in the introduction in footnote 12, as well as the literally *hundreds* of hot takes scattered across the internet. Admittedly part of my keeping away from this element of Peterson is because it has been done to death by now, and rather than simply adding more fuel to the flames, I'd prefer to orient myself in territory not yet sufficiently covered.

lectures,[6] is in the preface to *12 Rules* in a footnote, explaining that he'll be capitalizing the word *Being* "in part because of my exposure to the ideas of the 20th century German philosopher Martin Heidegger."[7] Peterson's own brief account of Heidegger is problematic, and even misunderstands Heidegger's capitalizing of *Being*. Peterson sees Being as indicating our own psychological experience of reality, as opposed to the factual reality we're surrounded with and that can be objectively measured. While not the worst take on Heidegger, it's clear from the beginning that his reading is some-what superficial. The capitalization of the word *Being* in the translation of *Being and Time* by MacQuarrie and Robinson that I've been relying on is attempting to differentiate between the verb *sein* (to be) and the proper noun *Sein* (being), which is always capitalized in German for grammati-cal reasons. They explain this on the first footnote of the first page of the text. This move has had mixed reception in English commentaries, since it misleads many people into thinking that Heidegger was doing something unique in capitalizing the term, and has also led some to think of *Being* in more mystical terms than intended, some critics even complaining that it seems to points towards the highly misleading spectre of 'Big Being'.[8] In her later translation, Stambaugh decided not to go with the capitalization, a move I've tended to follow. Peterson then throughout *12 Rules* proceeds to capitalize *Being*, as well as words as a way of emphasizing their psychologi-cal, rather than literal significance.

If we ignore this weird little mishap and let their two main texts speak in parallel, however, things will start to open up, and we'll be able to see both where they overlap and eventually diverge, and the significance of those divergences more clearly.

Peterson's main task in *Maps of Meaning* is to synthesize several differ-ent fields, including modern psychology and neuroscience, psychoanalysis and depth psychology, comparative mythology and religion to gain insights into the underlying causes of human motivations, so as to better understand fields such as history and politics. While it's been called many things, I'll be borrowing Cadell Last's term 'psychological realism'[9] to describe Peter-son's position. This view actually seems to come largely from Jung, albeit in slightly different terminology. Jung himself was heavily indebted to Kant's splitting of reality in two, into *phenomena* and *noumena*, and that we only

6. Peterson, "2017 Personality 12"; Peterson, 2016 "Personality Lecture 09"

7. Peterson, *12 Rules for Life*. xxxi.

8. Wheeler, "Martin Heidegger."

9. Last, "Žižek and Peterson," 6.

had access to the former. Jungian psychology takes this as its starting point, as Jung wrote in 1927;

> The only things we experience immediately are the content of consciousness. In saying this I am not attempting to reduce the 'world' to our 'idea' of it. . .My point of view is naturally a psychological one, and moreover that of a practicing psychologist whose task it is to find the quickest road through the chaotic muddle of complicated psychic states. . .I also differ from the metaphysician, who feels he has to say how things are 'in themselves,' and whether they are absolute or not. My subject lies wholly within the bounds of experience.[10]

This emphasis on the psychological significance would be developed and popularized by Joseph Campbell, who cut his academic teeth with a co-authored commentary on James Joyce's *Finnegan's Wake*,[11] and then with his book *The Hero With a Thousand Faces*,[12] although the real explosion in mainstream popularity would come in 1988 when PBS aired a collection of interviews between Campbell and Bill Moyers, later published as a book.[13]

Following Jung, Campbell saw the importance of various mythological and religious narrative structures and motifs for the way they helped cultivate a fully developed human subject. Breaking things down further, he offers four primary functions of mythology:

> The first function is that of reconciling consciousness to the preconditions of its own existence—that is, of aligning waking consciousness of the *mysterium tremendum* of this universe, *as it is.*[14]

> The second function of mythology is interpretive, to present a consistent image of the order of the cosmos.[15]

> The third function of a traditional mythology is to validate and support a specific moral order, that order of the society out of which that mythology arose.[16]

---

10. Jung, "The Structure of the Psyche," 24.

11. Campbell and Robinson, *A Skeletons Key to Finnegans Wake*. To tie the circle around these figures even tighter, Joyce's daughter even underwent psychoanalytic treatment with Carl Jung.

12. Campbell, *The Hero With a Thousand Faces*.

13. Campbell and Moyers, *The Power of Myth*.

14. Campbell, *Thou Art That*, 2.

15. Campbell, *Thou Art That*, 3.

16. Campbell, *Thou Art That*, 5.

> The fourth function of traditional mythology is to carry the individual through the various stages and crises of life—that is, to help person's grasp the unfolding of life with integrity.[17]

So the function of mythology and religion is to give the subject a comprehensible picture of the world around them and help them navigate it. One of the issues then facing today is a detachment from traditional wisdom that mythology offers, as Campbell explained to Moyers.

> Moyers: What happens when a society no longer embraces a powerful mythology?
>
> Campbell: What we've got on your hands. If you want to find out what it means to have a society without any rituals, read the *New York Times*.
>
> Moyers: And you'd find?
>
> Campbell: The news of the day, including destructive and violent acts by young people who don't know how to behave in a civilized society.[18]

It's here that Peterson's own work kicks off, since he shared a similar concern to Campbell, but on a much larger scale. His first BA was done in political science, with one of his main areas of concern being large-scale political atrocities such as the Soviet Gulags, the Nazi Holocaust, and the potential for nuclear annhialation posed by the Cold War. His turn to psychology was largely motivated by a desire to understand what could lead people to do (or come to precipice of doing) such horrific things.

> I couldn't understand the nuclear race: what could possibly be worth risking annihilation—not merely of the present, but of the past and the future? *What could possibly justify the threat of total destruction?* Bereft of solutions, I had at least been granted the gift of a problem. I returned to university and began to study psychology.[19]

His turn to Jungian thought to solve the question of political atrocities might seem surprising, but Jung himself was actually deeply concerned with the spectre of totalitarianism, writing much of his work in response to it.[20] Like Jung and Campbell, Peterson adopts the emphasis on psycho-

17. Campbell, *Thou Art That*, 5; also see Jung, "The Stages of Life."
18. Campbell and Moyers, *The Power of Myth*, 8-9.
19. Peterson, *Maps of Meaning*, xv.
20. See for example Jung, "Answer to Job"; for an in-depth analysis of Jung's thought

logical significance, although he arguably takes it further than Jung did. Bear in mind Jung's quotation above in which he cordones off study of material reality so as to better focus on psychological reality: "*My* subject lies wholly within the bounds of experience."[21] This leaves the world untouched, something Peterson doesn't do in his own theories: "I discovered that beliefs make the world, in a very real way—that beliefs *are* the world in a more than metaphysical sense."[22] His conception of *world* actually has two planes: "The world can be validly construed as a forum for action, as well as a place of things."[23] His emphasis will be on the former, the world of action, which has three primary pillars:

> First is unexplored territory—the Great Mother, nature, creative and destructive, source and final resting place of all determinate things. Second is explored territory—the Great Father, culture protective and tyrannical, cumulative ancestral wisdom. Third is the process that mediates between unexplored and explored territory—the Divine Son, the archetypal individual, creative exploratory Word and vengeful adversary.[24]

The complaint that the descriptions here lean towards a certain metaphorical abstraction miss the point Peterson is trying to get at, that these mythic images and motifs actually tap into certain impulses embedded deeply in human nature, and help us navigate those impulses, rather than being dominated by them. He shares the concern of Campbell, that societies without proper mythology will go off the rails: "the world-that-is-belief is orderly. . .there are moral absolutes. . .I believe that individuals and societies who flout these absolutes—in ignorance or willful opposition—are doomed to misery and eventual dissolution."[25]

In reanimating Jungian theories of narrative and their importance for conscious development, Peterson is attempting to give us a clearer framework to understand our own lives and the twists and turns they take. An example shows up early in *Maps of Meaning*, in the section titled 'Revolutionary Life'.[26] The story focuses on a young man attempting to climb the corporate ladder, only to be fired. After spending several weeks in a deep

---

as it applies to totalitarian ideology, see Johnson, *Ideological Possession and the Rise of the New Right*.

21. Jung, "The Structure of the Psyche," 24 (my emphasis).

22. Peterson, *Maps of Meaning*, xx.

23. Peterson, *Maps of Meaning*, xxi.

24. Peterson, *Maps of Meaning*, xxi.

25. Peterson, *Maps of Meaning*, xx.

26. Peterson, *Maps of Meaning*, 29-32.

depression, the main character eventually comes to realize that they maybe didn't really care for that job as much as they thought they had; maybe they have other passions they'd rather pursue, and now they're finally free to pursue them. "You start imagining a new future—one where you are not so 'secure,' maybe, but where you are doing what you actually want to do. . .You are a man recovering from a long illness—a man reborn."[27]

This is classic 'hero's journey' stuff right here, with the call to adventure, followed by a descent into the underworld or the belly of the whale, followed by a spiritual rebirth where one has gained a deeper insight into the nature of things.

As one digs further into the text, one will actually start seeing various parallels between it and *Being and Time*. Peterson and Heidegger share a similar appreciation for the way people find themselves in certain social orders and situations. *Maps of Meaning* uses the language of Jungian psychology and comparative mythology to try and describe the underlying elements that constitute our experience as subjects, which finds its most advanced expression in fully developed human societies, which "shelters, protects, trains and disciplines the developing individual—and places necessary constraints on his thought, emotion and behavior."[28] Following Jung, Peterson sees individual development as being, initially dependent but slowly working towards psychological independence. Initially, "childhood dependency entails adoption of ritual behavior and incorporation of a morality,"[29] but eventually the individual expands beyond its parentally created bubble and moves to adolescence; "Successful transition from childhood to adolescence means *identification with the group*, rather than continued dependency upon the parents."[30] What both these groups provide, on different scales, is a known environment, as well as protection from the unknown. It also provides the individual with a sense of identity, and the sorts of options available to the individual, options which have slowly acquired throughout the groups history. This analysis of a group, as something that the individual identifies with and which helps the individual discover its possible paths in life, is similar to Heidegger's analysis of the They. *Being and Time*, like *Maps of Meaning*, is in large part a study of everyday existence as experienced from the first-person human perspective, and one of the central points Heidegger makes is that we always initially experience ourselves as part of a larger social whole. The others, as with Peterson's socializing group, are those whom you identify

27. Peterson, *Maps of Meaning*, 32.
28. Peterson, *Maps of Meaning*, 216.
29. Peterson, *Maps of Meaning*, 221.
30. Peterson, *Maps of Meaning*, 221.

with. The Others amidst which Dasein, Heidegger's term for the human sub-ject, finds itself aren't simply the place Dasein finds itself, aren't simply those physically next to you, but are your very possibilities that are available to you for modes of existence. Both Peterson's heroic individual and Heidegger's *Dasein* then find themselves, initially, embedded in a social milieu which helps them understand who they are and how they ought to act.

Eventually, however, the individual begins to find itself trapped in the current social order. For Peterson, social order, which he identifies with the masculine king, eventually will reach a point of decay, but will not give up its power, leading to tyranny, both literal and spiritual. For Heidegger, Dasein often finds itself trapped by the They, who can simultaneously give it its own possibilities for how to exist, but can also close off alternative possibilities. In both cases, the subject being discussed finds itself wrestling against a so-cial structure where they do not fit. But both are given narratives by which to escape. Peterson's hero undergoes a breakdown which "re-exposes him to the unknown—previously covered, so to speak, by culture."[31] This is also the starting point of Joseph Campbell's monomythic structure, experienced as a call to adventure which "reveals an unsuspected world, and the individ-ual is drawn into a relationship with forces that are not rightly understood." Heidegger's Dasein experiences an ambiguous call which "calls Dasein forth (and 'forward') into its ownmost possibilities, as a summons to its ownmost *potentiality*-for-Being-its-Self."[32] In all cases, it's a journey of self-discovery that saves one from the entrapment in a social milieu.

The similarities between the two shouldn't be a surprise, given the shared background of influence. Both were heavily influenced by similar philosophers (Nietzsche being a key point of reference for both of them), and each have developed combinations of antimodernist pessimism about social trajectory, and attempted in various ways to combat it with bits of existentialism and romantic thought.[33]

Before further developing the comparison between them, let's briefly turn to focus on Peterson's theory of the subjects transition, which gets its most thorough analysis in chapter 4 of *Maps of Meaning*, 'The Appearance of Anomaly: Challenge to the Shared Map.'

Following along with Thomas Kuhn's theory of scientific paradigms, Peterson argues that "Human culture has, by necessity, a paradigmatic structure—devoted not toward objective description of what is, but to

31. Peterson, *Maps of Meaning*, 274.

32. Heidegger, *Being and Time*, 273.

33. For a discussion of the political and cultural context in which monomythic the-ories were developed, see Ellwood, *The Politics of Myth*. For a discussion of Heidegger's context, see Wolin, *The Politics of Being*, ch. 1-2 and Weitz, *Weimar Germany*.

description of the cumulative affective relevance, or meaning, of what is."[34] These cultures then have layers, like a Matryoshka doll, with each level having a 'story', the more specific ones at the center relying on the implicit ones at the broader edges of knowledge. The doll-structure of culture

> presents the 'personality' of a typical Western individual—in this case, a middle-class businessman and father. His individual life is nested within an increasingly transpersonal, shared 'personality', with deep, increasingly implicit historical roots. The 'smaller stories', nested within the larger, are dependent for their continued utility on maintenance of the larger—as the middle-class family, for example, is dependent for its economic stability on the capitalist system, as the capitalist system is nested in humanistic Western thought, as humanism is dependent on the notion of the inherent value of the individual (on the notion of 'individual rights'), and as the inherent value of the individual is dependent on his association, or ritual identification, with the exploratory communicative hero.[35]

So the individual subject has layers that help properly individuate them.[36] This implicit set of layers is usually fairly stable and predictable, but eventually anomalies start to appear. Peterson has three forms of anomaly: the strange, the stranger and the strange idea. What unites them all is the "capacity to threaten the integrity of the known, to disrupt the 'familiar and explored.'"[37] The introduction of anomalies into a culture can cause a variety of reactions, such as attempting to bury and 'lock away' unknown elements in order to preserve a certain way of life.[38] Others will descend into nihilism, while others may go the route of conservative or reactionary backlash.[39] However, while the group can at times protect from random intrusions and help both societies and individuals maintain some sort of stable identity over time, there is also the danger that "in that integration—stable, hierarchically organized structure—is inflexible, and therefore brittle. This means the group, and those who identify with it, cannot easily develop new modes of perception or change direction when such change or development

---

34. Peterson, *Maps of Meaning*, 236.

35. Peterson, *Maps of Meaning*, 241.

36. *Individuation* is the proper Jungian term, referring to one's "movement toward greater psychological wholeness." (Erickson, *Imagination in the Western Psyche*, 94). pg. 94)

37. Peterson, *Maps of Meaning*, 245.

38. Peterson, *Maps of Meaning*, 248.

39. Peterson, *Maps of Meaning*, 250.

is necessary."[40] In the face of this brittleness, we get the revolutionary hero, "the agent of change" and, ironically enough, the one "upon whose actions all stability is predicated."[41]

Peterson uses the example of the shaman to illustrate revolutionary activity, although it's clearly meant as an umbrella-concept to encompass a variety of figures, from philosophers, poets and artists.[42]

> These creative individuals detect emergent anomaly, and begin the process of adaptation to it, long before the average person notices any change whatsoever in circumstance. In his ecstasy the shaman lives the potential future life of his society. This dangerous individual can play a healing role in his community because he has suffered more through experience through his peers.[43]

Shamanesque individuals exist as anomalies to their surrounding culture, but it's a necessary challenge, as otherwise a society may fail to adapt to certain challenges, although this is itself a challenge, since by their very nature the shaman lives in a disjointed fashion with it's milieu, and is exposed to various sorts of antagonisms of that society in a much more raw and visceral fashion:

> The future shaman is in fact tormented by the incomplete or self-contradictory state of his cultural structure, as it is intra-psychically represented; is undergoing a breakdown induced by some aspect of personal experience, some existential anomaly, that cannot be easily integrated into that structure. This break-down re-exposes him to the unknown—previously covered, so to speak, by his culture.[44]

The problem is every society has limits to what it can handle, and eventually every cultural paradigm runs into anomalies it can't handle, so a new way of existential paradigm is required. The importance of the heroic individual is that they detect the need for change before most others do, and start living in ways that try and respond to the need for something new.

> He may also be the only person who is presently capable of perceiving that social adaptation is incompletely or improperly structured in a particular way . . . In taking creative action, he

40. Peterson, *Maps of Meaning*, 271.
41. Peterson, *Maps of Meaning*, 271.
42. Peterson, *Maps of Meaning*, 272.
43. Peterson, *Maps of Meaning*, 273.
44. Peterson, *Maps of Meaning*, 274.

(re)encounters chaos, generates new myth-predicated behavioral strategies, and extends the boundaries (or transforms the paradigmatic structure) of cultural competence. The well-adapted man identifies with what has been, conserves past wisdom, and is therefore protected from the unknown. The hero, by contrast, author and editor of history, masters the known, exceeds its bounds, and then subjects it to restructuring. . .[45]

As important as this transition is, the hero isn't always welcomed or recognized as such, since their very existence exists as a challenge to the dominant paradigm, and people will naturally feel a certain fear and hostility towards their own potential savior: "The hero is the first person to have his 'internal structure' (that is, his hierarchy of value and his behaviors) reorganized as a consequence of contact with an emergent anomaly. His 'descent into the underworld' and subsequent reorganization makes him a savior—but his contact with the dragon of chaos also contaminates him with the forces that disrupt tradition and stability."[46] However, the hero must weather this storm, because the inflexibility of societies is what eventually leads to their own demise in the face of change.

> The future brings with it the unknown; inflexibility and unwillingness to change therefore brings the certainty of extinction. . .If resolution is not reached in time of crisis, mental illness (for the individual) or cultural degeneration (for the society) threatens. This 'mental illness' (failure of culture, failure of heroism) is return to domination by the unknown—in mythological terms, expressed as involuntary incest (destructive union) with the Terrible Mother.[47]

So the hero is a desperately needed figure that revolutionizes our way of being in the face of a changing world. As certain social paradigms begin to crumble, something new is needed. One can see how this narrative might have clicked so well with the young people described in the previous chapters, strung out by long hours and low pay, debt, impending climate catastrophe and an intensification or the marginalization of various minority populations. Petersons own story of a society that begins to consume itself as a way of avoiding transition has certain vague thematic parallels to Karl Marx's description of how societies are forced to slowly cannibalize themselves in order to maintain profits (to say nothing of continuing to

---

45. Peterson, *Maps of Meaning*, 278.
46. Peterson, *Maps of Meaning*, 279.
47. Peterson, *Maps of Meaning*, 289.

burn fossil fuels in the face of impending climate change). So naturally the question must be asked, why isn't Peterson a revolutionary?

The story of radical change Peterson seems to have here is one of radical social change and reformulation of values and orientations. The shaman could be a political radical, an environmental activist or even someone who's transgender.[48] So why isn't Peterson advocating green and gay Communism?[49]

The obvious reason for his anti-Marxism would be that he hasn't bothered to read Marx beyond the pamphlet *The Communis Manifesto*, as opposed to the multi-volume *Capital* or *The Grundrisse* or one of Marx's more systematic works. Beyond that, his main understanding of Communism seems to come from Alexander Solzhenitsyn's 3-volume *Gulag Archipelago*, which, whatever its merits, is far from a rigorous debunking of Marxist theory. So yes, it's true that Peterson's politics seem to be somewhat poorly informed. However, there are other mechanisms at work in the stories we've been outlining that are at work in his resistance to radical political change.

To start us off, let's return to the story of a man who gets fired, only to eventually find a better place for himself in some other line of work. The story is kicked off by a meeting with the boss, who tells him she has some bad news. "'Look,' she says, 'I have received a number of very unfavorable reports regarding your behavior at meetings. All of your colleagues seem to regard you as a rigid and overbearing negotiator. Furthermore, it has become increasingly evident that you are unable to respond positively to feedback about your shortcomings. Finally, you do not appear to properly

---

48. "The archaic shamanic initiate was commonly someone uniquely marked by fate, by the 'will of the gods'—by particular heredity, 'magical' (novel) occurrence in early childhood or later in life (birth in a caul; survival of a lighting strike), or by intrapsychic idiosyncrasy (epileptic susceptibility, visionary proclivity). His unique personality or experiential history, in combination with presently extant social conditions, doomed him to experience so anomalous that it could not simultaneously be accepted as actually occurring—as real—*and* as possible with the confines determined by ruling social presumption. The existence of this experience, if 'admitted' and 'processed,' therefore presented a potentially fatal challenge to the perceived validity of the axioms currently underlying the maintenance of normal 'sanity'—the sociohistorically determined stability of mutually determined behavioral adaptation and experiential significance. The existence of this distinct experience served as a gateway to the unknown, or as a floodgate, a portal, through which the unexpected could pour, with inevitably destructive and potentially creative consequences. The shaman is the individual who chooses to meet such a flood head on." (Peterson, *Maps of Meaning*, pg. 274)

49. This is to be contrasted with gray and heteronormative Communism, a counter-evolutionary betrayal of authentically Marxist-Leninist principles.

understand the purpose of your job or the function of this corporation."[50] The story continues:

> You are shocked beyond belief, paralyzed into immobility. Your vision of the future with this company vanishes, replaced by apprehensions of unemployment, social disgrace and failure. You find it difficult to breathe. You flush and perspire profusely; your face is a mask of barely suppressed horror. You cannot believe your boss is such a bitch. 'You have been with us for five years,' she continues, 'and it is obvious that your performance is not likely to improve. You are definitely not suited for this sort of career, and you are interfering with the progress of the many competent others around you. In consequence, we have decided to terminate your contract with us, effective immediately. If I were you, I would take a good look at myself."[51]

Harsh, but possibly fair. The way this critique is interpreted and responded to is telling however. The encounter with the unknown has certainly "shaken the foundations of your worldview"[52] but in a certain sense, it's been completely missed. The fact that the hero here seems to be largely at fault, with his boss even explaining the issues that lead to the firing, gets largely ignored. In fact, the actual content of what she's seeing seems largely irrelevant; what's important is that from the hero's perspective, he has begun the disintegrating descent into the realm of chaos. The eventual rebirth won't be a result of reflecting on his own bad behavior; it'll be because he decides he didn't like the job in the first place, and he'd rather find a good job he actually likes. This is retroactively rewriting the past as a way to justify present plans, while also ignoring the historical problems that led you there in the first place.

To illustrate this a little more clearly, suppose the story had been written slightly differently here. Instead of happening in 1999 when *Maps* was first published, suppose it had been written in 2010, shortly after the 2008-fiscal crisis, and the hypothetical boss has brought the hero in to fire him, but under different circumstances.

> "Look," she says, "I have received word that we need to start making budgetary cuts. Much as we've appreciated the effort you've put in over the last few years, it's been decided that due to you being such a recent hire and still occupying a relatively inessential position, we're going to let you go. We don't want

50. Peterson, *Maps of Meaning*, 30.
51. Peterson, *Maps of Meaning*, 30.
52. Peterson, *Maps of Meaning*, 30.

to, but we're hoping doing this can allow us to weather out this
storm, and we'll be more than happy to hire you back if things
are better in a few years, and you're more than welcome to use
me as a reference." You are shocked beyond belief . . .

The story here could have continued in the same way it was originally written
and the meaning would be the same, because the actual reasons one was fired
aren't relevant; learning from those reasons, be they personal or systemic,
is irrelevant, because the ultimate reason you were fired isn't really either of
those; instead, it's chaos, and the way actual worldly phenomenon are translated by Peterson into his psychological language doesn't help us reflect any
more clearly on them; in fact, it prevents just such reflection from taking
place. When everything is to be understood as part of some deeply natural
binary, then fighting it is impossible; coping is our only option.

In parallel with this is the development of a very particular sort of
solipsism, an issue that seems to come up in monomythic approaches to
mythology and religion in general, since more, this approach always focuses
on the individual hero and their personal story and psychology, turning
traditional fields of scholarship into a slightly more developed version of
traditional self-help. However, if one is supposed to see themself as the lead
character in a story, what happens to everyone else? We've already seen the
boss get largely ignored, and then there's the treatment by the hero of his
family during his depression; just a brief mention that he snaps at them,[53]
and nothing else. Of course, this gets glossed over rather quickly, and isn't
ever apologized for. Neither does the man ever reflect on why he was fired
in the first place, making a self-fulfilling prophecy of the claim that "you are
unable to respond positively to feedback about your shortcomings". That Peterson considers this to be a prime archetypal example of how we navigate
our lives, failing to consider other perspectives and abusing those around
us, tells us a lot more than he seems to realize about how he sees himself as
the main character in some larger story.

Peterson, for example, lived out a real-world parallel of the story told
above in 2018, where he encountered criticism from a female-figure. Kate
Manne's review of his book *12 Rules for Life* was a rather harsh but fair
critique that pointed out several problematic blindspots in the book, such
as the ways in which Peterson doesn't seem aware of the ways in which
his feelings of a sort of 'cultural vertigo' might be partially determined
by his social position: "we should ask" Manne writes, "who in the world
is likeliest to be experiencing vertigo at the moment? Peterson does not
consider this question, but its answer is not far to seek: those with furthest

---

53. Peterson, *Maps of Meaning*, 30.

to fall, given their historically great expectations. Privileged white men, all else being equal, who also happen to number disproportionately among Peterson's loyal readers."[54] She also points out the ways in which Peterson takes quotes from mass-shooters out of context, often interpreting them as existential antiheroes who experience modernity too intensely, writing that "these murderous individuals had a problem with reality that existed at a religious depth."[55] Manne points out what Peterson has a tendency to either downplay or omit entirely:

> he ignores a few distinctive facts about those who commit such violence. First, he fails to acknowledge that these killers are overwhelmingly male, typically white, and otherwise privileged (straight and cis, in particular). Second, they often betray an obsession with being top lobster (many, for example, have also committed acts of intimate partner violence, which typically function to express and enforce male dominance). This makes them members of the very group to which Peterson's book is chiefly offering advice. The resulting discussion is not good, to put it mildly; it is highly irresponsible and deeply deceptive by omission."[56]

Later on, in an interview with Vox's Sean Illing, Manne says that certain aspects of the book could be described as sexist, due to their naturalization of patriarchal order, and also that his comments on enforced monogamy are misogynistic, since it hints at channeling women's behavior as a way of satisfying male desires and curbing male violence. In these instances, she's actually very precise, using the words 'sexism' and 'misogyny' in more careful ways than most (she did, after all, write a whole book on how misogyny functions).

In response to these comments, similar to the ones the hero from *Maps of Meaning* received from a female colleague (being rigid and overbearing, and misunderstanding ones place in a broader social artifice), Peterson threatened a lawsuit, demanding the statements be retracted and an apology issued. The irony of these demands coming from someone who's fame originated from a refusal to use transgendered students preferred pronouns because it was seen as an example of 'compelled speech' was apparently lost on Peterson, but it's telling that he seems to not have taken the criticism as a chance to reflect. Instead, he's rooted himself firmly in his own perspective, and sees Manne as a sort of intellectual combatant rather than a viable alternative perspective, although she's not to be combatted

54. Manne, "Reconsider the Lobster."
55. Peterson, *12 Rules for Life*, 147.
56. Manne, "Reconsider the Lobster."

intellectually, but with lawsuits. He did write a blog piece on the topic, pointing out that he hadn't actually written glorifying the mass shooters he'd written of, although it's hard to take such a claim seriously, given that he contextualizes their struggles (the ones occurring at a "religious depth") with passages from Goethe's *Faust*, Tolstoy's *Confessions*, and drops pieces from Nietzsche and Solzhenitsyn. He describes the story of Carl Panzram, who experienced a childhood filled with abuse, which led to his own violence and abuse of those around him.

> He started by hating the individuals who had hurt him. His resentment grew, until his hatred encompassed all of mankind, and he didn't stop there. His destructiveness was aimed in some fundamental manner at God Himself. There is no other way of phrasing it. Panzram raped, murdered and burned to express his outrage at Being. He acted as if Someone was responsible. The same thing happens in the story of Cain and Abel. Cain's sacrifices are rejected. He exists in suffering. He calls out God and challenges the Being He created. God refuses his plea. He tells Cain that his trouble is self-induced. Cain, in his rage, kills Abel, God's favourite (and, truth be known, Cain's idol). Cain is jealous, of course, of his successful brother. But he destroys Abel primarily to spite God. This is the truest version of what happens when people take their vengeance to the ultimate extreme.[57]

The actual victims here are barely present in Peterson's telling; instead, the anger is *actually* directed at Someone, God and Being, all capitalized to highlight that this is a struggle between Panzram and Something Bigger; the human victims simply got caught in the crossfire. It's unclear what makes this the 'truest version' of Panzram's story, or why a professor of psychology needs a collection of religious imagery and randomly capitalized words to make sense of Panzram, but it *is* clear why Manne found these passages among other objectionable. And they also betray Peterson to be, like the Red Pill-audience, obsessed with the first-person perspective to the point where one could justifiably call him a solipsist, albeit of an existential sort. That they all appeal to classical mythology is only a similarity in form; the underlying content is a set of theories and assumptions that justify their inability to take seriously that there are others around them.

This solipsism has two sides, however. The first we've been discussing is the emphasis on one's own experience as having a far more profound depth than it may have in reality. This was on full display at the recent (and much overhyped) Peterson v. Žižek debate. Peterson first demanded a debate on

---

57. Peterson, *12 Rules for Life*, 151-2.

Twitter in February 2018 in response to an article he didn't much care for. The debate was then announced in February 2019 for April, giving Peterson a couple months from the announcement (and over a year from his first demand for debate) to prepare on a debate on Marxism and Capitalism. His opening statement, after briefly bragging about how expensive the tickets had been for some people, went as follows:

> Alright, so how did I prepare for this? I went, I familiarized my-self to the degree that it was possible with Slavoj Žižek's work and, that wasn't that possible because he has a lot of work and he's a very original thinker, and this debate was put together in relatively short order, and what I did instead was returned to what I regarded as the original cause of all the trouble, let's say, which was the *Communist Manifesto*; and what I attempted to do, because that's Marx and we're here to talk about Marxism, let's say, and what I tried to do was read it. And to read some-thing, you don't just read all of the words and follow the mean-ing, but you take apart the sentences and you ask yourself: at this level of phrase, and at the level of sentence, and that the level of paragraph, is this true? Are there counter arguments that can be put forward that are credible, is this solid thinking?[58]

He then proceeded to give what amounted to a high schoolers response to *The Communist Manifesto*, written originally as a pamphlet to inspire the uneducated working class to revolt, making claims that Marx and Engels had never considered the possibility that they were wrong, which is true if you only read their pamphlets while ignoring the voluminous other writing they did. What's amazing though is that Peterson managed to show up for a debate he'd been demanding for over a year, admitted he wasn't terribly familiar with his interlocutor's work, and then proceeded to give some of the most superficial critique of the work possible, often stumbling over his own sentences as he searched for the right words, and all the while he seemed convinced that he was delivering some profound take no one had ever considered. What's on display here is a profoundly inflated sense of ego that assumes far more of one's own wisdom than is actually there.

But the flip-side of this self-inflation is a deflation of the other. The classicist Donna Zuckerberg experienced this deflation firsthand when she published the article "How to Be a Good Classicist under a Bad Emperor", which focused on the importance of paying attention to the Alt-Right's

---

58. It will no doubt be brought up that in my discussion of Žižek, I took his com-ments at the debate as worth listening to, something I am not doing in my discussion of Peterson. While true, this is largely in Petersons favor, given his lack of preparedness at that debate.

appropriation of classics, and the importance of fighting it with a diverse array of viewpoints and perspectives. That she was sent a wave of insults and threats was unsurprising to her, but "That response, alarming as it was, did not surprise me as much as the more substantive response articles accusing me of hating and wanting to destroy the Classics. One writer wrote, 'Had Zuckerberg her way, the ancient wisdom of Athens and Rome would likewise be consigned to the flames.' Another speculated, 'I think that deep down, you despise these books.' The idea of a feminist who enjoys and finds meaning in studying the ancient world is so inconceivable to these writers that they can more easily believe I have spent over a decade studying material I secretly despise."[59] This systematic deflation of Zuckerberg's own take as being driven by a one-dimensional resentment of a topic is an impressive feat, especially when we remember she has a PhD from an ivy-league university, and then started an online journal dedicated to the topic. Flipping through her book, one will find references to texts by Marcus Aurelius and Ovid, often dealing with them in their original languages, something no casual reader can pull off.

This deflation of the feminine perspective also happens again in Peterson's work. We've already seen his heroic figure in *Maps of Meaning* ignore the criticism of a female colleague, and then in *12 Rules* aggrandize the male perspective, regardless of its content, to being a sort of mythic hero. But the inverse was the deflated perspective of the female victims, largely forgotten in his telling. This deflationary perspective shows up in his own therapeutic practice, when he works with a patient he names Miss S.

> Miss S knew nothing about herself. She knew nothing about other individuals. She knew nothing about the world. She was a movie played out of focus. And she was desperately waiting for a story about herself to make it all make sense . . . I knew about all this when Miss S came to talk to me about her sexual experiences. When she recounted her trips to the singles bars, and their recurring aftermath, I thought about a bunch of things at once. I thought, 'You're so vague and so non-existent. You're a denizen of chaos and the underworld. You are going ten different places at the same time. Anyone can take you by the hand and guide you down the road of their choosing.'[60]

It was in response to these and other comments that Manne raised many of her objections, pointing out that to describe one's client in this way is highly suspect, since describing anyone as a 'a denizen of chaos and the

---

59. Zuckerberg, *Not All Dead White Men*, 187.

60. Peterson, *12 Rules for Life*, 236, 238.

underworld' is an odd way for anyone to describe anyone else, never mind a therapist describing their own client. But the questionability continues when he responds to the situation in a state of exasperation: "'Who are you? What did you do? What happened?' What was the objective truth? There was no way of knowing the objective truth. And there never would be. There was no objective observer, and there never would be. There was no complete and accurate story. Such a thing did not and could not exist. There were, and are, only partial accounts and fragmentary viewpoints."[61] It's odd that someone who's built a career railing against postmodernism's emphasis over the fragmented and subjective at the expense of the objective would decide to be at his most postmodern when listening to his own clients, but mystification of women is hardly new; Peterson would say it's a divine archetype, going back as far as recorded history, and perhaps further. Simone de Beauvoir also called attention to this phenomenon in *The Second Sex*, writing that of all the myths about women,

> none is more firmly anchored in masculine hearts than that of the feminine 'mystery'. It has numerous advantages. And first of all it permits an easy explanation of all that appears inexplicable; the man who 'does not understand' a woman is happy to substitute an objective resistance for a subjective deficiency of mind; instead of admitting his ignorance, he perceives the presence of a 'mystery' outside himself: an alibi, indeed that flatters laziness and vanity at once . . . in the company of a living enigma man remains alone . . . [this] is for man a more attractive experience than an authentic relationship with a human being.[62]

Beauvoir's account here points towards a mystification of women which has concrete effects, as we've been seeing. Their own needs and desires are generally neglected or ignored, their perspectives are not taken as seriously, and often they have ulterior motives assumed by others who claim to know them better than they know themselves.

This two-sided phenomenon of self-inflation and other-deflation happens along a number of lines, gendered and otherwise. Kate Manne, in her book *Down Girl*, looked at the credibility surpluses and deficits that men and women get, and the ways people of color and gender nonconforming people also are lacking in the 'credibility hierarchy'.[63] Peterson's client clearly was suffering from a credibility deficit, while his 'neutrality' was seen as a result or

---

61. Peterson, *12 Rules for Life*, 238-9.
62. Beauvoir, *The Second Sex*, 256.
63. Manne, *Down Girl*, 190-6.

expression of his surplus. Zuckerberg, in spite of obtaining a PhD, was accused of bad faith in her work by random posters on the internet.

That this happens along gendered lines is really an extension of the underlying point here, that the monomythic perspective encourages thinking of oneself as the star of reality, with other people relegated to playing the role of side-characters and NPC's.

Adding to all this is Peterson's over-spiritualization of everything. As we saw with Ayn Rand, Peterson's work functions to translate everyday reality into something much more spiritually significant, and even edifying. The goal of Petersons revolutionary life is to become what Joseph Campbell called the 'master of two worlds,' still engaged in the world while also realizing the *phenomenal* nature of it: "The problem of the theologian is to keep his symbol translucent, so that it may not block out the very light it is supposed to convey."[64] As we saw earlier, this translation of everyday activities, even those pushed for and demanded by capitalism, can be seen as some manifestation of a deep spiritual impulse. This obviously makes it difficult to demand socioeconomic change, since that level is fundamentally 'less real' for Peterson, and it also leads him to make some rather bizarre claims, such as when he implies many of the genocidal activities of the 20th century were carried out due to a *lack* of moral certainty on the part of the actors,[65] or that most attempts to do good in the world are driven by selfish delusions.[66] With such a solipsistic (and also pessimistic) view of humankind, it should ultimately be unsurprising that, since the "world and self are not different places,"[67] then Petersons opposition to social change comes into full view. All there is for him is personal psychological redemption, which is really just "identification with this eternal image, his active incarnation of the mythological role . . . "[68] It's a theory of subjectivity that demands a certain passivity, accepting the destruction around you as 'not really real,' a phantasm that you're supposed to see through. The emphasis on the psychological element also encourages thinking in purely personal or moral terms, at the expense of systematic deconstruction. This is a frequent issue in much writing about corruption today, which tends to see issues of financial corruption as a result of personal greed. While technically true in many cases, this obscures the way certain other objective economic and legal dynamics

64. Campbell, *The Hero With a Thousand Faces*, 202.

65. Peterson, *Maps of Meaning*, 342.

66. Peterson, *Maps of Meaning*, 455-6.

67. Peterson, *Maps of Meaning*, 443

68. Peterson, *Maps of Meaning*, 435.

actually encourage (and even reward) that sort of behavior.[69] It also leaves the reader conceptually stranded, offering lots of ways in to study affective realities, but without much capacity to study the conditions that design and condition those realities.[70]

However, suppose one were to identify with the role of the *revolutionary*, the one who flips the world on its head and inaugurates something new? Even Peterson gives much time and attention to the revolutionary hero. Is there a possibility for identifying with the more radical elements of the text? It seems unlikely, and a turn to his actual theory of revolutionary change should clarify why. But first, a short detour is needed.

It has become something of a running cliche to talk about Peterson in relation to lobsters. Part of this is because the lobster-passages have been chopped up and decontextualized, so let's put it back in context. The discussion of lobsters takes place near the beginning of *12 Rules*, which implores readers to 'stand up straight with your shoulders back.' Using lobsters, wrens and chickens as examples, his main goal is to pick animals "obsessed with status and position,"[71] who inhabit what he calls a 'dominance hierarchy.' The thing that unites your standard human suburbanites with these animals is that we live in some form of togetherness with one another, and there's a pecking order. Lobsters and wrens fight for better territory, and chickens want to be queens of their coop.

What's worth noting is the way Peterson jumps from various animal behaviors to human ones, looking for parallel appearances. For example:

> If a contagious avian disease sweeps through a neighbourhood of well-stratified songbirds, it is the least dominant and most stressed birds, occupying the lowest rungs of the bird world, who are most likely to sicken and die. This is equally true of human neighbourhoods, when bird flu viruses and other illnesses sweep across the planet. The poor and stressed always die first, and in greater numbers. They are also much more susceptible to non-infectious diseases, such as cancer, diabetes and heart disease. When the aristocracy catches a cold, as it is said, the working class dies of pneumonia.[72]

69. See Chambers, *There's No Such Thing as 'The Economy'*, ch. 1.

70. Those interested in a more dynamic approach to subjectivity and the 'inner life' under late capitalism should find Jason Read's *The Politics of Transindividuality* invaluable for this sort of project.

71. Peterson, *12 Rules for Life*, 3.

72. Peterson, *12 Rules for Life*, 4.

The key thing that's happened here is the naturalization (in the Darwin-ian biological sense) of fundamentally *un*natural phenomenon, in this case different classes.[73] Some birds being more prone to certain diseases might be a natural phenomenon; people are a different case, especially when you bring class into things, since that affects access to things like good medica-tion, healthy food or a lack of financial stress, which can contribute to one's physical well-being. But Peterson goes further in naturalizing some very *un*-natural phenomenon. Reflecting on the competition for territory between lobsters, he writes: "It's a winner-take-all in the lobster world, just as it is in human societies, where the top 1 percent have as much loot as the bottom 50 percent—and where the richest eighty-five people have as much as the bottom three and a half billion."[74] He continues:

> That same brutal principle of unequal distribution applies outside the financial domain—indeed, anywhere that creative production is required. The majority of scientific papers are published by a very small group of scientists. A tiny proportion of musicians produces almost all the recorded commercial mu-sic. Just a handful of authors sell all the books. A million and a half separately titled books (!) sell each year in the US. However, only five hundred of these sell more than a hundred thousand copies. Similarly, just four classical composers (Bach, Beethoven, Mozart, and Tchaikovsky) wrote almost all the music played by modern orchestras. Back, for his part, composed so prolifically that it would take decades of work merely to hand-copy his scores, yet only a fraction of this prodigious output is commonly performed. The same thing applies to the output of the other three members of this group of hyper-dominant composers: only a small fraction of their work is still widely played. Thus, a small fraction of the music composed by a small fraction of all the classical composers who have ever composed makes up almost all the classical music that the world knows and loves.[75]

So we've moved, in the span of a couple pages, from lobster neurochemistry to inequity in finances and music-composition. We've come a long way, and obviously I'm very proud of all of you for sticking with us through these enormous leaps from one disparate field of study to another. Pat yourselves on the back.

---

73. See Das, *Marxist Class Theory for a Skeptical Audience*, 266.
74. Peterson, *12 Rules for Life*, 8.
75. Peterson, *12 Rules for Life*, 8.

Once you've done that, let's think through what's happened. We started with brain chemistry, and ended up with financial markets. While one could hypothetically connect brain sciences and market forces to understand where certain trends come from,[76] Peterson is bypassing that more complicated dynamic to show that the social structure emerges directly from the neurochemical one. The difference in financial wealth is made out to be a product of natural forces and dynamics, as well as the differences in book sales or musical popularity. It's worth reflecting briefly on the various factors that get skipped over in these passages. Let's use the example of music. Peterson mentions that most classical orchestras play the same stuff over and over again. Some names such as Beethoven or Mozart are even more famous than the music itself, with many people knowing who Beethoven or Mozart are without having ever heard any of their music, or having heard it without realizing that *that* is what Mozart's *Requiem* sounds like. As with our discussion of James Joyce's work earlier, once certain figures achieve a certain level of notoriety, their importance is simply assumed without ever being argued for, and everyone at cocktail parties simply acknowledges their genius without much actual reason to back such a claim up. Mozart is great, perhaps even the great*est*, and everyone just sort of goes along with it, until that one person shows up who studied musical composition and history in college, and they start giving you a long explanation about how Italian composition is generally more fine-tuned and has been unfairly neglected, and if you want to listen to *real* music, you need to check out composers like Giovanni Pierluigi de Palestrina, Claudio Monteverdi or Carlo Gesualdo.

The point is that on this view, everything is a product of anonymous, natural forces. Resistance is not only futile, but perhaps even dangerous. Following this naturalization to its base, we get to Peterson's ultimate *grund*, the *real* reality underlying reality. Peterson is worth quoting at length.

> It is no simple manner for the limited subject to formulate an accurate representation of the unlimited unknown, of nature, the ground of existence. The unknown is the matrix of everything, the source of all birth and the final place of rest. *It hides behind our personal identity and our culture; it constantly threatens and engenders all that we do, all the we understand, and all that we are.* It can never be eliminated permanently from consideration, since every solution merely provides the breeding place for a host of new problems. The unknown is *Homo sapiens'* everlasting enemy and greatest friend, constantly challenging individual facility for adaptation and representation, constantly pushing

76. Salzinger, "Sexing Homo Economicus."

men and women to greater depths and more profound heights. The unknown as Nature appears as paradoxical formidable overwhelming power, applied simultaneously in one direction and its opposite. Hunger, the will to self-preservation, drives living creatures to devour each other rapaciously, and the hunters have no mercy for the hunted. Sexuality bends the individual will inexorably and often tragically to the demand of the species, and existence maintains itself in endless suffering, transformation and death. Life generates and destroys itself in a pitiless cycle, and the individual remains constantly subject to forces beyond understanding or control. The desire to exist permeates all that lives, and expresses itself in terrible fashion, in uncontrollable impulse, in an endless counterpoint of fecundity and decay. The most basic, fundamental and necessary aspects of experience are at the same time most dangerous and unacceptable.[77]

There isn't much explanation that seems necessary here; humans are composed of desires, fears, anxieties, impulses and drives that we are always being pushed and pulled by. These manifest themselves in our (often terrible) behavior. This condition cannot be escaped, but things go further than this, since this actually feeds into his interpretation of certain stories as well. Turning to *12 Rules*, he writes "Perhaps primordial Eve had more reason to attend to serpents than Adam. Maybe they were more likely, for example, to prey on her tree-dwelling infants. Perhaps it is for this reason that Eve's daughters are more protective, self-conscious, fearful and nervous, to this day (even, and especially, in the most egalitarian of modern human societies)."[78] What Peterson is trying to do is argue connect his belief in an underlying nature, and an extremely brutal one at that, to certain mythological motifs, in this case the story of Eve in the garden of Eden. If we take this as more than just a metaphor, then what we get is that the monomyth that Campbell and Peterson elaborate isn't just a narrative structure; it's a biological reality. These stories are products and descriptions of biological realities, and if that biology is unchangeable, then the stories are as well, which is why contemporary stories need to follow the right steps and those that fail to do so, such as Disney's *Frozen*, are "deeply propagandistic."[79] As with the use of spiritual themes we found in Rand and others, Petersons use of biology here functions to argue that capitalism is 'in human nature,' so to speak, and as with Rand, Peterson is here part of a broader trend, as Jason Read explains: "at the level of ideology or discourse, the rise of neoliberalism has led to

77. Peterson, *Maps of Meaning*, 159.
78. Peterson, *12 Rules for Life*, 48.
79. Peterson, *12 Rules for Life*, 324.

capitalism being defended on primarily anthropological grounds. Capital is no longer simply justified through the efficiency of the invisible hand, the efficiency of the market as an institution, but as an expression of our truly competitive nature. Homo sapiens has become homo economicus."[80] (And as we've seen, *Homo Economartist*).

Having established that, let's look at the actual way in which transformations occur in Petersons view. Given that these stories are expressions of biological truths, it should come as no surprise that change happens as slowly as evolution does. A number of passages demonstrate this.

> The group is the current expression of a pattern of behavior developed over the course of hundreds of thousands of years.[81]

> Customs—that is, predictable and stable patterns of behavior—emerge and are stored 'procedurally' as a consequence of constant social interaction, over time, and as a result of the exchange of emotional information that characterizes that interaction. You modify me, I modify you, we both modify others, and so on, in a cycle that involves thousands of individuals, over thousands of years.[82]

> Human moral knowledge progresses as procedural knowledge expands its domain, as episodic memory encodes, ever more accurately, the patterns that characterize that knowledge; as the semantic system comes to explicitly represent the implicit principles upon which procedural knowledge and episodic representation of that knowledge rest—and, of course, as the consequences of this second- and third-order representation alter the nature of procedure itself. Thus the democratic political theorist, for example, can finally put into words the essence of religious myth after the myth had captured in image the essence of adaptive behavior; can talk about 'intrinsic rights' as if the notion were something *rational*. This process of increasing abstraction and representation is equivalent to development of 'higher' consciousness (especially if the ever-more enlightened

---

80. Read, "Radicalizing the Root," 312. It should also be noted that this connection between particular political conditions, such as free market capitalism, moral values and 'Western civilization' has been developed in much neoliberal discourse, with many neoliberal theorists developing a moral justification for defending markets (see for examples Elyachar, "Neoliberalism, Rationality, and the Savage Plot,"; Whyte, *The Morals of the Market*) and excluding those with worse moral and financial portfolios (see Cooper, *Family Values*; Kotsko, *Neoliberalism's Demons*).

81. Peterson, *Maps of Meaning*, 222.

82. Peterson, *Maps of Meaning*, 252.

words are in fact—utopian wish—transformed back down the hierarchy to the level of action).[83]

This last passage offers us another element of this position, since it shows how culture emerges out of evolutionary processes, slowly but surely. The underlying biological dynamics are expressed via myth and religion, which then becomes more explicitly rendered in philosophical and political systems. This is what he means when he describes social structures "as a consequence of the 'battle of the gods'. . ."[84] Peterson elsewhere writes: "the simplistic promotion of 'cultural diversity' as panacea is likely to produce anomie, nihilism and conservative backlash. It is the molding of these diverse beliefs into a single hierarchy that is the precondition for the peaceful admixture of all."[85] It might be asked why cultures can't be pluralistic or hold multiple orientations in them. The reason would be that in Peterson's view, cultures are monolithic.

> Culture is therefore the sum total of surviving historically determined hierarchically arranged behaviors and second- and third-order abstract representations, and more: it is the integration of these, in the course of endless social abstract representations, and more: it is the integration of these, in the course of endless social and intrapsychic conflict, into a single pattern of behavior—a single system of morality, simultaneously governing personal conduct, interpersonal interaction and imagistic/semantic description of such. This pattern is the 'corporeal ideal' of the culture, its mode of transforming the unbearable present into the desired future, its guiding force, its central personality.[86]

So culture is a monolithic representation of biological realities that are rendered in mythological narratives. It cannot change too fast, because at that point we get ahead of our own biology, and social issues occur. Peterson could be seen elaborating this to Eric and Donal Jr. Trump (yes, *those* Trumps) regarding sexual morality:

> People are very upset about the manner in which sexual activity is occurring, especially among young people. They're upset on the left and they're upset on the right. . .I think it's partly a consequence of the fact that we haven't adapted to the birth

83. Peterson, *Maps of Meaning*, 260.

84. Peterson, *Maps of Meaning*, 198.

85. Peterson, *Maps of Meaning*, 250.

86. Peterson, *Maps of Meaning*, 192.

control pill yet. It was a major technological revolution, the birth control pill, and it's only been fifty years, and we haven't figured out what it means for women to have control over their reproductive function, or what the consequences of that should be socially. The leftist types, especially in the 60's thought you could just blow sexual morality apart completely because now people were free to do what they want, but that isn't working, there's a backlash against that, on the left as well.[87]

Whatever specific policy Peterson advocates, it should be clear that it probably won't be highly accessible birth control for all.

This isn't to say societies don't change, but that change happens slowly, and anonymously. Even the revolutionary shaman is "carried away by spirits"[88] rather than given, well, agency. Change also has its own conditions of possibility. As Marc Champagne puts it: "The only claim that Peterson is willing to make in an unqualified way is that if the preconditions for positive change are not present, such a change will certainly not come."[89] But since that change comes at at the pace of a Darwinian (r) evolution, the most we can hope for is personal psychological salvation, which won't be in the form of communal solidarity, but inward and personal. The result is what we discussed before, about the subject needing to fill a role already written, just now with a biological twist: "What happens has a pattern; the pattern has a biological, even genetic, basis, which finds its expression in fantasy; such fantasy provides subject material for myth and religion. The propositions of myth and religion, in turn, help guide and stabilize revolutionary human adaptation."[90]

So having unpacked these issues with Peterson, let's bring him back in dialogue with Heidegger. The final topic to be addressed is the potential overlap with Heidegger's concept of *authenticity* with Peterson's, although the latter might prefer the term *responsibility*. We brought up the ways in which the individual gets caught in a social milieu, only to experience a disjointedness with their world, a call that pulled them out, and a new life waiting for them on the other side. I will actually argue that there are a couple different forms authenticity, in Heidegger's reading can take, with Peterson and Campbell taking a former version, and Žižek taking a latter one.

Peterson's view points us towards authentic repetition, where "everything 'good' is a heritage and the character of 'goodness' lies in making

---

87. Peterson, "Exclusive."

88. Peterson, *Maps of Meaning*, 275.

89. Champagne, *Myth, Meaning and Antifragile Individualism*, 82.

90. Peterson, *Maps of Meaning*, 405.

authentic existence possible."[91] Petersons belief elaborated in *Maps of Meaning* is that culture as we currently know it has been slowly developed out
of a slow and complex process. Deviating too far from the cultural norms
that have been developed leads to chaos, so authenticity, even for the revolutionary shaman, involves coming back and engaging with one's society, even
while they realize that society is a purely *phenomenal* expression of something deeper. For Campbell this comes from the 'master of two worlds thesis,'
as well as the idea that marriage is actually a matter of one person being
reunited with their lost half,[92] to say nothing of the importance of atonement
with one's father, symbolic or not: "One must have faith that the father is
merciful, and then a reliance on that mercy."[93] This re-unification of the self
with society being the goal of Jungian therapy[94] also helps explain Peterson's
general opposition to social change; it's not his goal. His basic orientation is
to help people get their lives together, not to help change the circumstances
that may have pulled them apart in the first place. He says in a 2017 Q&A ses-
sion on YouTube that his goal is to help his clients, readers and listeners 'walk
in the light,' to find things within themselves that they're passionate about
and pursue them.[95] Champagne summarizes his message again: "Chances are
that if you manage to bring your own actions into conformity with what you
think is right, you will emerge from your house only to realize that the world
around you no longer needs any interference."[96]

　　While I actually like the message of walking in the light and exploring
oneself and one's passions, I need to now put him in dialogue with the last
several chapters; how does one 'walk in the light' and explore themselves
and their passions when they're working 50-hour weeks during varying
schedules set by an algorithm? How does one pursue their passions when
they need to constantly work overtime, either due to the demands of their
company, their financial needs, or both? If, as I've argued, the rise in various
forms of mental health and other personal issues are a result of systemic
financial dynamics, then what does taking responsibility look like, if not
working to change those dynamics? In a way, Peterson might not even care
to differentiate, as we saw with the businessman trying to climb the corporate ladder; his reasons for struggling were interpreted in entirely personal,
inner psychological terms; the *actual* reason for his being fired was largely

91. Heidegger, *Being and Time*, 383.

92. Campbell, *The Hero With a Thousand Faces*, 240.

93. Campbell, *The Hero With a Thousand Faces*, 110.

94. Fontelieu, *The Archetypal Pan*, 7.

95. Peterson, "Q & A 2017."

96. Champagne, *Myth, Meaning and Antifragile Individualism*, 102.

irrelevant. Peterson generally would prefer we not focus on the systemic, as he sees that as a way of avoiding personal responsibility.

> Each person's private trouble cannot be solved by a social revo-
> lution, because revolutions are destabilizing and dangerous. We
> have learned to live together and organize our complex societies
> slowly and incrementally, over vast stretches of time, and we do
> not understand with sufficient exactitude why what we are do-
> ing works. Thus, altering our ways of social being carelessly in
> the name of some ideological shibboleth (diversity springs to
> mind) is likely to produce far more trouble than good, given the
> suffering that even small revolutions generally produce.[97]

Here he has assumed things are 'working', which is fairly vague, but he's also painted with a rather broad brush, that ethical development happens slowly and incrementally, rather than with bold (and sometimes violent) steps. I'm not sure what he thinks of the emancipation of slavery in the United States (or the marches for civil rights a century later), but if history teaches us anything, it's that there have always been people willing to say things like this in the face of radical demands for justice, whether they be called as-similationists[98] or liberals.[99] In spite of Petersons warning that the dangers of conservatism involves a worship of culture that turns from respect[100] to an overly rigid idolization,[101] he refuses to jump on board with demands for social justice, both out of some vague, poorly argued belief that things are ultimately pretty amazing in spite of what you may think, but also a Jungian complex, a fear of any sort of radical social change. As we've seen in unpacking his work, it's not just that he thinks we shouldn't change, but that we can't, that the world we have now is too embedded, too solid and too deep for us to resist, so the best we can do is cope. The best he ultimately has to offer us is authenticity as an opiate, a way to make the bitter pill that is the 'terrible burden of Being' go down easier. If we put this in dialogue with what we explored in chapters 4 and 5, we can also see how his spiritual-ized monomythic rhetoric functions to make the fatalism of his view seem more palatable. Robin James' idea of the 'conceptual jacquemart' may be of use here. She describes it as "a clock equipped with mechanical bell-ringing puppets that are supposed to disguise a sound made by an ugly machine as

97. Peterson, *12 Rules for Life*, 118-9.
98. Kendi, *Stamped From the Beginning*.
99. Zevin, *Liberalism at Large*; Losurdo, *Liberalism*.
100. Peterson, *Maps of Meaning*, 230.
101. Peterson, *Maps of Meaning*, 203.

one made by an aesthetically pleasing one."[102] While there is a difference between Peterson and the earlier work of Rand or Campbell, who tended to have significantly more optimism about the human condition, they all offer high-minded rhetoric to subvert attention to people's actual material conditions, or to turn shitty conditions into an adventure, while also turning aloof indifference to them into a sort of spiritual virtue. This explains both the popularity of Peterson, but also the limits. He appeals to people by describing our current situation with some level of accuracy, at least at the psychological level. He argues that we're now lost in chaos, speaking to people at the personal affective level, giving words to what a lot of them are feeling, and to some degree he is right: things are chaotic right now. However, he then closes off our capacity to act, to try to change our situation, but also to think it beyond certain mystified dynamics. Stagnant wages, rising costs of living, schedules that change from one week to the next and his readers receive nothing beyond various forms of busywork, as well as not being told not to complain until they've gotten their own shit together.

If we could change things, it seems fair to say Peterson might encourage us to try. After all, even he describes your existence as being miserable.[103] He just thinks that any attempt at larger social transformation is futile, bound to make things worse rather than better.[104] Even ignoring this, his commitment to a particular biological realism has cut off the possibility of change. Biology becomes a way of passing off responsibility for who one is and how one will lead their life, a way of pointing at some particular piece of matter and saying 'That's who I am!' without needing to reflect up on it further. This works at the level of both individual and larger sociological forms of identity. Solidarity isn't a possibility; people are too brutal and individualistic, and we know this because so are lobsters, finches, and chimpanzees.[105] The result is subjects are actually cut off from addressing the call, from heeding their own calls to adventure beyond maintaining the status quo. Change will happen, but it will be carried out by phylogenetic angels; until then, we're stuck cleaning the psychological rooms we've been locked in.

Unless of course, the door is unlocked. . .

---

102. James, *The Sonic Episteme*, 169.

103. Peterson, *12 Rules for Life*, 64.

104. Peterson, *12 Rules for Life*, 79.

105. Peterson, *12 Rules for Life*, 120-1.

Chapter 10—**Žižek**

We can strip down reality, layer by later, and never reach its core, for what the last layer covers over is the most unreal of all, the greatest fiction of them all, the true nature of things.

—Karl Ove Knausgaard, *My Struggle Vol VI*

A nd so, finally, we get to Žižek. As with Peterson, any attempt to engage with Žižek's work means picking certain themes and emphasizing them, while leaving others behind. This is partly because, like Peterson, Žižek's work touches on just about everything, from psychoanalysis, philosophy, history, politics, literature and theology. The superficial similarities continue into their use of various narrative and cultural examples to illustrate their underlying philosophical points, often resulting in the accusation that underneath the myriad of examples and digressions, there's nothing actually there. I tried to show this would be a mistake in Peterson's case, although in Žižek's it ironically hits the core (or lack thereof) of his ontology, even if unwittingly.

This final chapter on Žižek will offer up an account of his core philosophical project, but it will be more in the service of criticizing Petersons own project. There were a few comments at the debate between the two where it was clear that Žižek was dropping subtle critiques of Peterson, although for reasons that will be explained, he decided not to offer up any direct attack, leaving things implicit and direct. This chapter will be directed towards unpacking his critique, and contextualizing it within his larger philosophical project. He'll also be put in dialogue with Heidegger in order to explicate a second possible reading of *authenticity*, which will be contrasted with Peterson's reading of it in the previous sections. This is then less an introduction to Žižek and more a 'use and abuse' of him, albeit one that will hopefully do justice to his thought and work.

Perhaps the best place to start in order to put Žižek in dialogue with Heidegger would be Žižek's interpellated subject. He gets the term from

Althusser, who argues that subjects are *called* or *interpellated* into an ideological field.[1] Althusser often uses the example of Yahweh calling to Moses, to which Moses replied 'Here I am!' In Moses' response, he recognizes himself as a subject, one who occupies a certain place within a symbolic network, who has a role to play, demands to keep up with.[2] A number of things follow from this interpellation.

> The subject is always fastened, pinned, to a signifier which represents him for the other, and through this pinning he is loaded with a symbolic mandate, he is given a place in the inter-subjective network of symbolic relations. The point is that this mandate is ultimately always arbitrary since its nature is performative, it cannot be accounted for by reference to the 'real' properties and capacities of the subject. So, loaded with this mandate, the subject is automatically confronted with a certain '*Che vuoi?*', with a question of the Other. The Other is addressing him as if he himself possesses the answer to the question of why he has this mandate, but the question is, of course, unanswerable. The subject does not know why he is occupying thi place in the symbolic network. His own answer to this '*Che vuoi?*' of the Other can only be the hysterical question: 'Why am I what I'm supposed to be, why have I this mandate? Why am I [a teacher, a master, a king. . .or George Kapan]?' Briefly: '*Why am I what you [the big Other] are saying that I am?*'[3]

So as with Heidegger's Dasein, always-already in a world that has been established with certain ways of understanding oneself, Žižek's subject is interpellated, called into a world with various demands and expectations.

A difference appears here, however, regarding the predominant expectation of the day. Heidegger's primary concern was that we were living in an epoch of boredom, an age where we had no task or calling that could help bring us into any sort of authentic life. Žižek sees us as living in an era defined by a similar, but slightly different mood, that of cynicism. Unlike boredom, which cannot find a cause, cynicism subverts the very possibility of attaching oneself to a cause. It's 'part of the game,'[4] so to speak. How does it function?

1. Althusser, "Ideology and Ideological State Apparatuses," 130-1.
2. Rehmann, *Theories of Ideology*, 156.
3. Žižek, *The Sublime Object of Ideology*, 125-6.
4. Žižek, *The Sublime Object of Ideology*, 24.

Following Peter Sloterdijk,[5] Žižek sees cynics taking into account the fact that the ruling narrative, be it totalitarian or democratic, will contain lies, and yet not caring. This is to be contrasted with *kynicism*, the rejection of the ruling narrative via satire or sarcasm, such as when one points out how a speech about the nobility of sacrifice is being given by someone profiteering from war. Cynicism "recognizes, it takes into account, the particular interest behind the ideological universality, the distance between the ideological mask and the reality, but it still finds reasons to retain the mask."[6] This subverts the possibility of traditional ideological critique, which attempted to show that the ruling narrative was a lie meant to prop up the powerful and replace it with a more honest or just structure. The cynic might be willing to point out the lie, the gap between the truth and the mask, but has nothing to replace it with.

> In this situation parody finds itself without a vocation; it has lived, and that strange new thing pastiche slowly comes to take its place. Pastiche is, like parody, the imitation of a peculiar or unique, idiosyncratic style, the wearing of a linguistic mask, speech in a dead language. But it is a neutral practice of such mimicry, without any of parody's ulterior motives, amputated of the satiric impulse, devoid of laughter and of any conviction that alongside the abnormal tongue you have momentarily borrowed, some healthy linguistic normality still exists. Pastiche is thus blank parody, a statue with blind eyeballs: it is to parody what that other interesting and historically original modern thing, the practice of a kind of blank irony, is to what Wayne Booth calls the 'stable ironies' of the eighteenth century.[7]

Cynicism, like Jameson's pastiche, is then a way for the ruling powers to take into account their own deceitful character in advance, and subvert the possibility of losing their legitimacy on the basis of that critique. After all, how does one criticize a politician's dishonesty when they never made any serious claims to honesty in the first place?

The cynical subject doesn't actually seek out any long-term ground to stand on and justify their lives; instead, rules change every now and then, and so the subject moves along with them, adapting as they need to. Beyond being a dominant affect, this may also be a coping mechanism for life under late capitalism, which consists of lots of short-term projects rather than any

---

5. Sloterdijk, *Critique of Cynical Reason*.
6. Žižek, *The Sublime Object of Ideology*, 26.
7. Jameson, *Postmodernism*, 17.

sustained sense of *what it's all about*.[8] The short-termism made possible by cynicism is actually a necessary element of late capitalism, which needs to constantly revolutionize itself in order to survive.[9] It also prevents any actual transition or demand for something new, since cynics obviously cannot commit to any particular cause.

> Things look bad for great Causes today, in a 'postmodern' era when, although the ideological scene is fragmented into a panoply of positions which struggle for hegemony, there is an underlying consensus: the era of big explanations is over, we need 'weak thought,' opposed to all foundationalism, a thought attentive to the rhizomatic texture of reality; in politics too, we should no longer aim at all-explaining systems and global emancipatory projects; the violent imposition of grand solutions should leave room for forms of specific resistance and interventions.[10]

So is Jordan Peterson a cynic? This would be an ambitious and questionable claim, as he seems to genuinely believe most of the things he says. One could oscillate between trying to put Peterson in either the role of the cynic or the ever-delaying obsessional, always waiting for the 'right moment,'[11] and while this latter option does speak to Petersons evolutionary incrementalism, it also implies Peterson actually wants a revolution, which is far from clear. However, since we saw Peterson believes change emerges at the pace of biological evolution, it might be best to call him a bio-obsessional, one who is waiting for us to evolve in the right direction. Untangling this, from a Žižekian standpoint, will mean challenging the narrative that has us waiting for the right phylogenetic moment. We'll proceed here in two stages; first, we'll offer up an account of Žižek's subject. Second, we'll connect Žižekian thought to biology.

To turn back to Žižek's interpellated subject, we've seen how subjects are called into an ideological field, one which produces demands in order to generate certain sorts of behavior and activity.[12] What is 'ideology' for Žižek then? He borrows Marx's definition, that ideology is something people do, even though they don't know it.[13] But what is *ideology*? For Žižek, it is a

8. Read, *The Politics of Transindividuality*, 213.

9. Žižek, *The Sublime Object of Ideology*, 53-4.

10. Žižek, *In Defense of Lost Causes*, 1.

11. Žižek, *The Sublime Object of Ideology*, 63.

12. Žižek, *The Sublime Object of Ideology*, 92.

13. Žižek, *The Sublime Object of Ideology*, 24.

multitude of 'floating signifiers', of proto-ideological elements, is structured into a unified field through the intervention of a certain 'nodal point' (the Lacanian *point de capiton*) which 'quilts' them, stops their sliding and fixes their meaning. Ideological space is made of non-bound, non-tied elements, 'floating signifiers', whose very identity is 'open', overdetermined by their articulation in a chain with other elements—that is their 'literal' signification depends on their metaphorical surplus-signification.[14]

Ideology then is a constellation that holds a variety of terms and themes together. Contra Petersons Jungian definition of ideology as an 'incomplete myth',[15] ideology is closer to Heidegger's world, a collection of meanings that offer up certain goals so as to compel one towards certain behaviors. It is the place in which one finds their identity, their sense of who they are and what it means to be *them*. Ideologies are held together by various *quilting points*, major signifiers that hold together a variety of free-floating secondary signifiers. In previous chapters, we've discussed how the contemporary ideology of *homo economartist* involves a combination of themes and threads around biology and spirituality, which act as master signifiers that ground our current ideological/worldly constellation, meaning any attempt at ideological critique means attempting to reclaim said terms, or at least dislodge them from their centrality in the current framework. To quote Žižek at length:

> What is at stake in the ideological struggle is which of the 'nodal points', *points de capiton*, will totalize, include in its series of equivalences, these free-floating elements. Today, for example, the stake of the struggle between neo-conservatism and social democracy is 'freedom': neo-conservatives try to demonstrate how egalitarian democracy, embodied in the welfare state, necessarily leads to new forms of serfdom, to the dependency of the individual on the totalitarian state, while social democrats stress how individual freedom, to have any meaning at all, must be based upon democratic social life, equality of economic opportunity, and so forth. In this way, every element of a given ideological field is part of a series of equivalences: its metaphorical surplus, through which it is connected with all other elements, determines its very identity. . .But this enchainment is possible only on the condition that a certain signifier—the

14. Žižek, *The Sublime Object of Ideology*, 95.

15. Peterson, *Maps of Meaning*, 216.

Lacanian 'One'—'quilts' the whole field and, by embodying it, effectuates its identity.[16]

Ideology, like Heideggerian worlds, have accents, moods and affects that taint them in a variety of directions. New works of art or master-signifiers can shake our ideological constellation. How does one 'found' a new world, or switch to a new master-signifier?

Žižek's Lacanian influence is important here. Where Petersons Jungianism has him trying to essentially get people to see how they are playing out some deeper, noumenal role, Žižek's Lacanianism is intended to get us to see that there is no role. Let's remember that ideology calls us, gets us to perform certain behaviors. But what calls us? Who are we performing for? To repeat Žižek's question, "*Why am I what you [the big Other] are saying that I am?*"[17] The big Other is a Lacanian term, standing in for whatever grounds or *guarantees* ones way and reason for existing in such and such a way.[18] The big Other can take a number of forms, an obvious one being any sort of religious deity, but it can take other secularized forms, from Adam Smith's invisible hand of the market to Stalin's *diamat*.[19] When we perform a role, we are performing for said big Other, attempting to justify ourselves by it, recognizing that the mask is only the phenomenal representation of some deeper significance.[20] This big Other behind the mask can be evolutionary biology, markets, gender roles, spiritual expressions, or as we've seen some combination of all of them. So where does Žižek leave us with regards to big Others? How does he answer the question *What am I for the big Other?* The Lacanian answer is subjective destitution; "the final moment of the psychoanalytic process is, for the analysand, precisely when he gets rid of this question—that is, when he accepts his being as *non-justified by the big Other.*"[21] There is, in Žižekian ontology, nothing behind the appearances with which we are confronted, no god or invisible hand or arc of history that guarantees this will all work out in the end. This point comes from both Lacan as well as Žižek's other primary reference point, Hegel, but we'll start with the former. In his previously cited seminar, Lacan recalls an ancient Greek myth.

---

16. Žižek, *The Sublime Object of Ideology*, 96.

17. Žižek, *The Sublime Object of Ideology*, 126.

18. Lacan, *Seminar XI*, 36.

19. Žižek, *Less Than Nothing*, 71; Johnston, *Prolegomena* Vol 2, 129-30.

20. One should be reminded of Kierkegaard's description in *Works of Love* of life being an 'outer garment' or 'disguise' through which the eternal shines through. (Kierkegaard, "Works of Love," 298-300).

21. Žižek, *The Sublime Object of Ideology*, 126.

In the classical tale of Zeuxis and Parrhasios, Zeuxis has the advantage of having made grapes that attracted the birds. The stress is placed not on the fact that these grapes were in any way perfect grapes, but on the fact that even the eye of the birds was taken in by them. This is proved by the fact that his friend Parrhasios triumphs over him for having painted on the wall a veil, a veil so lifelike that Zeuxis, turning towards him said, *Well, and now show us what you have painted behind it.*[22]

Žižek unpacks this, writing that

> We can deceive animals by an appearance imitating reality for which it can be a substitute, but the properly human way to deceive a man is to imitate the dissimulation of reality—the act of concealing deceives us precisely by pretending to conceal something. In other words, there is nothing behind the curtain except the subject who has already gone beyond it.[23]

In other words, appearance *appears* in such a way that it appears to be hiding something, when in fact there's nothing. However, this leaves us with a problem; if there is nothing more than the material world, how do we account for subjects with agency, capable of stepping out of and changing our situation, and not end up stranded via Heidegger's technological or Peterson's phylogenetic fatalism? If material reality is all there is, then that would seem to imply a such a hard determinism that any serious social, political or even personal transformation would be impossible.

The Žižekian answer to this is the Lacanian *desunivers*. "[Lacan] stipulates that the discursive realities inhabited by (and inhabiting) speaking beings constitutes a "*desunivers*," namely, a detotalized, disunified multiplicity without set limits—and this by contrast with the universe as One-All (i.e. 'uni-')."[24] The *desunivers* is an updated version, for Žižek, of the key conclusion of German idealism, particularly the transition from Kant to Hegel, or as Žižek would put, Hegel's ontologization of Kant. Kant's philosophical project, particularly in his *Critique of Pure Reason*, was to set limits around what we can know. He begins thus, "Human reason has a peculiar fate in one species of its cognition that it is burdened with questions which it cannot dismiss, since they are given to it as problems by the nature of reason itself, but which it also cannot answer, since they transcend every capacity

---

22. Lacan, *Seminar XI*, 103.

23. Žižek, *The Sublime Object of Ideology*, 223. Also see Johnston, *Žižek's Ontology*, 139.

24. Johnston, *Adventures in Transcendental Materialism*, 66-7.

of human reason."[25] Kant tried to draw boundaries about what reason could actually address, so that it wouldn't wander into antinomies.

The standard reading of Hegel is that he then managed to rise above the Kantian contradictions and get to the thing itself, via a series of thesis, antithesis and synthesis, progressive steps towards greater knowledge in which the essential character of reason leads us to absolute knowledge. A standard summary of this account might read something like this:

> Starting with 'sense certainty', the most basic form of sensory consciousness, Hegel shows how consciousness evolves through a series of transformations towards increasingly developed forms. Each form of consciousness (like each stage of history) contains tensions or contradictions which render it incomplete and unstable, so that it is ultimately bound to give way dialectically to more adequate forms. The scope of Hegel's enterprise is daunting. He traces not only the development of sensory or empirical consciousness but also the emergence of self-consciousness and reason through a variety of forms of moral, religious and philosophical thought. In fact, he attempts to compress the entire history of morality, art, religion and philosophy into the stages of his phenomenology of mind. The ethical community of the modern state, art and religion are identified as stages on the way to 'absolute knowledge'. The dialectic culminates with the self-reflective appropriation of the whole process of spirit's dialectical development by philosophy or, more precisely, Hegel's own philosophy. Philosophy brings spirit to the fullest and most fully rational self-consciousness—a self-consciousness without further internal contradiction or incompleteness. . .[26]

Hegel then is often thought to have 'overcome' Kant's epistemological limitations, and managed to give us a philosophical method of getting to reality as it is. Žižek takes this narrative and flips it on its head. Kant argued that the contradictions we find in our opinions (and between the opinions of different people) was a result of reason extending beyond what it could adequately grasp, reality-in-itself. Instead we could only engage with phenomena, things that our minds can actually perceive and engage with. What this move does, and that (Žižek's) Hegel calls into question, is assumes that there is a coherent reality-in-itself out there. Adrian Johnston explains at length:

> Kant assumes—he simply takes it for granted—that contradictions dwell within the confines of subjective cognition alone.

25. Kant, *Critique of Pure Reason*, 99 (A vii).
26. West, *Continental Philosophy*, 42-3.

According to this presupposition, only thinking can harbor antinomies and antagonisms; substantial being must be internally at one with itself and without contradiction. Žižek, departing from Hegel's observation that Kant's assumption regarding the contradiction-free nature of Real being is just an article of dogmatic faith, frequently portrays Hegel as taking the small but enormously significant step of transforming Kant's epistemology into ontology. (In fact, Hegelian dialectics is both an epistemology and an ontology, namely, a mobile, dynamic knowledge-process that, in its functioning [and, more importantly, malfunctioning], simultaneously reveals the very configuration of being itself.) Through this move, being becomes something incomplete and inconsistent, a sphere penetrated by divisions and ruptures.[27]

This is how Žižek sees the move from *understanding* to *reason*, the former usually understood as engaging with sense data and, as a result, producing contradictory information that a dialectically informed reason is able to get above and beyond. Žižek flips this:

> For Hegel, Reason is not another, 'higher' capacity than that of 'abstract' Understanding: what defines Understanding is the very illusion that, beyond it, there is another domain (either the ineffable Mystical or Reason) which eludes its discursive grasp. In short, to get from Understanding to Reason, one does not have to *add* anything, but, on the contrary, to *subtract* something: what Hegel calls 'Reason' is *Understanding itself*, bereft of the illusion that there is something Beyond it.[28]

This idea gets repeated some years later, as Žižek points out how Kant made a profoundly radical break, but attempted to retreat from it rather than follow through with it:

> With his philosophical revolution, Kant made a breakthrough the radicality of which he was himself unaware; so, in a second move, he withdraws from this radicality and desperately tries to navigate into safer waters of a more traditional ontology. Consequently, in order to pass 'from Kant to Hegel,' we have to move not 'forward' but backward: back from the deceptive envelope to identify the true radicality of Kant's breakthrough—in this sense, Hegel was literally 'more Kantian than Kant himself.'[29]

27. Johnston, *Žižek's Ontology*, 129.
28. Žižek, *The Ticklish Subject*, 97.
29. Žižek, *Less Than Nothing*, 280-1.

He clarifies again elsewhere that Hegel's 'radicalization' of Kant is not to overcome the gap left by Kant, but to assert it as such.[30] The core point here that Žižek is making is that reality itself is fundamentally *incomplete*, a Non-All. This is what is meant when Žižek argues that Hegel *ontologized* Kant, taking the epistemological cracks and arguing that the cracks and gaps were themselves *the* discovery made in Kant's *Critique*.

> The statement 'material reality *is not all there is*' can be negated in two ways, in the form of 'material reality *is not all there is*' and 'material reality *is non-all*.' The first negation (of a predicate) leads to standard metaphysics: material reality is not everything, there is another, higher, spiritual reality. As such, this negation is, in accordance with Lacan's formulae of sexuation, inherent to the positive statement 'material reality is all there is': as its constitutive exception, it grounds its universality. If, however, we assert a non-predicate and say 'material reality *is non-all*,' this merely asserts the non-All of reality without implying any exception—paradoxically, one should thus claim that the axiom of true materialism is not 'material reality is all there is,' but a double one: (1) there is nothing which is not material reality, (2) material reality is non-All.[31]

Žižek opts for the second option, where there is nothing that is not material reality, but that material reality is non-All. What is meant by this? He offers an example to elucidate what he means by referring to digital realities and video-games.

> If we want to simulate reality within an artificial (virtual, digital) medium, we do not have to go all the way: we just have to reproduce those features which will make the image realistic from the spectator's point of view. For example, if there is a house in the background, we do not have to program the house's interior, since we expect that the participant will not want to enter the house; or, the construction of a virtual person in this space can be limited to his exterior—no need to bother with inner organs, bones, etc.[32]

Anyone who's ever worked in video-game design is possibly feeling called out at this moment, because Žižek is on to them; programmers cheat! Houses are often designed with doors and windows that are unopenable and opaque, covering up the fact that there's actually nothing inside them.

30. Žižek, *Less Than Nothing*, 267.
31. Žižek, *Less Than Nothing*, 742.
32. Žižek, *Less Than Nothing*, 743.

They're large blocks with doors painted on the outside to give one the impression that they're houses, but if one could somehow get through the wall, there would be nothing in them.

Reality then for Žižek is filled with various gaps, holes and inconsistencies, but it has the superficial appearance of being complete. Gamers are caught in the same trap as Zeuxis, imagining there to be various things behind those walls and doors, but after Parrhasios reveals his trick, we've "discovered the real secret: beyond the door is only what your desire introduces there . . . "[33] Parrhasios remains a Kantian here, still pressusping "that the Thing-in-itself exists as something positively given beyond the field of representation."[34] Ideology then is an attempt to smooth out reality's inconsistencies and wrinkles,[35] to give reality the appearance of some sort of consistency.

Another critical element of this picture is the *objet a*, the disjointed object that the subject needs to put back into place in order for everything to feel complete again. Of course, this completeness is a fantasy, but if we pay attention to fantasies, we can learn a lot about the subjects who live them out. A question we ought to raise regarding Peterson is what his missing object is, what drives him? A hint can be found early in *Maps of Meaning*, where he writes:

> Prior to the time of Descartes, Bacon and Newton, man lived in
> an animated, spiritual world, saturated with meaning, imbued
> with moral purpose. The nature of this purpose was revealed in
> the stories people told each other—stories about the structure of
> the cosmos and the place of man. But now we think empirically
> (at least we think we think empirically), and the spirits that once
> inhabited the universe had vanished.[36]

This repeats the idea from both Campbell and Jung that myths once had an intuitive truth to them that we could learn from, although that capacity is to some degree lost since the symbols are no longer alive, and neither is the world around us. The Petersonian desire could then be said to be a desire to return to the world in such a way that it makes an intuitive sense to him, one where he doesn't have to think critically but can simply *feel* it. As we saw throughout the last few chapters, this nostalgia is questionable for a number of historical and political reasons, and for Marx economically

33. Žižek, *The Sublime Object of Ideology*, 70.
34. Žižek, *The Sublime Object of Ideology*, 232.
35. Žižek, *The Sublime Object of Ideology*, 137-8.
36. Peterson, *Maps of Meaning*, 5.

impossible under current economic circumstances, but Žižek offers his own response to the issue here.

The goal of Lacanian psychoanalysis, as well as Žižek's connected political work, is to achieve what is called *subjective destitution*, where one recognizes reality in all its utter contingency and stupidity. This explains his brief but biting quip from his opening remark contra Peterson, that one should not assume their suffering is proof of their authenticity. In subjective destitution, one no longer experiences the demands made of their world with the same force.

> What is at stake in this 'destitution' is precisely the fact that *the subject no longer presupposes himself as subject*; by accomplishing this he annuls, so to speak, the effects of the act of formal conversion. In other words, he assumes not the existence but the *non-existence* of the big Other, he accepts the Real in its utter, meaningless idiocy; he keeps open the gap between the Real and its symbolization. The price to be paid for this is that by the same act he also *annuls himself as subject. . .*[37]

Two objections will likely be brought up in response to this. The first will be that this can only lead to some sort of hedonistic absolution of any sort of responsibility or morality. Žižek would counter that, in fact, this is the very starting possibility for responsibility. The other option is to continuously transpose our abilities onto some other force, alienating oneself from one's own creative capacities.[38] Our ability to act is in fact always-already at work in a way, we just often fail to recognize it, because our acts are unconscious, although this term receives a new twist for Žižek, who follows the Lacanian wordplay when he translates Freud's German *Unbewusste* (*unconscious*) to *une bevue* (*a blunder*). The Lacanian unconscious is "an overlooking: we overlook the way our act is already part of the state of things we are looking at, the way our error is part of the Truth itself."[39]

A political example may be of assistance to see how this works. The United States often portrays itself as intervening only in *response* to provocation; it doesn't like to think of itself as the initial aggressor. World Wars I and II are exemplary of this, since they give Americans two clear instances of being forced into action, both of which only work if you ignore the Lusitania's munitions delivery, or the deliberately provocative nature of the American embargoes on Japan.[40] There's also the presentation of the world as increas-

---

37. Žižek, *The Sublime Object of Ideology*, 263.
38. Žižek, *The Sublime Object of Ideology*, 256-7.
39. Žižek, *The Sublime Object of Ideology*, 62.
40. Losurdo, *War and Revolution*, 118-9.

ingly peaceful, largely in thanks due to US hegemony,[41] which often ignores the way American military intervention often does so now in more clandestine fashion, be it violent interventions that are never officially declared as 'wars',[42] economic transitions that are imposed from without on developing nations,[43] or some combination. The first Gulf invasion by the United States in 1991 is a rather illustrative example, since it had spent the previous decade egging Iraq on and providing assistance in its war with Iran. At the end, Iraq was left largely bankrupt, and invaded Kuwait to make up for its losses, only to find it had misinterpreted the US's lenience, leading to an invasion that not only involved tipping weapons with depleted uranium, leading to high levels of medical complications and birth-deformities for decades after, but also the use of smart-bombs to destroy water treatment plants and hospitals. Following the war, the United States imposed sanctions, blocking equipment and medicine, forcing the country to wither for a decade. The *Washington Post* reported in 1996 that half a million children had died of starvation, never mind the various other reasons for death in a country ripped apart from the outside and then denied the opportunity to heal.[44] Blame Saddam Hussein all you want; it doesn't justify the collective punishment enforced on an entire nation. Several years later on September 11, the United States largely seemed uninterested in examining why anyone could be driven to such hatred for them, the last several decades of international atrocities committed abroad largely forgotten in a moment of collective amnesia, and any retaliation justified as a defensive response. A more "innocent" but disturbingly similar example can be found in a collection of books written for children, the now-famous series of biographies by Laura Ingalls Wilder, a girl who documented her life with her family living in the American woods and great plains, often marvelling at how alone they were in forging a new life in an undiscovered world. The 'discovery' here was only made possible, however, because of the way in which she consistently left out the fact that they were occupying land recently occupied by indigenous people, recently forced out by violent or 'legal' (law-stere) means.[45]

This is the Hegelian 'beautiful soul,' which

41. Pinker, *Enlightenment Now.*

42. Losurdo, *War and Revolution*, 135. Also see Chomsky and Herman's 2-volume *Political Economy of Human Rights* for a detailed examination of the relation between these interventions and how they are (or aren't) depicted in mainstream media.

43. See Klein, *The Shock Doctrine.*

44. Losurd, *War and Revolution*, 325.

45. For a detailed deconstruction of the mythology Ingalls constructed of the frontier, see Fraser's *Prairie Fires.*

Structures the 'objective' social world in advance so that it is able to assume, to play in it the role of the fragile, innocent and passive victim. This, then, is Hegel's fundamental lesson: when we are active, when we intervene in the world through a particular act, the real act is not this particular, empirical, factual intervention (or non-intervention); the real act is of a strictly symbolic nature, it consists in the very mode in which we structure the world, our perception of it, in advance, in order to make our intervention possible, in order to open in it the space for our activity (or inactivity). The real act thus *precedes* the (particular-factual) activity; it consists in the previous re-structuring of our symbolic universe into which our (factual, particular) act will be inscribed.[46]

This brings us again back to Heidegger, albeit in a much more explicitly political direction, that we are always-already immersed in a particular interpretation of the way things are, that said interpretation has a development that is ultimately composed of various contingencies that appear as a unified story. We are also here forced, destitute of any reference to some final goal we can appeal to in order to justify the way things are, to uncover the world in our own way, and to stand by it.[47]

This doesn't mean it will be easy, and even Žižek has expressed a pessimism about our chances for actually creating change. Part of this is for ideological reasons, the assumption that we are locked into certain ways of being that cannot be changed. An example of this was given to us by George W. Bush, who refused to curb fossil fuel consumption on the grounds that doing such a thing ran against the 'American way of life,' a true wall of grapes if there ever was one.[48] But beyond the allure of certain ideological fantasies is the addictive power of ideology, the way we get hooked on our fantasies, capital being a prime one, bringing us another Žižekian-Lacanian lesson.

One of the overlaps between (Lacanian) psychoanalysis and (Marxist) economic critique is that both see a surplus as throwing things off-balance, but in a particular way that can not only be destructive but, if not addressed and handled properly, endlessly so. It's worth recapping what we learned about capitalism earlier in chapter 6. The formula Marx gives for capital, money used not just to purchase goods and services (what he calls 'use-values') but to increase the money-supply is M-C-M', where $M'=M+\Delta M$ where ΔM is the change in the amount of money. Δ is the amount one gains off of an investment, the surplus money, and capitalism is driven by the

46. Žižek, *The Sublime Object of Ideology*, 244-5.
47. Heidegger, *Being and Time*, 129.
48. Johnston, *Badiou, Žižek and Political Transformations*, 102.

need for this surplus. Marx will go on to show a host of issues that arise from the need of this little extra hit, but very quickly after bringing up this formula,[49] he will point out how this is not circulation-as-usual. "The simple circulation of commodities—selling in order to buy—is a means to a final goal which lies outside circulation, namely the appropriation of use-values, the satisfaction of needs. As against this, the circulation of money as capital is an end in itself, for the valorization of value takes place only within this constantly renewed movement. The movement of capital is therefore limitless."[50] The issue here is that, while one can in theory have enough food or shelter to have those needs satisfied, money doesn't satisfy a particular need. The attempts at acquiring money, when they replace attempts to use it to satisfy actual human needs by purchasing various use-values, never actually succeed at acquiring *enough* so that the operations will stop; instead, the surplus gets recirculated again and again and again with no actual end in sight. One might wonder what this has to do with theories of psychology. The key here is Lacan's notions of desire and drive. Where desire is always for a contingent, historical object (such as surplus value), drive actually has a fourfold structure, being composed of pressure, aim, object and source. It's intuitive to think that drives aim at their desired object, but Lacan's understanding is a bit more complicated than that: "the drive is actually inhibited as to its aim, inasmuch as no object can satisfy it: paradoxically, the real (unconscious) aim of the drive is to repeat incessantly the circuit around the missed object."[51] This surplus that we chase, in a psychological or nonfinancial sense, is not things themselves, or use-values. Instead, we are always chasing that little extra *je ne sais quoi*. Much advertising is actually based on getting us to chase this ever-elusive extra, often by situating a product in a larger context that we wish to be a part of. The difference between Coke and Pepsi is illustrative of this; the two drinks are almost exactly the same, and yet their advertising pulls in opposite directions. Coke's logo often includes the *Classic Coca-Cola* in somewhat fancier lettering, giving it the aura of being part of a long-running tradition. It is the drink of 'the good ol' days'. I remember a SuperBowl ad once had two large parade balloon-characters, Underdog and Stewie Griffin, fighting over a large inflated bottle of coke. They flew around the city, bouncing off one another until a large inflatable Charlie Brown flew in to claim the prize, and with no Lucy in sight we are left with the thought that Charlie Brown won for once. What this ad does, with the orchestral music and cartoon characters set against the backdrop of the

49. Marx, *Capital* Vol 1, 251.
50. Marx, *Capital* Vol 1, 253.
51. Vighi, "Capitalist Bulimia," 427.

Macy's day parade is it associates the product with a variety of other ambiguous elements of classic American life. When you drink an ice-cold Coke, you are participating in the American dream, with all its shitty cartoons and consumerism that comes along with it. Pepsi, on the other hand, often goes for a more 'modern' feel to it, encouraging its consumers to join the 'Pepsi generation'. The fonts and logos are much more modern, and it's ads tend to tap into a more progressive feel. In one, a series of protests in a major city are occurring, a bunch of young people carrying signs with ambiguous slogans such as 'Join the Conversation'. Musicians and photographers come out to join them, break-dancers do their thing and people of all genders and ethnicities join in. All seems to be going well until they come up to a police line, with some rather intense looking riot-police blocking their way. It looks like a confrontation is inevitable, until Kendall Jenner shows up with an ice-cold Pepsi, giving one to one of the police. Crisis averted!

Of course, these products will not ever do what they promise; drinking Coke will not bring the good ol' days back, and drinking Pepsi will not stop police from shooting unarmed people of color only to be exonerated by a mostly white jury. But this failure is not a weird aberration of drives and desires; it is constitutive of them. The inability to get that *je ne sais quoi* is actually the unconscious goal. As Žižek puts it, "desire is grounded in its constitutive lack, while the drive circulates around a hole, a gap in the order of being."[52] These attachments go beyond 'things' however; one can find themself attached to various sorts of ideological signifiers, deriving a *enjoyment* from their participation in a particular ideological constellation, which is part of why it can become so hard to untie someone enmeshed in a way of life, even one that causes them pain.[53]

This desire for completeness is what drives much of our behavior, and even though that sense of completeness may never actually be achieved, that isn't entirely a bad thing. Žižek himself provides a perfect example of this with even a cursory glance at his bibliography. Just starting with his English bibliography, *The Sublime Object of Ideology* first appeared in 1989, and was followed up over the next several years with a variety of texts on Kant, Hegel, Schelling, Lacan, and their implications for a revived left-politics. This all came to a conclusion in 1999 with the publication of his theoretical magnum opus *The Ticklish Subject*, where he set down the core elements of his ontology of the subject, and finally giving critics a core text to say was emblematic of 'Žižekian philosophy'. This was, of course, until the publication in 2006 of *The Parallax View*, which stood in as his crowning theoretical achievement.

52. Žižek, *Less Than Nothing*, 496.
53. For more on this, see Berlant's *Cruel Optimism* and Delay's *Against*.

Until, of course, the 1000-page tome *Less Than Nothing*, which he later admitted he felt didn't *quite* convey what he wanted to, so he wrote the shorter reformulation *Absolute Recoil*. One could then add *Disparities, Sex and the Failed Absolute*, and by the time I finish writing this I'm sure something new will have been announced.[54] Each time the offer is that with *this* text, Žižek will have completed his system (and maybe that part of him that *wants* to feel complete), and each time, he misses what he's aiming for. This is desire and drive at work, missing the mark each time, but nonetheless productive in its own way, since it's need to achieve some semblance of balance pushes it to do what it does. This is what pushes human creativity to write, paint, design and build. The trouble Žižek is calling attention to is that capitalism has commodified the ceaseless need for 'something' and commodifies it, turning it into a ceaseless drive to increase profits.

Subjective destitution is an attempt to intervene in this repetitive cycle, to get help us intervene in our own ideological constellation and rewire ourselves towards new ends. The question of Lacanian and Žižekian therapy is not to eliminate our desire, but to help cultivate it in more productive directions.[55] As Adrian Johnston puts it, the political-therapeutic question and task set for Žižek is this: "how does one get people to stop being seduced into a stupor by the anesthetizing sounds of over-synthesized siren songs, to unplug from fantasies of eliminating disharmonious discord constitutive of subjectivity, and start listening to the sounds of a new sort of music?"[56]

An objection may be raised, however, that will lead us on to our second point to be made regarding Žižekian ontology; isn't there a limit to what we can expect of people regarding change and transformation? Does Žižek demand too much change here? Does Peterson's biological foundation prevent some fundamental barrier to the sort of political change and transformation that's needed to escape the hypercompetitive individualism and start building solidarity? And if subjects are so capable of transformation, why can't they adjust to neoliberal capitalism? Why can't they live out the flexibility that's demanded of them?

I wouldn't be attempting to address this if I didn't think there was something fundamentally wrong with Petersons use and abuse of biology to try and legitimate the status-quo (to say nothing of the way in which it closes off alternative possibilities), and have already addressed a possible neurological starting point for demanding a more socialized subject

54. In the time I spent writing this book, Žižek actually managed to produce both *Hegel and the Wired Brain* and *Pandemic*.

55. For a more positive and productive perspective on our strange psychological compulsions, see Ruti's *The Call of Character*.

56. Johnston, *Žižek's Ontology*, 268.

of solidarity.[57] Here I want to address the synthesis of Žižekian ontology, particularly as it has occurred in Adrian Johnston and Catherine Malabou with neuroplasticity, a term that might imply the capacity of the subject to change in any direction possible. However, Malabou differentiates neuro-*plasticity* with neuro*flexibility*. Plasticity is obviously opposed to rigidity, but for two reasons rather than one. Plastic is able to receive and change forms, as opposed to rigid structures, but it is also able to *give* form; "Talking about the plasticity of the brain thus amounts to thinking of the brain as something modifiable, 'formable,' and formative at the same time."[58] This gives Malabou the gateway into her paraphrasing of Marx; "Humans make their own brain, but they do not know that they make it."[59] Our brains are capable of receiving, giving and rejecting form, and they often shape themselves, even without realizing it, giving us Hegelain 'beautiful brains': "The word *plasticity* thus unfolds its meaning between sculptural modeling and deflagration, which is to say explosion. From this perspective, to talk about the plasticity of the brain means to see in it not only the creator and receiver of form but also an agency of disobedience to every constituted form, a refusal to submit to a model."[60] This is to be contrasted with *flexibility*, which is only capable of receiving form, but cannot give or reject it.[61] And late capitalism demands flexibility, demands we adjust to Boltanski and Chiapello's post-Fordist capitalism, Malabou even drawing connections between neuroflexibility and their projective and connective city, in constant flux, but also at the constant whim of capital (or any other supra-human force, be it biological or historical), as opposed to historical agents.

> One notes that many descriptions of plasticity are in fact unconscious justifications of a flexibility without limits. Sometimes it seems as though in nervous systems, form the aplysia to the human, a faculty is deployed—a faculty described precisely in terms of synaptic plasticity—to fold., to render oneself docile vis-a-vis one's environment, in a word, to adapt to everything, to be ready for all adjustments. It is as though, under the pretext of describing synaptic plasticity, we were really looking to show that flexibility is inscribed in the brain, as though we knew more about what we could stand than about what we could create. That said, securing a true plasticity of the brain means insisting

57. Dozeman, "Mythic Individualism."
58. Malabou, *What Should We Do With Our Brain?*, 5.
59. Malabou, *What Should We Do With Our Brain?*, 1.
60. Malabou, *What Should We Do With Our Brain?*, 6.
61. Malabou, *What Should We Do With Our Brain?*, 12.

on knowing what it can do and not simply what it can tolerate. By the verb *to do* or *to make* we don't mean just 'doing' math or piano but making its history, becoming the subject of its history, grasping the connection between the role of genetic nondeterminism at work in the constitution of the brain and the possibility of a social and political nondeterminism, in a word, a new freedom, which is to say: a new meaning of history.[62]

Our brains are more capable of shaping themselves around new sorts of habits than we often realize, but they also have the capacity to break, as well as explode in revolt.[63] Our brains actively shape our world and themselves, giving us more agency in *acting* than we often realize. As Žižek himself puts it; "our mind does not only reflect the world, it is part of a transformative exchange with the world, it 'reflects' the possibilities of transformation, it sees the world through possible 'projects,' and this transformation is also self-transformation, this exchange also modifies the brain as the biological 'site' of the mind."[64] This biological contingency goes beyond individual ontogenesis, however; it also goes into the *big* narrative, the larger set of evolutionary steps that got us to where we are, and where we might go.

Contra the standard idea that we were designed to be perfectly adapted to our surroundings, Žižekian evolution eliminates a past of developments upwards to get us to where we are now as some sort of pinnacle achievement, but instead as the result of a million evolutionary mistakes: "This is what is so unbearable about Darwin's discovery: not that man emerged out of a natural evolution, but the very *character* of this evolution—chaotic, nonteleological, mocking any 'attunement of mind to world.'"[65] This is the evolutionary version of the fundamental Lacanian lesson, that we are *dis-* and *mal-*adapted to our surroundings,[66] contra the Jungian idea of some deep down harmony that we might be able to return to.[67] Lacking any final ground to point to, we are left with both more agency, and more responsibility, than we previously realized, something Žižek made a point of in his opening statement contra Peterson, and reiterated in a later essay.[68]

62. Malabou, *What Should We Do With Our Brain?*, 13

63. Malabou points out that plastic is also an explosive substance (*What Should We Do With Our Brain?*, 5).

64. Žižek, *The Parallax View,* 209.

65. Žižek, *The Parallax View,* 164.

66. Žižek, *The Parallax View,* 231.

67. Žižek, *The Parallax View,* 195-7.

68. Žižek, "Jordan Peterson as a Symptom. . .of What?" pg. 8-9.

Beyond this antagonized material subjectivity, there's also the destabilizing effect Malabouian plasticity can have on broader cultural narratives. If we accept our evolutionary history as a collection of contingencies
that cobble themselves together, then we're left with a certain level of
freedom in how we respond to our influences. Following along with all
the figures we've discussed, we see how subjects are interpellated with a
set of values and expectations that help to shape them, something even
Žižekian contingency doesn't deny. The twist is that references to biology
don't have the same sort of orienting power, as they do in Peterson's constant reference to an underlying brutality in nature to legitimate the more
brutalistic individualism enabled and encouraged by capitalism with his
constant references to the violent natures of lobsters, wrens or chimpanzees.[69] Since apparently any old example in the animal kingdom is valid
as an example to base one's biopolitics on, I'll use ants. While writing this
book, I often took breaks by watching tv, and at one point I felt like watching documentaries about ants. Netflix didn't have any, so I tried just typing
'ant documentaries' on YouTube to see what happens, and two stood out.
One of the first I watched was a BBC show titled 'Killer Ants', which focused on various species like the Australian myrmecia or African dorylus
ants, all of which use aggressive means of acquiring food and defending
their territory. Obviously hierarchies come into play here, both within the
colony itself and between the colony and surrounding environment, and
could've easily fit into *12 Rules for Life* as an argument for both the inherent
violence in nature, and perhaps also the impossibility of solidarity. Another
documentary came up, 'Empire of Ants,' narrated by David Attenborough,
where he found a mountain covered in colonies of wood ants. Warfare between ant colonies of course does happen, but what Attenborough found
that many of these colonies actually worked cooperatively, having traded
domination for solidarity, leading to one of the largest insect societies in
the world. This doesn't simply mean we can flip a switch and turn solidarity on, but it does reveal that even in some creatures substantially more
'simple' than humans that there is a certain instability regarding how they
will live their lives and how their society at large will play out. Reference to
biology and evolution, interestingly enough, ends up *opening up* questions
of who we are rather than *closing it off*.

One can also see the Žižekian dialectical subject that to some degree
creates itself in Darwinian evolutionary theory itself, as Stephen Jay Gould
draws our attention to:

69. Peterson, *12 Rules*, ch. 1 and 120-1.

if Darwin required Malthus to grasp the central role of continu-
ous and severe struggle for existence, then he needed the related
school of Scottish economists—the laissez-faire theorists, centered on Adam Smith and the Wealth of Nations (first published
in the auspicious revolutionary year of 1776) — to formulate the
even more fundamental principle of natural selection itself. But
the impact of Adam Smith's economics did not strike Darwin
with the force of eureka; the concepts crept upon him in the
conventional fashion of most influences upon our lives.[70]

In unpacking the parallel structure of Smith's *laissez-faire* economics and
various elements of Darwinian evolution, Gould argues that in large part, "the
theory of natural selection is, in essence, Adam Smith's economic transferred
to nature."[71] What's more is that one can find in Darwin's work defenses of
gentleness, love and kindness, since he also saw such traits as these as being
somehow peculiar, and essential, to human nature. Our desire for things like
community and solidarity, as well as our ability and desire to protect those
in need, isn't some aberration in our nature; it's an essential part of it. This is
not to say that aggression and desire for domination aren't also part of our
natures, but instead that 'human nature' is more multifaceted, diverse and
dynamic than either of these binaries can properly account for.

All this brings us back to Žižek's claim that while we are always indebted to certain influences, interpellated by a certain *tune*, we are still responsible for what elements of our (evolutionary, cultural, etc) history we'll
be interpellated by. Autonomy for Žižek is not going beyond narratives to
help guide our actions, but deciding what narratives we'll pick up and allow
to guide us, be it in alternative approaches to history, politics, religion, or
even the substance that we make ourselves out of.

One can detect a similar search for the responsibility weaker substance
seems to imply in Heidegger as well, albeit in a much more fragmentary
nature. Returning to Heidegger's account of authenticity in *Being and Time*
might be a good place to start. He writes at length:

> The more authentically Dasein resolves—and this means
> that in anticipating death it understands itself unambigu-
> ously in terms of its ownmost distinctive possibility—the
> more unequivocally does it choose and find the possibility of
> its existence, and the less does it do so by accident. Only by
> the anticipation of death is every accidental and 'provisional'
> possibility driven out. Only Being-free *for* death, gives Dasein

70. Gould, *The Structure of Evolutionary Theory*, 121.
71. Gould, *The Structure of Evolutionary Theory*, 122.

its goal outright and pushes existence into its finitude. Once one has grasped the finitude of one's existence, it snatches one back from the endless multiplicity of possibilities which offer themselves as closest to one—those of comfortableness, shirking, and taking things lightly—and brings Dasein into the simplicity of its *fate*. This is how we designate Dasein's primordial historizing, which lies in authentic robustness and in which Dasein *hands* itself *down* to itself, free for death, in a possibility which it has inherited and yet has chosen.[72]

The point where a lot hinges is in the second to last sentence, where the endless possibilities 'brings Dasein into the simplicity of its *fate*,' a possibility Dasein is handed but also chooses for itself. This would seem to imply that Heidegger is out of sync with Žižek here, given Žižek's emphasis on an agency that emerges from fracture and a lack of a monomythic big Other. Things get more complicated when we turn to Heidegger's essay on technology, where he brings *fate* back, talking about the prevalence of technology as a "fate that compels."[73] There is, unfortunately, not a whole lot we can do about fate, especially one that has "already been guided in advance . . . "[74] This anti-humanist techno-pessimism[75] is certainly not to be taken lightly, given Heidegger's political engagement. One can even see a preamble to Heidegger's political engagement in these passages from 1927, where he talks about a 'generation' that 'struggles' to free the 'power of destiny.'[76] The later talk of fate and destiny in his technology-essays seems to imply a certain fatalism where Dasein "does not have control over unconcealment itself,"[77] a resigned despair in the wake of a failed transformation that did nothing but reinstate the reign of efficiency, now in the form of mass-consumerism of advertisements where one "merely responds to the call of unconcealment."[78] But is this fatalism really a fair reading of Heidegger? Or is it, in fact, closer to Žižek than first glance might indicate?

The German words Heidegger use for fate (*Schicksals*) and destiny (*Geschick*) both relate to *Schicken, to send*. The latter term, *Geschick* is also similar to *Geschicklichkeit*, often rendered as one's *talent* or *skill*, or more abstractly, one's possibility for doing a certain thing or being a certain way.

72. Heidegger, *Being and Time*, 384.

73. Heidegger, "The Question Concerning Technology," 25.

74. Heidegger, *Being and Time*, 384.

75. Berardi, *Futurability*, 59-60.

76. Heidegger, *Being and Time*, 384-5.

77. Heidegger, "The Question Concerning Technology," 18.

78. Heidegger, "The Question Concerning Technology," 19.

What's more, we can even see Heidegger wrestling with this term in his essay on technology, seeing if there was a possible split with the compulsion it seems to imply, writing that "destining is never a fate that compels. For man becomes truly free only insofar as he belongs to the realm of destining and so becomes one who listens and hears, and not one who is simply constrained to obey."[79] He continues further down to contrast the two:

> The essence of modern technology lies in Enframing. Enframing belongs within the destining of revealing. These sentences express something different from the talk that we hear more frequently, to the effect that technology is the fate of our age, where 'fate' means the inevitableness of an unalterable course. But when we consider the essence of technology, then we experience Enframing as a destining of revealing. In this way we are already sojourning within the open space of destining, a destining that in no way confines us to a stultified compulsion to push on blindly with technology or, what comes to the same thing, to rebel helplessly against it and curse it as the work of the devil. Quite to the contrary, when we once open ourselves expressly to the *essence* of technology, we find ourselves unexpectedly taken into a freeing claim.[80]

Even on its own here, *destiny* is being weakened by Heidegger's approach, something that doesn't confine or compel us in the same way fate does, but we could go even further on Žižekian grounds.

Freud famously quipped that *Die Anatomie ist das Schicksal*, "anatomy is destiny". This would seem not only to support a sort of biological essentialism in terms of, say, gender roles, but also could also be used to support a Darwinian defense of people as *homo economicus*, or in more aggressively competitive Machiavellian terms as a way of cutting of the possibility of solidarity. Žižek flips this again, taking an inverted lesson to say that "the 'truth' of anatomy is 'destiny', in other words a symbolic formation. In the case of sexual identity, an anatomic difference is 'sublated', turned into the medium of appearance/expression—more precisely, into the material support—of a certain symbolic formation."[81] Adrian Johnston connects 'destiny' here to Hegelian 'possibility', while 'actuality' gets connected with 'anatomy.'

> In this association, Hegel and Freud share in common, contrary to widespread, prevailing misunderstandings and caricatures of these two figures, rejections of mechanistic materialisms,

79. Heidegger, "The Question Concerning Technology," 25.
80. Heidegger, "The Question Concerning Technology," 25-6.
81. Žižek, *Less Than Nothing*, 216.

reductive naturalisms, scientistic determinisms, and the like. In Hegel's logic of modal categories, as already witnessed, a given actuality tends to generate a bandwidth of multiple corresponding real possibilities; Hegelian necessity is nothing other than the whole formed by an actuality and its accompanying possibilities. Likewise, in Freud's metapsychology of libidinal life, a given anatomy tends to generate a bandwidth of multiple corresponding real destinies. However, by contrast with the English *destiny*, the German *Schicksal* does not automatically connote the deterministic necessitarianism of fate, instead allowing for a plurality, albeit constrained, of possible courses of subsequent vicissitudes.[82]

This weakening of destiny opens up new ways of thinking about it beyond biology as well. John McCumber, for example, has demonstrated in extraordinary detail how the history of western philosophy has produced various theories of substance, going all the way back to Aristotle, that legitimate various forms of oppression, with Heidegger's work offering a surprising counter to this tendency.[83] The counter-turning Heidegger found in *Antigone*, as well as the poetry of Holderlin could also be linked up with the Lacanian-Žižekian death-drive, a breaking out of stabilizing habits.[84] A synthesis of Heidegger and Marx can also be a starting point for thinking about the role of interpretation in creating and legitimating imperialism. Part of this can come from the weakening role of Heideggerian hermeneutics, and the way it *de*-naturalizes what you often assume to be a sort of natural development.

> Hermeneutics is a way of looking at Being as an inheritance that is never considered as ultimate data. Capitalism has always grown by considering, or forcing another to consider, as a 'natural' possession what is inherited. The great dominating families are really the inheritors of the strongest pirates, thieves, and bandits, and they consider themselves entitled to command through a divine or natural law, when they really are only the result of a forgotten 'violence.'[85]

---

82. Johnston, *A New German Idealism*, 103. Also see chap 5 and the conclusion, as well as his *Adventures in Transcendental Materialism*, chap 5–7 and 12 for more analysis of the weakening of biological destiny.

83. McCumber, *Metaphysics and Oppression*.

84. Withy, *Heidegger on Being Uncanny*.

85. Vattimo and Zabala, *Hermeneutic Communism*, 93. Also see Marx, *Capital* Vol 1, ch. 26-33 and Malm's *Fossil Capital*.

Even at the level of identity, there's a certain destabilizing liberation at play. This weakening of fate and opening up to a weak-destiny also finds itself, if we turn back to the beginning of this chapter, in the call Moses receives. Rather than see the call as addressed to a subject-already-composed, the Lacanian reading encourages a shift towards a subject that *will* be, like Heidegger's *Ding* as the jug that *will be* filled.[86] Lacan's translation of the bush's response when Moses asks who calls him, *Eye Asher Eyeh*, shifts our perspective. "Lacan insists that we refuse to read the divine name in the manner prescribed by Greek metaphysics: 'I am what I am'—a reading that points us toward the self-coincidence of Being, the pure *ipseity* of God—in favor of sticking close to the sense of the original Hebrew: 'I will be what I will be'—a rendering that suggests a non-coincidence that corresponds to a temporal scansion."[87] The shift destabilizes any attempt to reference not only oneself but any Other that might legitimate who one is, and Boothby points out this remark comes from a section titled "From an Other to the other."[88] It also points to Lacan's observation that, while subjects arise as a response to a call, the call-response dynamic often contains various contingencies and accidents that only appear necessary in retrospect.[89]

What's more is that we can realize that certain possibilities may appear as *im*possibilities because of a sustained effort to demonize those alternatives, whether it be by hegemonic constellation, military and economic intervention, or both.[90] The destiny we have is then a collection of possible ways for us to be, and what's more, it's one we need to *struggle* to uncover.[91] This term naturally has some troubling connotations, a major one being it's appearance in the title of Hitler's autobiography, *Mein Kampf*, or *My Struggle*. It is tempting then to retreat from the struggle for authenticity, although this would be mistaken for a couple reasons. For one, while it is definitely possible to see *Being and Time* as leaving Heidegger open to throw his weight behind Nazism,[92]

86. Heidegger, "The Thing."

87. Boothby, "On Psychoanalysis and Freedom," 25.

88. Boothby, "On Psychoanalysis and Freedom," 24.

89. See Lacan, "The Subversion of the Subject," as well as Finkelde, *Excessive Subjectivity*, 167-8 and Žižek, *The Sublime Object of Ideology*, ch. 3.

90. Vattimo and Zabala, *Hermeneutic Communism*, ch. 4; Losurdo, *War and Revolution*.

91. Heidegger, *Being and Time*, 384-5.

92. See Fritsche, "National Socialism, Anti-Semitism, and Philosophy in Heidegger and Scheler."

the danger in reading these passages in retrospect is that such
an interpretation reduces the possibilities of Heidegger's text to
the actuality in which they were realized in 1933. A possibility
is recognized as such only when it is maintained as possibility; it
cannot be reduced to the particular acts or happenings in which
it becomes manifest. *Being and Time* opens possibilities; it does
not call for a particular choice or act, but encourages its readers
to ask how their community can be defined.[93]

Beyond that, struggle here can also connote a constant self-interrogation, a
constant asking of the question 'Who am I?' and in broader political terms,
'Who are *we*?' Heidegger's disillusionment with the Nazi part was that in its
appeal to biology, it tried to offer up a simple answer that closed off interroga-
tion rather than opened it up, and then reduced struggle to physical violence.
Struggle can also happen at the ideological level, as I've been attempting to
do for the last several chapters. It can be a matter of attempting to fight over
the ways certain terms are used and abused, the way our experience of our
own reality is either mystified or clarified, which brings our Žižekian reading
into contact with recent Leninist scholarship as well[94] in the way we seek to
expand people's consciousness to understand themselves and their place in
history.[95] This isn't a simple matter of closing down possibilities to a single
possibility (i.e. class, gender, race, etc.) but opening up alternative ways of
thinking about ourselves and our politics beyond questions of profitability,
of salvaging the *artist* from *homo economartist*.

Doing so on Heideggerian, Žižekian or even Marxist grounds offers
no true guarantee, nor even a unified system for thinking about how we'll
get to the other side (or even what side we'll get to). In Heidegger's works,
we have *paths, not positions*, wandering reflections about various possibilities for thinking and being. In Marx, we have frameworks for thinking about
certain social and economic dynamics and possibilities for subverting them,
and a vague sense of what we ought to aim for.[96] And in Žižek's work, we see
that the past is a collection of contingencies, constantly being rewritten as an
unstable amalgamation of events and dynamics that lead to our precarious
present, leaving us open to start thinking about what sort of future we want
to occupy. If this sounds utopian, then perhaps it's because it is, but I'd argue
that we get a very qualified utopia here. If we've learned anything from Žižek's
inspiration from Lacan, it's that people are fractured and antagonized to their

93. Polt, *Time and Trauma*, 53.

94. Shandro, *Lenin and the Logic of Hegemony*, 135-8.

95. Shandro, *Lenin and the Logic of Hegemony*, 194; Lih, *Lenin Rediscovered*, 49.

96. See Hudis, *Marx's Concept of the Alternative to Capitalism*.

cores, although this doesn't have to be the only way to look at this, as this fracture can be a great source of artistic creativity. The search for emotional stability can be what drives us to explore ourselves and our surroundings, so long as we are able to engage with them productively.

So now that we are coming to an end, we might ask Žižek 'What is to be done?' This question has plagued Žižek for some time, since he often fails to offer what seem to be actual solutions, or at other times seems to flirt with a rather dangerous political irrationalism,[97] reminding us again of his constant engagement with Heidegger, documented in greater detail elsewhere.[98] A different question has then popped up when the first one failed to produce an answer: 'What is Žižek for?'[99] A similar question popped up in the wake of his debate with Peterson, where it was argued (or complained) that he'd treated Peterson with kid-gloves. Some final remarks should address these concerns, before we finally leave.

First, to the point about a synthesis of Heidegger and Žižek to develop a new politics being a risky endeavor, this is absolutely true. Both flirt in various ways with a sort of irrational, overly emotional politics at times, idolizing violences of various sorts as ways of disrupting the status-quo. However, the response here should be to accept this but also flip things around; we need to remember that violence is always already happening, just usually to 'others' somewhere 'over there', or in invisible (i.e. legal) forms, such as evictions, putting people into debt for needed medication or food. To protest 'violence' so that the status-quo can be maintained is a way of maintaining violence without taking responsibility for it, inauthentically transposing our agency onto some other story or narrative while denying we're making the choice at all, rather than demanding a new interpretation and attempting to see it through.

'But doesn't this risk degenerating into violence?' one might ask, and with perfectly good reason. 'Isn't hermeneutic and/or political transition too risky?' Given that we've been grounding ourselves for most of this book on Heidegger's *Being and Time*, a text written only a few short years before his enthusiastic joining of the Nazi party, this question ought to weigh heavily on us, and there are lessons we should learn about Heidegger's mistake; his idolization of the *Volk*-wisdom, his failure to listen or include other perspectives, his constant obsession with the politician as a solitary artistic or poetic figure.[100] One could try, and I long considered, switching our key point of

---

97. Sharpe and Boucher, *Žižek and Politics*, ch. 5.

98. Brockelman, *Žižek and Heidegger*; Vaden, *Heidegger, Žižek and Revolution*.

99. Moller-Neilson, "What is Žižek For?"

100. Polt, *Time and Trauma*; Knowles, *Heidegger's Fascist Affinities*.

reference from Heidegger to Gadamer, Arendt, or Sartre, all of whom had much in common with Heidegger, but failed to make the same horrific error with their own lives. There are lessons here that we can, and ought to learn about how to maintain the integrity of a political transformation so that it doesn't find itself derailed from its hopeful aspirations.

However, I also think we ought to bite the bullet here and also embrace the fact that, yes, even the best-intentioned transformations may end up finding themselves derailed and failing to bring about the better world they desire. Contra the constant fear that we might end up taking a wrong step, it's important we remember here that we are surrounded by a social inertia that already has a direction, that is already moving at breakneck speed. The Heideggerian lessons are a constant reminder that we are always-already interpreting, and the synthesis with Žižek forces us to acknowledge our destitution, and take responsibility for our interpretations, and possibly start finding some new ways of interpreting.

This still doesn't answer the question of what Žižek was doing debating Peterson, or what he's been doing throughout the last several decades, if he's been unable to articulate any clear alternative to our current situation. Having gone through all this, I would encourage a re-reading of Žižek's opening statement. One can hear him at various points dropping subtle counters to Peterson, about the contingency of biological development, the way certain economic antagonisms are often shifted to cultural battles, or the way optimism and pessimism often see the same thing but in different ways. In all this, Žižek doesn't offer a direct fact-checking of Petersons work (and for the most part I've followed this strategy) because Lacanian therapy is not about simply handing over 'the truth' to the patient; it's a matter of subtle and patient listening, and offering subtle hints that help the analysand slowly untie their own knots of *jouissance,* to work themselves into their own emancipatory destitution. Both at the debate and throughout his work, Žižek's project has been a matter of untying knots, albeit from a distance. A passage from Lacan himself should be illuminating here:

> Shouldn't the true termination of an analysis. . .in the end confront the one who undergoes it with the reality of the human condition? It is precisely this, that in connection with anguish, Freud designated as the level at which its signal is produced, namely, *Hilflosigkeit* or distress, the state in which man is in that relationship to himself which is his own death. . .and can expect help from no one. At the end of a training analysis the subject should reach and should know the domain and the level of the experience of absolute disarray. It is a level at which anguish is already a protection, not so much *Abwarten* (waiting)

as *Erwartung* (expecting). Anguish develops by letting a danger appear, whereas there is no danger at the level of the final experience of *Hilflosigkeit* (helplessness).[101]

This bringing the analysand to the point of realizing a certain helplessness is a goal Žižek seems to have picked up and translated into his political writings, attempting to get us to realize the danger and precarity of our predicament, but also eliminating the obstacles to taking action. Johnston connects this to Heidegger's authentic anticipation of being-towards-death, writing

> In a state of complete helplessness before death as the 'absolute master,' the lone individual has to realize that nobody can come to his or her rescue. The transferential relationship to the analyst, as an Other related to in this manner precisely in part because of anticipations and expectations regarding the salvation supposedly promised by the end of analysis (i.e. 'the cure,' conceived in any number of different fashions), must dissolve in this confrontation prompting a 'subjectification of death,' a confrontation in which the analysand-subject must accept that neither the analyst-Other nor anyone else finally can provide a saving absolution from the condition of being condemned to moral finitude. The 'anguish' of this concluding moment of analysis arises from the profound sense of isolation and solitude that the renunciation of faith in the powers of all forms of the big Other brings about ('You are utterly alone. Nothing can help you now'). In a manner of speaking, the analyst, through the consummated act of assisting in bringing the analysis to a close, commits suicide, eliminating his or her position as an addressable Other for the analysand in the transference.[102]

In short, in the same way that Heidegger sees us as having a moment where we're left anxiously alone, without justification for our mode of existence, the Lacanian analysand finds themself eventually at a point where they realize their analyst doesn't have 'the cure' waiting for them at the end. Speaking to our broader political scenario, one of Žižek's favorite phrases now is that the light at the end of the tunnel may turn out to be the light of an oncoming train. But we're not left with nothing, or to borrow Žižek's phrase, we're left with (or *as*) *Less than Nothing*, destitute in a world that was driving us to personal and collective suicide, but also realizing that the world is substantially less substantial than we often imagine, and more capable of saving it than we may have realized, a combination of anxiety and adrenaline as we

---

101. Lacan, *Seminar VII*, 303-4.
102. Johnston, *Badiou, Žižek and Political Transformations*, 153.

discover 'the terrible lightness of being.'[103] In other words, we're left capable of responding to the call to *be* something fundamentally new.

103. This phrase is the title of the concluding chapter in Adrian Johnston's *Žižek's Ontology*, although it can also be found in Sloterdijk's *Spheres* trilogy, where he connects existential lightness, or a lack of an existential burden to bear, to Heidegger's politics. He argues that Heidegger's fascism might be an attempt to resecure being to certain roots in the face of the horror of boredom, (Sloterdijk *Spheres* Vol 3, 663-81) arguably a parallel to much of what Peterson has tried to do (bear in mind his reported appraisal of Hungarian Prime Minister Victor Orban's attempt to "reinstitute the metaphysical foundations of Hungarian culture" (Cseko, "A meaningful purpose in life keeps a person in times of disaster")).

Conclusion—The Wisdom of Being (Un)cool

"It was so much easier to carry despair than hope."

—Karl Ove Knausgaard, *My Struggle, Vol VI*

One question that came up a lot in my time in college was varieties of the formula 'What is X for?' with X often representing the particular topic at hand, or education more broadly. I imagine STEM students didn't feel quite as pressured to answer such questions as me and many of my humanities-classmates did, my minor in art history often presenting me with something of a challenge.[1] Majoring in philosophy didn't put me on much more solid ground, possibly because philosophers themselves have struggled to come up with any sort of consensus, the continental-analytic divide not helping since it meant much of the 20th century involved every philosopher spending all their time claiming half the philosophy professors today weren't even doing proper philosophy. However having studied philosophy and relied on it to help me make sense of my life and the world around me, I want to draw attention to two things philosophy and the humanities more broadly *can* do.

It's often been said by critics that Jordan Peterson seems to have a number of repressed anxieties and fears that he's struggling to keep from bubbling up, many of which come up in his recollections of his various dreams.[2] There is, however, a deeper fear that he is trying to keep at bay that I haven't seen discussed, and that is his fear of a lack of meaning. On the surface, this might seem like an odd claim, but it's worth elucidating. As I argued above, much of the work of Peterson (and Joseph Campbell) is designed around using various myths to try and make sense of themselves and their lives, to take our everyday lives and imbue them with some deeper

1. Luckily one of my professors gave me an excellent answer by making us read Wu Hung's excellent *Remaking Beijing*.

2. Peterson, *Maps of Meaning*, 163-4.

significance. It's Heidegger's phenomenology of everyday life pumped up to literally mythic proportions, where every single object and choice is a part of some cosmic play, and your job is essentially to understand your role in it all. Things like getting through a work-shift, grocery shopping, a trip to the dentist and getting dumped are all connected back to 3,000 year old myths and stories about warriors fighting demonic monsters. It's certainly creative and entertaining at times, and without this sort of synthetic work we would certainly be poorer for it in my opinion, but it can reach its limits at a certain point, for a variety of reasons already pointed out, but here I want to zoom out and discuss the subjective or affective response one might have if they absorb too much of this uncritically. If there is a subject that is likely to result from this view that everything is part of some cosmo-mythic play, I'd argue that Heidegger is surprisingly close, and I don't simply say this to make a pivot to arguing that Peterson is a reactionary mystic, as some have done. Instead, Heidegger and Peterson share a similar distaste for Nazism, seeing it as swallowing up individual creativity and closing off our possibilities for developing ourselves. Heidegger's *Black Notebooks* have in fact revealed a figure who regularly expressed various ambivalences about the movement, even saying in one lecture that "what is peddled about nowadays as the philosophy of National Socialism, but which has not the least to do with the inner truth and greatness of this movement [namely, the encounter between global technology and modern humanity], is fishing in these troubled waters of 'values' and 'totalities.'"[3] What Heidegger had hoped for was that Nazism might represent a sort of cultural reanimation; what he found was that all the cultural aesthetics was simply masking the same technological dynamics he was starting to work through, and which would be expressed in some of his later essays. Obviously there are shortcomings to how much we can forgive him, especially considering his early commitments meant ignoring the violence being committed by actual Nazis in the streets, and diverting questions about Hitler's ability to lead by pointing out that he had wonderful hands.[4] But Heidegger's response to disillusionment about Nazism should also give us pause, and the *Black Notebooks*, private journals kept secret until rather recently, allow us to see his intellectual and emotional trajectory over the 30's and 40's. One might imagine his disillusionment about Nazism would lead to a celebration of its defeat at the hands of the liberal and democratic forces of America, or even perhaps the Communist forces of the Soviet Union, but one would be wrong. Instead, his tone throughout might be described as 'sour' or 'bitter,' a certain frustrated

---

3. Heidegger, *Introduction to Metaphysics*, 222.

4. Ullrich, *Hitler*, 384.

disdain running through many of them. Throughout the 30's, his frustration often gets thrown at just about any intellectual current he stumbles upon, occasionally managing to throw together Marxism, Judeo-Bolshevism, Christianity as all representing the same underlying closure of possibilities.[5] Also falling into his sights are liberalism and democracy, the obsession with biology, and the enlightenment.[6] The result is a figure who seems determined throughout this time to remain uncommitted, above the ideological fray going on below him being carried about by a dull and gullible 'public' that he has lost all patience for.

What this indifference shares with figures like Peterson and Campbell is that it is deeply committed to not caring about the nuances of reality, instead translating everything into some highly abstract master-narrative which must simply be allowed to play itself out in order to make way for the next beginning. Heidegger's comments throughout the war often reveal a cruel indifference to the destruction going on around him. Every political leader is simply a puppet for forces beyond their superficial comprehension,[7] and the best we can do is welcome the destruction, as Polt summarizes:

> It may be gratifying to see Heidegger, even before the war, condemning feature after feature of the National Socialist worldview. It seems safe to say that by the late thirties, he was no Nazi anymore. But we should remember that he does not crticize Nazism as morally inferior to any other contemporary political movement. His criticism is not ethical at all, but purely *seynsgeschichtlich*. His refrain is that Nazism is machination - but so is all else. There is no nonmachinational alternative. And as we have seen, he thinks that Nazism must be 'affirmed' because it will accelerate the necessary apocalypse.[8]

While it can hardly be said that Peterson is looking forward to social collapse, the overlap I'm trying to draw out here is in the cold indifference to the reality of the world, and the retreat into abstract narratives when threatened with confusion. As we saw in his story of the fired worker, he's generally uninterested in the details of reality and more in looking for ways to translate it into a wide-ranging and abstract narrative about which he can theorize from a distance. The reason for the firing is left untouched; instead it is the entrance of chaos and the conquest of it by the hero.

5. Heidegger, *Contributions*, 44.
6. Polt, *Time and Trauma*, 110.
7. Polt, *Time and Trauma*, 118.
8. Polt, *Time and Trauma*, 153.

This indifference to reality and turn to the abstract isn't for nothing though, especially in the situation I've tried to describe. Times are tough, and with climate change coming in they are about to get a lot tougher as the earth heats up. Trying to fight for necessary social changes is a daunting task, and I can say from experience usually unrewarding. For every one step forward, there are often at least two steps back and a dozen in every other direction, which can lead to one trying to do the political splits in order to keep up. What monomythic theories of subjectivity offer is a place to retreat, where one no longer has to worry about it all and instead can create a bubble in which nothing can really touch your 'true self,' or whatever might be left of it when all is said and done.

But beyond a place of ideological escape, there's a deeper thing on offer in the work of Heidegger, Peterson and Campbell, a protection from what I think is the greatest fear of all in many people, and that is the growing sense that the situation we're in is actually incredibly stupid. By placing our current moment in an enormous 'history of Being' or the eternal dance of various archetypal forces, one can turn a truly horrific situation into something to be idolized as part of some larger plan. As Žižek writes in response to much of Heidegger's later writings,

> Here we find Heidegger at his worst, perfectly fitting the "cool" postmodern attitude. The greatest Occidental wisdom is supposed to reside in the ability not to simply withdraw from the world, but to participate in its affairs with an inner distance, to "do it without doing it," without being really engaged in it. Ironically, this version of *Gelassenheit* finds its equivalent in today's expression "cool" - a "cool" person does everything with an air of indifference or inner distance.[9]

While this may be an understandable response that helps some people cope, the underside of this anesthetizing affect is it can cultivate a certain indifference to the suffering we see around us, and sometimes experience ourselves. In this way, Marxist theory can offer a counterpush to this by giving us a systematic way of understanding where much (though not all) suffering today comes from. While this can be an existential relief in some ways, since it gives us a sense of possibility when we realize much suffering can be alleviated by changes in policy, it also brings with it a new sort of psychological burden when you realize how utterly pointless so many of our problems are.

As I write this, COVID-19 has been ravaging the world for several months, leaving many not only ill, but also unemployed and wondering where their next meal and rent-check will come from. I've been helping

---

9. Žižek, *Less Than Nothing*, 896.

organize rent-strikes, organizing tenants and educating them on their legal rights and tactics to avoid eviction. While many of the problems we're facing are intertwined, there's a way they should also be separated. A pandemic might be natural, but an entire group of people suddenly finding homelessness to be a very real prospect as the economy grinds to a halt is not; it's the result of a very particular way of organizing things.

A similar way of thinking about this could come from Jordan Peterson's own life; in the finale chapter of *12 Rules*, he writes about his daughter Mikhaila's struggle with various medical conditions. Several pages tell us of her struggle with various medications, surgeries and related struggles such as learning to drive a motorcycle since her walking was severely impeded. It's an interesting enough story to read, and I applaud their whole family for coming together and supporting one another as they learned to cope with the condition. What never gets mentioned, however, is the cost of the various medicine's, surgeries and motorcycle, provided by Canada's socialized healthcare system and the salary afforded tenured professors at major universities. In many places, many families would've been thrown into debt by her condition, unable to see various specialists or schedule various surgeries or provide their daughter with personalized transport. In the United States, almost half of all cancer diagnosis result in bankruptcy within 2 years. Patients with diabetes regularly because they have to ration out their insulin, even though it's relatively cheap to produce. Tests for COVID can be somewhere between free and $2000 depending on various factors, and who knows how much the vaccine will cost whenever it comes out. To pretend that this is simply a natural thing that all people through history have had to deal with is a way of turning *away* from the issue. It might make for an interesting YouTube video to try and draw from ancient mythology to make various analogies, but it doesn't make these things affordable for most people; it's an emotional coping mechanism for a system that produces misery and anxiety on a massive scale, and this is all before we get to addressing debt, increased workloads and climate change.

To the degree that Žižek gives us a way of making sense of our reality, it is by encouraging us to see it in all its contingent stupidity, and to recognize that we *can* in fact do better. While he has struggled to articulate a sense of what he wants, usually floundering around when he tries to articulate his own political vision, he at least leaves us with a renewed sense of critical agency, a sense this is all incredibly stupid, but it doesn't have to be.

One idea I share with Peterson is that life is (or can be) incredibly meaningful. A lifetime spent reading, reflecting, engaging with others and wrestling with big questions about who we are is a life well spent. However, under our current setup, that lifestyle is available only to a select few, with most others working in various ways to make that very lifestyle possible. But it doesn't have to be this way. We can fight for a society that is built around various avenues of accessible and sustainable forms of low-carbon leisure, and where we have time to learn to be people rather than just workers.[10]

To try and close things off, I'll say that I've seen two things being posted about over the last couple days. On the one hand, in Portland, Oregon masked, unidentified and heavily armed federal agents have started kidnapping people off the streets in unmarked vans, disappearing them for who knows how long. On the other hand, in Seattle, Washington socialist activists recently managed to push for a tax that would help divert money to public housing initiatives and other forms of social infrastructure. I don't think I could've come up with a better and more illustrative real-life version of the 'Which way Western man?' meme if I tried, but it does illustrate the two things philosophy can do, or the two directions it can go rather starkly, whether it wants to defend the world or call it into question.[11] I can understand being scared and not wanting to get involved, to create a personal space where I simply tend to myself and those in my immediate circle, and maintain distance from anything that seems 'ideological'. I understand and empathize with the desire to do that. I cannot understand trying to spin such a lifestyle as 'virtuous' or 'responsible'. Being in a world comes with responsibilities, including deciding what we want to take a stand for, and what we'll do to make the world better. However, the world is slightly *less* than it often appears, and this is our lucky break; the gaps and cracks we find in this world may prove to be doorways into the next one.

10. See Aronoff, et, al. *A Planet to Win* and Hagglund, *This Life*.

11. For more on this, see Vattimo and Zabala, *Hermeneutic Communism*, ch. 1.

Bibliography

Althusser, Louis. "Ideology and Ideological State Apparatuses (Notes towards an Investigation)." In *Mapping Ideology*, edited by S. Žižek, 100–140. London: Verso, 1994.

Antunes, Ricardo. *The Meanings of Work: Essays on the Affirmation and Negation of Work*. Translated by E. Molinari. Chicago: Haymarket, 2013.

———. "The New Service Proletariat." *Monthly Review* 69, no. 11 (2018).

Aronoff, Kate, et al. *A Planet to Win: Why We Need A Green New Deal*. London: Verso, 2019.

Beauvoir, Simone. *The Second Sex*. Translated by H. M. Parsley. New York: Vintage, 1989.

Berardi, Franco 'Bifo'. *Futurability: The Age of Impotence and the Horizon of Possibility*. London: Verso, 2017.

Berkowitz, Edward. *Something Happened: A Political and Cultural Overview of the Seventies*. New York: Columbia University Press, 2006.

Berlant, Lauren. *Cruel Optimism*. Durham: Duke University Press, 2011.

Biebricher, Thomas. *The Political Theory of Neoliberalism*. Stanford: Stanford University Press, 2018.

Blattner, William. *Heidegger's* Being and Time: *A Reader's Guide*. London: Bloomsbury, 2013.

———. *Heidegger's Temporal Idealism*. Cambridge: Cambridge University Press, 1999.

———. "Temporality." In *A Companion to Heidegger*, edited by H. Dreyfus and M. Wrathall, 311–24. Oxford: Blackwell, 2005.

Boedeker, Edgar. "Phenomenology." In *A Companion to Heidegger*, edited by H. Dreyfus and M. Wrathall, 156–72. Oxford: Blackwell, 2005.

Boer, Dick. *Deliverance From Slavery: Attempting a Biblical Theology in the Service of Liberation*. Translated by R. Pohl. Chicago: Haymarket, 2017.

Boltanski, Luc and Eve Chiapello. *The New Spirit of Capitalism (New Updated Edition)*. Translated by G. Elliott. London: Verso 2018.

Boothby, Richard. "On Psychoanalysis and Freedom: Lacan vs. Heidegger." *Crisis and Critique* 6, no. 1 (2019) 10-27.

Borgmann, Albert. "Technology." In *A Companion to Heidegger*, edited by H. Dreyfus and M. Wrathall, 420–32. Oxford: Blackwell, 2005.

Braver, Lee. *A Thing of This World: A History of Continental Anti-Realism*. Evanston: Northwestern University Press, 2007.

Brockelman, Thomas. *Žižek and Heidegger: The Question Concerning Techno-Capitalism*. London: Continuum, 2008.

Brons, Lajos. *The Hegemony of Psychopathy*. Santa Barbara: Brainstorm, 2017.

Brown, Wendy. *Undoing the Demos: Neoliberalism's Stealth Revolution*. Brooklyn: Zone, 2015.

Burgis, Ben, et al. *Myth and Mayhem: A Leftist Critique of Jordan Peterson*. Winchester: Zero, 2020.

Burston, Daniel. *Psychoanalysis, Politics and the Postmodern University*. Cham: Palgrave Macmillan, 2020.

Campbell, Joseph. *The Hero With a Thousand Faces*. 3rd ed. Novato: New World Library, 2008.

———. *Thou Art That: Transforming Religious Metaphor*. Novato: New World Library, 2001.

Campbell, Joseph, and Bill Moyers. *The Power of Myth*. Edited by B. Flowers. New York: Anchor, 1991.

Cambell, Joseph, and Henry Robinson. *A Skeletons Key to Finnegans Wake: Unlocking James Joyce's Masterwork*. 3rd ed. Novato: New World Library, 2013.

Caputo, John. "A Commentary: Deconstruction in a Nutshell." In *Deconstruction in a Nutshell: A Conversation with Jacques Derrida*, edited by John Caputo and Jacques Derrida, 29–202. New York: Fordham University Press, 1997.

———. *Hermeneutics: Facts and Interpretation in the Age of Information*. New York: Pelican, 2018.

Carman, Taylor. "The Principle of Phenomenology." In *The Cambridge Companion to Heidegger*, edited by C. Guignon, 97–119. 2nd ed. Cambridge: Cambridge University Press, 2006.

Chambers, Samuel. *There's No Such Thing as 'The Economy': Essays on Capitalist Value*. Earth: Punctum, 2018.

Champagne, Marc. *Myth, Meaning, and Antifragile Individualism: On the Ideas of Jordan Peterson*. Exeter: Imprint Academic, 2020.

Chomsky, Noam and Ed Herman. *The Political Economy of Human Rights*. 2 vols. Chicago: Haymarket, 2014.

Cooper, Melinda. *Family Values: Between Neoliberalism and the New Social Conservatism*. Brooklyn: Zone, 2017.

Cox, Harvey. *The Market as God*. Cambridge: Harvard University Press, 2016.

Crary, Jonathon. *24/7: Late Capitalism and the Ends of Sleep*. London: Verso, 2013.

Crowell, Steven. "Heidegger and Husserl: The Matter and Method of Philosophy." In *A Companion to Heidegger*, edited by H. Dreyfus and M. Wrathall, 49–64. Oxford: Blackwell, 2005.

Cseko, Imre. "A Meaningful Purpose in Life Keeps a Person in Times of Disaster." *Magyar Nemzet*, June 1, 2019. https://magyarnemzet.hu/belfold/az-ertelmes-eletcel-tartja-meg-az-embert-katasztrofa-idejen-6982826/.

Das, Raju. *Marxist Class Theory for a Skeptical World*. Leiden: Brill, 2017.

Davis, Owen. "Class Warfare: What the Cottage Industry of Admissions Consultants Tells Us about American Higher Education." *The Baffler* no. 45 (May/June 2019) 96–106.

DeLay, Tad. *Against: What Does the White Evangelical Want?* Eugene, OR: Cascade, 2019.

Dozeman, Stephen. "Mythic Individualism - Stephen Dozeman on Jordan Peterson." https://www.youtube.com/watch?v=8ZOkhF1QLPc&list=LLKvu5Y9NdUmc_TGos51mwpg&index=.

Dreyfus, Hubert. *Being-in-the-World: A Commentary on Heidegger's* Being and Time, Division I. Cambridge: MIT Press, 1991.

———. "Being-with-Others." In *The Cambridge Companion to Heidegger's* Being and Time, edited by M. Wrathall, 145–56. Cambridge: Cambridge University Press, 2013.

———. "Heidegger's Ontology of Art." In *A Companion to Heidegger*, edited by H. Dreyus and M. Wrathall, 407–19. Oxford: Blackwell, 2005.

Duggan, Lisa. *Mean Girl: Ayn Rand and the Culture of Greed.* Oakland: University of California Press, 2019.

Ellwood, Robert. *The Politics of Myth: C.G. Jung, Mircea Eliade and Joseph Campbell.* New York: SUNY Press, 1999.

Elyachar, Julia. "Neoliberalism, Rationality, and the Savage Plot." In *Mutant Neoliberalism: Market Rule and Political Rupture*, edited by W. Callison and Z. Manfredi, 177–95. New York: Fordham, 2020.

Erickson, Jonathon. *Imagination in the Western Psyche: From Ancient Greece to Modern Neuroscience.* London: Routledge, 2020.

Finkelde, Dominik. *Excessive Subjectivity: Kant, Hegel, Lacan, and the Foundations of Ethics.* Translated by D. Kemmis and A. Weigert. New York: Columbia University Press, 2017.

Fisher, Mark. *Capitalist Realism: Is There No Alternative?* Winchester: Zero, 2008.

———. "The London Hunger Games." In *K-Punk: The Collected and Unpublished Writings of Mark Fisher (2004-2016)*, edited by S. Reynolds, 511–14. London: Repeater, 2018.

———. "October 6, 1979: Capitalism and Bipolar Disorder." In *K-Punk: The Collected and Unpublished Writings of Mark Fisher (2004-2016)*, edited by S. Reynolds, 433–36. London: Repeater, 2018.

———."The Privatisation of Stress." In *K-Punk: The Collected and Unpublished Writings of Mark Fisher (2004-2016)*, edited by S. Reynolds, 461–68. London: Repeater, 2018.

Fleming, Peter. *The Death of Homo Economicus: Work, Debt and the Myth of Endless Accumulation.* London: Pluto, 2017.

Fontelieu, Sukey. *The Archetypal Pan: Hypermasculinity in America.* London: Routledge, 2018.

Foucault, Michel. *The Birth of Biopolitics: Lectures at the College de France, 1978–9.* Translated by G. Burchell. New York: Picador, 2004.

Frank, Thomas. "Monoculturalism." *The Baffler* no. 4 (Winter/Spring 1993) 5–11.

———. "Rock n Roll is The Health of the State." *The Baffler* no. 5 (Winter/Spring 1993) 5–14, 119–28.

———. *What's the Matter With Kansas: How Conservatives Won the Heart of America.* New York: Picador, 2004.

Fraser, Caroline. *Prairie Fires: The American Dreams of Laura Ingalls Wilder.* New York: Picador, 2017.

Fritsche, J. "National Socialism, Anti-Semitism, and Philosophy in Heidegger and Scheler: On Peter Trawny's *Heidegger and the Myth of a Jewish World Conspiracy*." *Philosophy Today* 60, no. 2 (2016) 583–608.

Gould, Stephen Jay. *The Structure of Evolutionary Theory.* Cambridge: Harvard University Press, 2002.

Greif, Mark. *The Age of the Crisis of Man: Thought and Fiction in America, 1933–1973.* Princeton: Princeton University Press, 2016.

Guendelsberger, Emily. *On the Clock: What Low-Wage Work Did to Me and How It Drives America Insane.* New York: Little, Brown, 2019.

Harris, Malcolm. *Kids These Days: Millennials and the Making of Human Capital.* New York: Back Bay, 2018.

Harvey, David. *A Brief History of Neoliberalism.* Oxford: Oxford University Press, 2007.

Heidegger, Martin. "Comments on Karl Jaspers *Psychology of Worldviews.*" In *Pathmarks*, edited by William McNeill, 1–38. Cambridge: Cambridge University Press, 1998.

———. *Being and Time.* Translated by J. MacQuarrie and E. Robinson. London: HarperPerennial, 2008.

———. *Being and Time.* Translated by J. Stambaugh. Albany: SUNY Press, 2010.

———. *Contributions to Philosophy (of the Event).* Translated by R. Rojcewicz and D. Vallega-Neu. Bloomington: Indiana University Press, 2012.

———. *The Fundamental Concepts of Metaphysics: World, Finitude, Solitude.* Translated by W. McNeill and N. Walker. Bloomington: Indiana University Press, 1995.

———. *Introduction to Metaphysics.* Translated by R. Polt and G. Fried. 2nd ed. New Haven: Yale University Press, 2014.

———. "Kant's Thesis about Being." In *Pathmarks* edited by W. McNeill, 337–64. Cambridge: Cambridge University Press, 1998.

———. "Letter on Humanism." In *Basic Writings: Key Selections from Being and Time to The Task of Thinking*, edited by D. F. Krell, 213–66. London: Harper Perennial, 2008.

———. "The Origin of the Work of Art." In *Poetry, Language, Thought*, edited and translated by A. Hofstadter, 15–86. New York: Harper Perennial, 2013.

———. "The Question Concerning Technology." In *The Question Concerning Technology*, edited and translated by W. Lovitt, 3–35. London: Harper Perennial, 2013.

———. "The Thing." In *Poetry, Language, Thought*, edited and translated by Albert Hofstadter, 161–84. New York: Harper Perennial, 2013.

Hosang, Daniel Martinez and Joseph Lowndes. *Producers, Parasites, Patriots: Race and the New Right-Wing Politics of Precarity.* Minneapolis: University of Minnesota Press, 2019.

Hudis, Peter. *Marx's Concept of the Alternative to Capitalism.* Chicago: Haymarket, 2013.

Iacoboni, Marco. *Mirroring People: The New Science of How We Connect with Others.* New York: Farrar, Straus and Giroux, 2008.

James, Robin. *The Sonic Episteme: Acoustic Resonance, Neoliberalism, and Biopolitics.* Durham: Duke University Press, 2019.

Jameson, Fredric. *Postmodernism or, the Cultural Logic of Late Capitalism.* Durham: Duke University Press, 1991.

Johnston, Adrian. *Adventures in Transcendental Materialism: Dialogues with Contemporary Thinkers.* Edinburgh: Edinburgh University Press, 2014.

———. *Badiou, Žižek and Political Transformations: The Cadence of Change.* Evanston: Northwestern University Press, 2009.

———. *A New German Idealism: Hegel, Žižek, and Dialectical Materialism.* New York: Columbia University Press, 2018.

———. *Prolegomena to Any Future Materialism* Volume 1: *The Outcome of Contemporary French Philosophy.* Evanston: Northwestern University Press, 2013.

———. *Prolegomena to Any Future Materialism* Volume 2: *A Weak Nature Alone.* Evanston: Northwestern University Press, 2019.

———. *Žižek's Ontology: A Transcendental Materialist Theory of Subjectivity.* Evanston: Northwestern University Press, 2008.

Johnson, Laurie. *Ideological Possession and the Rise of the New Right: The Political Thought of Carl Jung.* London: Routledge, 2019.

Jung, Carl. "Answer to Job." In *The Portable Jung*, edited by J. Campbell, 519–650. New York: Viking Penguin, 1971.

———. "The Stages of Life." In *The Portable Jung*, edited by J. Campbell, 3–22. New York: Viking Penguin, 1971.

———. "The Structure of the Psyche." In *The Portable Jung*, edited by J. Campbell, 23–46. New York: Viking Penguin, 1971.

Kant, Immanuel. *Critique of Pure Reason.* Translated by P. Guyer and A. Wood. Cambridge: Cambridge University Press, 1998.

Kaufer, Stephan. "Temporality as the Ontological Sense of Care." In *The Cambridge Companion to Heidegger's* Being and Time, edited by M. Wrathall, 338–59. Cambridge: Cambridge University Press, 2013.

Kendi, Ibram X. *Stamped From the Beginning: The Definitive History of Racist Ideas in America.* New York: Nation, 2016.

Kierkegaard, Søren. "Works of Love." In *The Essential Kierkegaard*, edited by H. Hong and E. Hong, 277–311. New Jersey: Princeton University Press, 2000.

Kisiel, Theodore. "The Paradigm Shifts of Hermeneutic Phenomenology: From Breakthrough to the Meaning-Giving Source." *Gatherings: The Heidegger Circle Annual* no. 4 (2014) 1–13.

Klein, Naomi. *The Shock Doctrine: The Rise of Disaster Capitalism.* New York: Picador, 2007.

Knausgaard, Karl Ove. *My Struggle* Book 6: *The End.* Translated by D. Bartlett and M. Aitken. New York: Farrar, Straus and Giroux, 2019.

Knowles, Adam. *Heidegger's Fascist Affinities: A Politics of Silence.* Stanford: Stanford University Press, 2019.

Knox, Robert. "Against Law-sterity." *Salvage* no. 6 (November 2018) 49–67.

Kotsko, Adam. *Neoliberalisms Demons: On The Political Theology of Late Capital.* Stanford: Stanford University Press, 2018.

Lacan, Jacques. *Seminar VII: The Ethics of Psychoanalysis.* Translated by D. Porter. New York: Norton, 1997.

———. *Seminar XI: The Four Fundamental Concepts of Psychoanalysis.* Translated by A. Sheridan. New York: Norton, 1981.

———. "The Subversion of the Subject and the Dialectic of Desire in the Freudian Unconscious." In *Ecrits: The First Complete Edition in English*, translated by B. Fink, 671–702. New York: Norton, 2006.

Lafont, Cristina. "Hermeneutics." In *A Companion to Heidegger*, edited by H. Dreyfus and M. Wrathall, 265–84. Oxford: Blackwell, 2007.

Last, Cadell. "Žižek and Peterson: Demonstrating the Importance of Higher Order Dialogue." *International Journal of* Žižek *Studies* 13, no. 2 (2019) 1–37.

Lazzarato, Maurizio. *The Making of Indebted Man.* Translated by J. D. Jordan. South Pasadena: Semiotext(e), 2012.

Leary, Jonathan Patrick. *Keywords: The New Language of Capitalism*. Chicago: Haymarket, 2018.

Liebenthal, Ryann. "The Incredible, Rage-Inducing Inside Story of America's Student Debt Machine." *Mother Jones*, September 2018. https://www.motherjones.com/politics/2018/08/debt-student-loan-forgiveness-betsy-devos-education-department-fedloan/.

Lih, Lars. *Lenin Rediscovered:* What Is To Be Done? *in Context*. Chicago: Haymarket, 2008.

LoRusso, James Dennis. *Spirituality, Corporate Culture, and American Business: The Neoliberal Ethic and the Spirit of Global Capital*. London: Bloomsbury, 2018.

Losurdo, Domenico. *Liberalism: A Counter-History*. Translated by G. Elliott. London: Verso, 2014.

——. *War and Revolution: Rethinking the Twentieth Century*. Translated by G. Elliott. London: Verso, 2015.

MacLean, Nancy. *Democracy in Chains: The Deep History of the Radical Right's Stealth Plan for America*. New York: Penguin, 2018.

Macy, David. *Frantz Fanon: A Biography*. London: Verso, 2012.

Malabou, Catherine. *What Should We Do with Our Brain?* Translated by S. Rand. New York: Fordham, 2008.

Malm, Andreas. *Fossil Capital: The Rise of Steam Power and the Roots of Global Warming*. London: Verso, 2016.

Manne, Kate. *Down Girl: The Logic of Misogyny*. New York: Oxford University Press, 2018.

——. "Reconsider the Lobster." *Times Literary Supplement*, 2018. https://www.the-tls.co.uk/articles/jordan-peterson-12-rules-kate-manne-review/.

Mann, Thomas. *The Magic Mountain*. Translated by J. Woods. New York: Vintage, 1996.

Marcuse, Herbert. *Heideggerian Marxism*. Edited by R. Wolin and J. Abromeit. Lincoln: University of Nebraska Press, 2005.

Marion, Jean-Luc. *God Without Being: Hors-Texte*. Translated by T. Carlson. Chicago: University of Chicago Press, 2012.

Martin, Wayne. "Semantics of 'Dasein' and Modality of *Being and Time*." In *The Cambridge Companion to Heidegger's* Being and Time, edited by M. Wrathall, 100–128. Cambridge: Cambridge University Press, 2013.

Marx, Karl. *Capital: A Critique of Political Economy* Volume I. Translated by B. Fowkes. London: Penguin, 1990.

Maslow, Abraham. "A Theory of Human Motivation." *Psychological Review* 50, no. 4 (1943) 370–96.

McCumber, John. *Metaphysics and Oppression: Heidegger's Challenge to Western Philosophy*. Bloomington: Indiana University Press, 1999.

——. *On Philosophy: Notes From a Crisis*. Stanford: Stanford University Press, 2013.

——. *The Philosophy Scare: The Politics of Reason in the Early Cold War*. Chicago: Chicago University Press, 2016.

McGowan, Todd. *Capitalism and Desire: The Psychic Cost of Free Markets*. New York: Columbia University Press, 2016

Meszaros, Istvan. *Beyond Capital: Towards a Theory of Transition*. New York: Monthly Review Press, 1995.

——. *The Work of Sartre: Search for Freedom and the Challenge of History*. New York: Monthly Review Press, 2012.

Midgley, Mary. *The Myths We Live By*. London: Routledge, 2004.

Miller, M. H. "Been Down So Long It Looks Like Debt to Me: An American Family's Struggle for Student Loan Redemption." *The Baffler* no. 40 (July/August 2018) 82–90.

Mitchell, Andrew. *The Fourfold: Reading the Late Heidegger*. Evanston: Northwestern University Press, 2015.

Modonesi, Massimo. *The Antagonistic Principle: Marxism and Political Action*. Translated by L. Goldsmith. Chicago: Haymarket, 2019.

Moller-Nielson, Thomas. "What Is Žižek For?" *Current Affairs*, October 18, 2019. https://www.currentaffairs.org/2019/10/what-is-Žižek-for.

Monbiot, George. *Out of the Wreckage: A New Politics for an Age of Crisis*. London: Verso, 2017.

Morgan, Ben. *On Becoming God: Late Medieval Mysticism and the Modern Western Self*. New York: Fordham University Press, 2013.

Pappenheim, Fritz. *The Alienation of Modern Man: An Interpretation Based on Marx and Tonnies*. New York: Monthly Review Press, 1959.

Petroff, ALanna and Oceane Cornevin. "France Gives Workers 'Right to Disconnect' from Office Email." *CNN*, January 2, 2017. https://money.cnn.com/2017/01/02/technology/france-office-email-workers-law/index.html.

Peterson, Jordan. "Exclusive: Jordan Peterson Talks to Donald Trump Jr. Behind The Scenes." https://www.youtube.com/watch?time_continue=196&v=K8_EY9WkV4A&feature=emb_logo.

———. *Maps of Meaning: The Architecture of Belief*. London: Routledge, 1999.

———. "Q & A 2017 07 July." https://youtu.be/1EmrMTRj5jc.

———. *12 Rules for Life: An Antidote to Chaos*. Toronto: Random House Canada, 2018.

———. "2016 Personality Lecture 09: Phenomenology: Heidegger, Binswanger, Boss." https://www.youtube.com/watch?v=539UQF6eT6I.

———. "2017 Personality 12: Phenomenology: Heidegger, Binswanger, Boss." https://www.youtube.com/watch?v=110BFCNeTAs.

Peterson, Jordan and Derek Robertson. "What I'm Doing Is Not Political. It's Psychological … And It's Working." *Politico*, September 2018. https://www.politico.com/magazine/story/2018/09/04/jordan-peterson-interview-politico-50-219620.

Piketty, Thomas. *Capital in the Twenty-First Century*. Translated by A. Goldhammer. London: Belknap, 2014.

Pinker, Steven. *Enlightenment Now: The Case for Reason, Science, Humanism, and Progress*. New York: Penguin, 2018.

Polt, Richard. *Time and Trauma: Thinking Through Heidegger in the Thirties*. London: Rowman & Littlefield, 2019.

Rand, Ayn. *The Fountainhead*. New York: New American Library, 2016.

Ratcliffe, Matthew. "Why Mood Matters." In *The Cambridge Companion to Heidegger's Being and Time*, edited by M. Wrathall, 157–76. Cambridge: Cambridge University Press, 2013.

Read, Jason. *The Politics of Transindividuality*. Chicago: Haymarket, 2016.

———. "Radicalizing the Root: The Return of Philosophical Anthropology to the Critique of Political Economy." *Crisis and Critique* 3, no. 3 (2016) 310–32.

Rehmann, Jan. *Theories of Ideology: The Powers of Alienation and Subjection*. Chicago: Haymarket, 2014.

Robinson, Nathan. "The Intellectual We Deserve." *Current Affairs*, March 14, 2018. https://www.currentaffairs.org/2018/03/the-intellectual-we-deserve.

Rouse, Joseph. "Heidegger's Philosophy of Science." In *A Companion to Heidegger*, edited by H. Dreyfus and M. Wrathall, 173–89. Oxford: Blackwell, 2005.

Ruti, Mari. *The Call of Character: Living a Life Worth Living*. New York: Columbia University Press, 2013.

Salzinger, Leslie. "Sexing Homo Economicus: Finding Masculinity at Work." In *Mutant Neoliberalism: Market Rule and Political Rupture*, edited by W. Callison and Z. Manfredi, 196–214. New York: Fordham University Press, 2020.

Sartre, Jean Paul. *Critique of Dialectical Reason* Volume 1. Translated by A. Sheridan-Smith. London: Verso, 2004.

Shandro, Alan. *Lenin and the Logic of Hegemony: Political Practice and Theory in the Class Struggle*. Chicago: Haymarket, 2015.

Sharpe, Matthew and G. Boucher. *Žižek and Politics: A Critical Introduction*. Edinburgh: Edinburgh University Press, 2009.

Sheehan, Thomas. "Reading a Life: Heidegger and Hard Times." In *The Cambridge Companion to Heidegger*, edited by C. Guignon, 70–96. 2nd ed. Cambridge: Cambridge University Press, 2006.

Slaby, Jan; et al. "Enactive Emotion and Impaired Agency in Depression." In *Depression, Emotion and the Self: Philosophical and Interdisciplinary Perspectives*, edited by M. Ratcliffe and A. Stephan, 17–36. Exeter: Imprint Academic, 2014.

Sloterdijk, Peter. *Critique of Cynical Reason*. Translated by M. Eldred. Minneapolis: University of Minnesota Press, 1987

———. *Spheres* Vol 3, *Foam (Plural Spherology)*. Translated by W. Hoban. South Pasadena: Semiotext(e), 2016.

Solomon, Andrew. *The Noonday Demon: An Atlas of Depression*. New York: Scribners, 2015.

Taylor, Keeanga-Yamahtta. *Race for Profit: How Banks and the Real Estate Industry Undermined Black Homeownership*. Chapel Hill: University of North Carolina Press, 2019.

Thomson, Iain. *Heidegger on Ontotheology: Technology and the Politics of Late Education*. Cambridge: Cambridge University Press, 2005.

———. *Heidegger, Art, and Postmodernity*. Cambridge: Cambridge University Press, 2011.

Tokumitsu, M. "Tell Me It's Going To Be OK: Self-care and Social Retreat under Neoliberalism." *The Baffler* no. 41 (September/October 2018) 6–11.

Tomsic, Samo. *The Capitalist Unconscious: Marx and Lacan*. London: Verso, 2015.

Trawny, Peter. *Freedom to Fail: Heidegger's Anarchy*. Trans. Moore, I.A. Cambridge: Polity Press, 2015.

Ullrich, Volker. *Hitler: Ascent 1889–1939*. Translated by J. Chase. New York: Knopf, 2016.

Vaden, Tere. *Heidegger, Žižek and Revolution*. Leiden: Brill, 2014.

Valencia, Adrian Sotelo. *The Future of Work: Super-Exploitation and Social Precariousness in the 21st Century*. Translated by A. Latimer. Chicago: Haymarket, 2018.

Vallega-Neu, Daniela. *Heidegger's Poietic Writings: From* Contributions to Philosophy *to* The Event. Bloomington: Indiana University Press, 2018.

Van Buren, John. *The Young Heidegger: Rumor of the Hidden King*. Indianapolis: Indiana University Press, 1994.

Vattimo, Gianni and Santiago Zabala. *Hermeneutic Communism: From Heidegger to Marx*. New York: Columbia University Press, 2011.

Vighi, Fabio. "Capitalist Bulimia: Lacan on Marx and Crisis." *Crisis and Critique* 3, no. 3 (2016) 414–32.

Weber, Max. *The Protestant Ethic and the Spirit of Capitalism*. Translated by T. Parsons. London: Routledge, 2001.

Weeks, Kathi. *The Problem with Work: Feminism, Marxism, Antiwork Politics, and Postwork Imaginaries*. Durham: Duke University Press, 2011.

Weitz, Eric. *Weimar Germany: Promise and Tragedy*. Princeton: Princeton University Press, 2007.

West, David. *Continental Philosophy: An Introduction*. 2nd ed. Cambridge: Polity, 2010.

Withy, Katherine. *Heidegger on Being Uncanny*. Cambridge: Harvard University Press, 2015.

Wrathall, Mark. "Heidegger on Human Understanding." In *The Cambridge Companion to Heidegger's* Being and Time, edited by M. Wrathall, 177–200. Cambridge: Cambridge University Press, 2013.

Wheeler, Michael. "Martin Heidegger." The Stanford Encyclopedia of Philosophy. Edited by Edward N. Zalta. https://plato.stanford.edu/archives/fall2020/entries/heidegger/.

Whyte, Jessica. *The Morals of the Market: Human Rights and the Rise of Neoliberalism*. London: Verso, 2019.

Wolin, Richard. *The Politics of Being: The Political Thought of Martin Heidegger*. 2nd ed. New York: Columbia University Press, 2016.

Zabala, Santiago. *Being at Large: Freedom in the Age of Alternative Facts*. Montreal: McGill Queens University Press, 2020.

Zevin, Alexander. *Liberalism at Large: The World According to the Economist*. London: Verso, 2019.

Žižek, Slavoj. "Appendix B: An Answer to Two Questions." in Johnston, A. *Badiou, Žižek and Political Transformations: The Cadence of Change*, 174-230. Evanston: Northwestern University Press 2009.

———. *In Defense of Lost Causes*. 2nd ed. London: Verso 2017.

———. *Disparities*. London: Bloomsbury 2016.

———. "Jordan Peterson as a Symptom . . . of What?" in Burgis, B., et al. *Myth and Mayhem: A Leftist Critique of Jordan Peterson*, 1-18. Winchester: Zero, 2020.

———. *Less Than Nothing: Hegel and the Shadow of Dialectical Materialism*. London: Verso 2012.

———. *The Parallax View*. Cambridge: MIT Press 2006.

———. *The Sublime Object of Ideology*. 2nd ed. London: Verso 2008.

———. *The Ticklish Subject: The Absent Centre of Political Ontology*. 2nd ed. London: Verso 2008.

Zuckerberg, Donna. "How to Be a Good Classicist under a Bad Emperor." Eidolon, November 21, 2016. https://eidolon.pub/how-to-be-a-good-classicist-under-a-bad-emperor-6b848df6e54a.

———. *Not All Dead White Men: Classics and Misogyny in the Digital Age*. Cambridge: Harvard University Press 2018.

www.ingramcontent.com/pod-product-compliance
Lightning Source LLC
Chambersburg PA
CBHW071052280326
41928CB00050B/2285